SPECIAL ISSUE
IS THE DEATH PENALTY DYING?

STUDIES IN LAW, POLITICS, AND SOCIETY

Series Editor: Austin Sarat

Volumes 1–2:   Edited by Rita J. Simon
Volume 3:   Edited by Steven Spitzer
Volumes 4–9:   Edited by Steven Spitzer and Andrew S. Scull
Volumes 10–16:   Edited by Susan S. Sibey and Austin Sarat
Volumes 17–33:   Edited by Austin Sarat and Patricia Ewick
Volumes 34–41:   Edited by Austin Sarat

STUDIES IN LAW, POLITICS, AND SOCIETY   VOLUME 42

SPECIAL ISSUE
IS THE DEATH PENALTY DYING?

EDITED BY

AUSTIN SARAT

Department of Law, Jurisprudence & Social Thought and
Political Science, Amherst College, USA

ELSEVIER
JAI

Amsterdam – Boston – Heidelberg – London – New York – Oxford
Paris – San Diego – San Francisco – Singapore – Sydney – Tokyo

JAI Press is an imprint of Elsevier

JAI Press is an imprint of Elsevier
Linacre House, Jordan Hill, Oxford OX2 8DP, UK
Radarweg 29, PO Box 211, 1000 AE Amsterdam, The Netherlands
525 B Street, Suite 1900, San Diego, CA 92101-4495, USA

First edition 2008

Notice
No responsibility is assumed by the publisher for any injury and/or damage to persons
or property as a matter of products liability, negligence or otherwise, or from any use
or operation of any methods, products, instructions or ideas contained in the material
herein. Because of rapid advances in the medical sciences, in particular, independent
verification of diagnoses and drug dosages should be made

British Library Cataloguing in Publication Data
A catalogue record for this book is available from the British Library

ISBN: 978-0-7623-1467-6
ISSN: 1059-4337 (Series)

For information on all JAI Press publications
visit our website at books.elsevier.com

Printed and bound in the United Kingdom

08 09 10 11 12 10 9 8 7 6 5 4 3 2 1

Working together to grow
libraries in developing countries

www.elsevier.com | www.bookaid.org | www.sabre.org

ELSEVIER   BOOK AID
            International   Sabre Foundation

CONTENTS

v

LIST OF CONTRIBUTORS

Molly Appel	Department of Government, Skidmore College, New York, USA
Susan A. Bandes	DePaul University College of Law, Chicago, IL, USA
Leigh B. Bienen	Northwestern University School of Law, Chicago, IL, USA
Beau Breslin	Department of Government, Skidmore College, New York, USA
Jesse Cheng	Department of Anthropology, University of California, Irvine, CA, USA
John J.P. Howley	Partner, Kaye, Scholar, LLP, New York, NY
Paul J. Kaplan	Department of Criminology, Law and Society, University of California, Irvine, CA, USA
Bharat Malkani	University of Bristol, Bristol, England, UK
Benjamin S. Yost	Harvard University, Cambridge, MA, USA

EDITORIAL BOARD

EVOLUTIONARY HISTORY: THE CHANGING PURPOSES FOR CAPITAL PUNISHMENT

Beau Breslin, John J. P. Howley and Molly Appel

ABSTRACT

This chapter explores how the principles of retribution and deterrence were framed and thus used to justify capital punishment in the early years of the Republic, and how the purposes for capital punishment have changed in the past two centuries. We ask several related questions: (1) Has our understanding of the morality and utility of retributive justice changed so dramatically that the historical argument tying justification for capital punishment to the past now ought to carry less weight? (2) Have our perspectives on the purposes for capital punishment changed in ways that now might call the entire experiment into question? and (3) What, in short, can we say about the historical similarities between arguments concerning retribution and deterrence at the Founding and those same arguments today?

As is often true of common law principles, the reasons for the rule are less sure and less uniform than the rule itself. (Justice Marshall's majority opinion in Ford v. Wainwright, 477 U.S. 399 (1986))

Special Issue: Is the Death Penalty Dying?
Studies in Law, Politics, and Society, Volume 42, 1–19
Copyright © 2008 by Elsevier Ltd.
ISSN: 1059-4337/doi:10.1016/S1059-4337(07)00401-2

INTRODUCTION

For almost half a century now, the members of America's Founding generation have found themselves at the axis of a fierce legal battle surrounding the legitimacy of capital punishment. Their involvement began in earnest in 1972 when several members of the Court's majority in *Furman v. Georgia* (408 U.S. 238) invoked the spirit of the Founding by building their individual opinions around the concept of the nation's historical and moral development. Justice Douglas was perhaps the most explicit. In rejecting the constitutionality of capital punishment, he noted that "the Eighth Amendment must draw its meaning from the *evolving standards of decency* that mark the progress of a maturing society" (*Furman v. Georgia*, at 242 (1972)). His point, of course, was that the perspective of the past is relevant (in the arena of capital punishment at least) only insofar as it provides a baseline for an "evolving" or developing conception of morality. We can recognize that the meaning of such terms as "cruel and unusual punishment" or "excessive" sanctions was different at the time of America's birth, and that since then our collective understanding of the concepts has "matured" or "advanced" – evolved over time, in other words. The Constitution's expansive clauses, Douglas inferred, take on more sophisticated meanings as the social, political, and legal realities of the American polity evolve.

The four jurists who dissented in *Furman* – Chief Justice Burger and Associate Justices Powell, Blackmun, and Rehnquist – were not convinced. They remarked that the views of eighteenth and nineteenth-century thinkers should not so easily be dismissed. They are not simply figures that mark the beginning of a society's maturation process. Instead, the thoughts of America's constitutional draftsmen, amenders, and ratifiers are themselves critical to comprehending the legitimacy of America's experiment with capital punishment. For jurists like former Chief Justice William Rehnquist, who never wavered from his belief that the death penalty was appropriately constitutional, a jurisprudence anchored to the notion of a changing or "evolving" definition is patently absurd. America's constitutional Founders should be consulted because they provide important insight into the *fixed* meaning of the constitutional text. To suggest that a polity's interpretation of the Eighth Amendment changes or matures over time is to ignore the simple fact that the Constitution is a *written* document. Its words do not change, and thus, the meaning of those words should not change. Those who crafted the original Constitution and its amendments, Rehnquist concluded, were authoritative, and since capital punishment was both a widespread practice in the eighteenth and nineteenth centuries and is explicitly anticipated in such constitutional additions as the Fifth Amendment, the Eighth Amendment cannot be interpreted as proscribing that practice now. Its continued use in the twenty-first century, Rehnquist insisted, is entirely justified.

Today, the debate continues. In fact, the evolutionary perspective that so animated the opinions in *Furman* and other cases of the time is just as present, and just as controversial, as it was 36 years ago. Consider one recent example. In *Roper v. Simmons*, a 2005 High Court case focused on whether the Eighth Amendment's prohibition against cruel and unusual punishment exempts minors below the age of 18 from facing the death penalty, five justices signed Justice Kennedy's majority opinion expressly adopting the "evolving standards of decency" rationale. This majority opined that the Eighth Amendment, as understood through a contemporary lens, prevents states from executing minors who were underage at the time of the crime. A sixth jurist, former Associate Justice Sandra Day O'Connor, dissented in the outcome of the case, but agreed with the majority that "it is now beyond serious dispute that the Eighth Amendment's prohibition of cruel and unusual punishments is not a static command" (*Roper v. Simmons*, at 1206 (2005)). She concluded her opinion by noting that because the "'basic concept underlying the Eighth Amendment is nothing less than the dignity of man,' the Amendment 'must draw its meaning from the evolving standards of decency that mark the progress of a maturing society'" (*Roper v. Simmons*, at 1207 (2005)).

Each of the opinions in *Roper* acknowledged that the interpretation of the Eighth Amendment in reference to evolving standards of decency is supported by a long line of Supreme Court precedents. The five justices who signed Justice Kennedy's opinion for the Court in *Roper* expressly adopted and applied the "evolving standards of decency" rationale to support the conclusion that the Eighth Amendment prohibits the execution of individuals who commit a capital offense before their 18th birthday (Justices Stevens, Souter, Ginsburg, and Breyer joined the opinion delivered by Justice Kennedy), as did the two concurring justices (Justice Stevens, concurring and joined by Justice Ginsburg). Justice O'Connor, although dissenting in the result in *Roper*, agreed that the Eighth Amendment must be construed in the context of evolving standards of decency (Id. at 1206–1207). With O'Connor's dissent, a total of six justices agreed at the time *Roper* was decided that not only "evolving standards of decency" is settled law, but also that it is a correct interpretation of the Eighth Amendment.

Even the remaining dissenting justices agreed that the "evolving standards of decency" standard applied by the majority was supported by a well-established Supreme Court precedent. Justice Scalia, in a dissenting opinion joined by Chief Justice Rehnquist and Justice Thomas, acknowledged that the Supreme Court has "long rejected a purely originalist approach to our Eighth Amendment" (Scalia, J., dissenting). While Justice Scalia expresses his own view that those cases were "wrongly" decided and "mistaken," he accepted that the established precedent requiring examination of "evolving standards of decency" when interpreting the Eighth Amendment "remains authoritative until (confessing our prior error) we overrule" prior precedent.

Notwithstanding their agreement on the status of the Supreme Court precedent, the three most conservative members of the Court issued a scathing dissent. Justice Scalia, in particular, registered his frustration. Scalia has long believed that the evolutionary method of interpretation is deeply flawed. One passage from a recent article reveals Scalia's position. He writes:

> If I subscribed to the proposition that I am authorized (indeed, I suppose compelled) to intuit and impose our 'maturing' society's 'evolving standards of decency,' this essay would be a preview of my next vote in a death penalty case. As it is, however, the Constitution that I interpret and apply is not living but dead – or, as I prefer to put it, enduring. It means today not what current society (much less the Court) thinks it ought to mean, but what it meant when it was adopted. For me, therefore, the constitutionality of the death penalty is not a difficult, soul-wrenching question. It was clearly permitted when the Eighth Amendment was adopted (not merely for murder, by the way, but for all felonies – including, for example, horse-thieving, as anyone can verify by watching a western movie). And so it is clearly permitted today. (Scalia, 2004, p. 565)

He continues in a separate article: A proper interpretation must acknowledge that the *"use [of the death penalty] is explicitly contemplated in the Constitution*. The Due Process Clause of the Fifth and Fourteenth Amendments says that no person shall be deprived of life without due process of law; and the Grand Jury Clause of the Fifth Amendment says that no person shall be held to answer for a capital crime without grand jury indictment" (Scalia, 1997, p. 46; italics in original). For Justice Scalia, the combination of clauses explicitly referencing capital punishment within the text and the historical reality that death was a popular penal option at the time of the Founding renders it almost unbelievable to conclude that the imposition of the death penalty on specific populations like minors is now unconstitutional.

The furor over the proper interpretation of constitutional clauses – with the majority in *Furman* and *Roper* embracing what we might call a "living" Constitution and the dissenters supporting an "originalist" view of the text – is hardly isolated to the controversy surrounding capital punishment. It is, however, critical to understanding the nuance of the continuing penal debate. What is unique about appealing to the practices of the Founding generation when considering the contemporary legality of capital punishment is that no one can contest the fact that executions *were* a common practice in the pre- and post-revolutionary periods of American history. The state regularly hanged criminal offenders. The event was very public and often resembled a carnival. Throngs of curious citizens would descend on the town square to witness the spectacle. Aside from a few objectors, most citizens in early America believed that executing serious felons represented an appropriate legal and moral response to certain deviant behavior. The general consensus was that the government had the right – indeed, the duty – to condemn, in a very public demonstration, any disruption of the social order that rose to the level of a capital offense. Stuart Banner's comprehensive historical account of capital punishment in early America attests to the common use of executions for advancing particular social objectives (Banner, 2002). "Capital punishment," he wrote, "could command widespread support in the seventeenth and eighteenth centuries as a punishment for all serious crimes because it served three important purposes. One was deterrence ... A second ... was retribution ... [and] the third was penitence" (Banner, 2002, p. 23).

This chapter explores some of the key arguments that connect the continued justification for capital punishment to the original purposes for the practice in the eighteenth and early nineteenth centuries. We set out to construct an argument that questions the continued appeal to early retributive purposes as a means to justify capital punishment. In other words, we are interested in how conceptions of retribution in the early years of the Republic have been used to legitimize capital punishment and how those conceptions have changed over the last two centuries.

What we found is that even though conceptions have not changed dramatically, the *purposes* behind exercising the death penalty are different now. Once we get below the surface of the main philosophical arguments about vengeance and retribution, it is clear that the goals the state now cites as reasons for carrying out executions are much different than they were at the Founding. And yet, unfortunately, so much of the continued rationalization for capital punishment by jurists such as Antonin Scalia is still tied to the argument that it was a common practice (based on moral and utilitarian considerations) throughout the early history of America. That, we argue, is not the point. We suggest that if the goals for capital punishment are now different, then continually tying it to the Founding renders the argument subject to criticism. Thus, the primary goal of this chapter is to examine if the historical connection to the Founding era is enough to justify state-sponsored executions now, especially when we consider that the Founding generation's *concerns* about criminal activity were far different than they are at present.

By implication, we will also ask if the need for capital punishment is still so compelling. In considering the principal question of this volume – Is the death penalty dying? – it is important to consider the main historical reasons for state-sponsored executions, and whether those reasons are still legitimate. During America's infancy in the late eighteenth and early nineteenth centuries, for example, it was necessary for state and federal government officials to use particular, and indelible, methods of punishment to demonstrate the power of the state. One of those important methods was the death penalty. One question we presently ask, therefore, is whether the need still exists to use capital punishment as the means to display the authority of the state. In the twenty-first century, does the death penalty still promote the legitimacy or credibility of the government as it did when the country was so nascent? Should it? In the end, then, we will use the frame of retributive justice – among the most important objectives of America's entire penal system – to explore conceptions of liberty, utility, proportionality, and order at the Founding and at the present.

Before turning to the historical and theoretical analyses, it is important that we offer a crucial admission: In focusing on the theme of retribution and asking hard questions about its continued role in capital punishment today, our goal is not to discredit either the retentionist or abolitionist positions, but rather to illuminate the ongoing debate by exploring the more subtle historical and philosophical arguments for the death penalty. In other words, our primary goal is not to derail the pro-death penalty position or the anti-death penalty position, but rather simply to suggest that both sides of the debate must consider that the penal landscape has changed since the Founding, and that such a change ought to become part of the overall dialogue about the future of capital punishment in America.

THE JUSTIFICATION FOR CAPITAL PUNISHMENT: RETRIBUTION

Unraveling the question of why certain jurisdictions still hold on to capital punishment as a penal option is well beyond the scope of this chapter. Some brief explanation, however, is probably warranted. In its most simplistic form, the justification for the continued use of the death penalty can be narrowed to a series of complex values, institutions, and beliefs, all of which fuel a jurisdiction's desire for the type of moral or practical expression of condemnation that comes only with execution. In other words, capital punishment remains a penal option in certain states (and the federal government) because it serves important moral and practical purposes. It provides comfort to those who believe the legal system is too soft on criminals, while simultaneously announcing to any future offenders that the community will not tolerate the most immoral behavior. Consider Jim Acker's reflections on the question of why capital punishment remains a part of the American legal landscape: The answers, he writes, "include a real or perceived lack of practical punishment alternatives, beliefs that executions are necessary to rid the community of dangerous people, or to set an example and thus discourage others from committing similar offenses..." (Sullivan, 2001, p. 371).

Acker's observations are accurate, and yet there is perhaps no clearer statement of the objectives for capital punishment in America than the one made by Justice Stewart in his majority opinion in *Gregg v. Georgia* (1976). He writes that the imposition of the death penalty should "serve two principal social purposes: retribution and deterrence" (*Gregg v. Georgia*, at 183 (1976)). He expands on the comment by citing his earlier concurring opinion in *Furman v. Georgia*. "The instinct for retribution," he notes, "is part of the nature of man, and channeling that instinct in the administration of criminal justice serves an important purpose in promoting the stability of a society governed by law" (*Gregg v. Georgia*, at 183 (1976)). He goes on to conclude that, even though retribution as a justification for capital punishment is not as fashionable as it once was, it still stands to reason that "the decision that capital punishment may be the appropriate sanction in extreme cases is an expression of the community's belief that certain crimes are themselves so grievous an affront to humanity that the only adequate response may be the penalty of death" (*Gregg v. Georgia*, at 184 (1976)).

DEFINING RETRIBUTION

A simple definition of retribution focuses on two related concepts: (1) just desserts for a criminal offender and (2) the process of moral correction for a political community that has undergone some criminal harm. A slightly more subtle reading of the concept would define retribution as the process through which a community re-affirms or renews itself against an offender who has damaged the social and moral fabric by exercising an unjust or immoral act.

This particular definition derives in part from the writings of Emile Durkheim and Adam Smith. They argued separately that the social contract, the core of society's identity and the foundation of conceptions of justice, consists of a polity's moral code combined with the sentiment of sympathy shared for each fellow citizen. In their estimations, a retributive philosophy is a bedrock principle of a legitimate and just polity. As Smith remarked in *The Theory of Moral Sentiments*, "Justice ... is the main pillar that upholds the whole edifice [of society]. If it is removed, the great, immense fabric of human society, that fabric which to raise and support seems in this world, if I may say so, to have been the peculiar and darling care of Nature, must in a moment crumble into atoms" (Smith, 1976, p. 86). Similarly, Durkheim writes in *Division of Labor in Society*, "Law and morality are the totality of ties which bind each of us to society, which make a unitary, coherent aggregate of the mass of individuals" (Durkheim, 1997, p. 136). According to Smith and Durkheim, retribution is necessary for a society's survival: it is the primary mechanism of reconstructing a polity's eroded "pillar" after a breach of the social contract. In essence, both say, it is the mechanism of moral repair.

Justice Stewart imagines the concept similarly: "The instinct for retribution," he writes, "is part of the nature of man, and channeling that instinct in the administration of criminal justice serves an important purpose in promoting the stability of a society governed by law" (*Furman v. Georgia*, at 308 (1972)). If a polity's governing body fails to lead it through an effective retributive process, therefore, justice is not restored and the social contract remains broken. Again, Stewart is helpful here. He speculates on the result of such a failure in *Furman v. Georgia*: "When people begin to believe that organized society is unwilling or unable to impose upon criminal offenders the punishment they 'deserve,' then there are sown the seeds of anarchy – of self-help, vigilante justice, and lynch law" (*Furman v. Georgia*, at 308 (1972)). Under a system of retributive justice, allowing an offender to escape the proportional consequences of his or her crime not only fails to restore the social order, but also denies the offender the human dignity of being able to choose his or her own actions. In brief, retribution is the process by which the state repairs a rupture in the social contract that resulted from a criminal transgression. The penal philosophy itself is not the end that the state desires to achieve but rather the means employed to return balance to the social fabric. In other words, punishment and its chosen form are the means used to achieve that end; it is the state's preferred mechanism through which the process of moral repair is carried out.

RETRIBUTION AT THE FOUNDING

America's conception of retributive justice was not so dramatically different during the years surrounding the nation's Founding, especially when applied to capital punishment. Stuart Banner accurately portrays the sentiment of many Americans in that period. He insists that the public believed that there was an almost organic connection – what Justice Stewart might describe as "part of the nature of man" – between capital punishment and the retributive need to punish certain felons. In response to abolitionist forces in Pennsylvania at the turn of the nineteenth century, for example, Banner notes that "the majority explained that capital punishment 'is so clearly a law of nature' that it would be futile to try to amend it" (Banner, 2002, p. 116). Retributive arguments of the time were invariably connected with the population's strong religious convictions, primarily because questions of morality at the time were so deeply rooted in religious teachings. "Retentionists' confidence in the death penalty's fitness for retribution," Banner writes, "was reinforced by the conviction that God was on their side. The Bible still played an important role in public life. Scriptural arguments in support of capital punishment received much wider circulation than they do today, and they were taken more seriously" (Banner, 2002, p. 116).

But, just the same, there was concern that a sentence of death was too severe for some crimes. Many at the Founding noted that because it serves the purpose of correcting a moral wrong, retributive justice requires a high degree of proportionality between the punishment and the crime. The oft-quoted biblical passage, "an eye for an eye, a tooth for a tooth" (Exodus 21:23–27) captures the essence of this principle: one does not take an eyelash for an eye, nor a life for an eye, but an eye for an eye – no more and no less than what is justly proportional. Richard Worsnop says it best. He writes, "an 'eye for an eye' [is] an attempt to make [punishment] proportionate to the offense. The passage [is] not a command to seek vengeance but a limitation on retribution" (Worsnop, 1990, p. 406). Since the process of retribution requires proportionality to achieve its end, the form of the means is the key factor in achieving that proportionality.

Thus when considering the thoughts of the Founding generation on the concept of retribution, the issue of proportionality is critical. And, as we shall see, it is far more nuanced than is reflected in the passage from the book of Exodus. There is, in addition to the obligation to repair the harm to the community, an equally powerful responsibility not to use the offender exclusively as a means to an end. Ensuring that the punishment matches the crime is a central component of the retributive philosophy because of the sense that the torn social fabric should not be further damaged as a consequence of any moral wrongdoing imposed on the offender. That is, just as the polity requires repair through the act of punishment, the state also has an obligation not to abuse the convicted felon by sentencing him to a punishment that is undeserved. That too would harm the carefully woven social fabric.

Montesquieu, the eighteenth-century French political philosopher whose perspectives on separation of powers and divided government profoundly influenced the Founding generation, understood this dynamic. In Book VI, Chapter 16, of *The Spirit of the Laws*, he wrote, "It is an essential point that there should be a certain proportion in punishments, because it is essential that a great crime should be avoided rather than a smaller, and that which is more pernicious to society rather than that which is less" (Montesquieu, 1987, p. 370). After citing countries around the world (including Russia and China) that shamelessly ignore the principle of proportionality, Montesquieu continues, this time hinting at the utilitarian benefit that comes from following a retributive philosophy. "It is a great abuse amongst us," he writes, "to condemn to the same punishment a person that only robs on the highway and another who robs and murders. Surely, for the public security, some difference should be made in the punishment" (Montesquieu, 1987, p. 370). Montesquieu recognized that a state willing to mete out punishments that were viewed by the public as wildly disproportional to the crime committed risked flirting with tyranny.

Thomas Jefferson also understood the complexity of retributive justice and the need for proportionality. In a letter to Edmund Pendleton dated August 26, 1776, Jefferson spoke about the moral requirement that a state inflict punishments only commensurate with the gravity of the offense. He wrote, "Punishments I know are necessary, and I would provide them, strict and inflexible, but proportioned to the crime" (Jefferson, 1987a, p. 374). He goes on to say that while executives ought to have the capacity for mercy, judges should be "mere machines," officers of the state whose singular duty is to apply appropriate sanctions to the specific crime. Two years later, Jefferson fashioned his famous "Bill for Proportioning Crimes and

Punishments," a lengthy document proposed to the Virginia legislature which outlines Jefferson's particular views on the subject of retribution. In it, he notes that the issue of proportionality is critical not only from the perspective of the state's moral obligation, but also as a mechanism to prevent further deviant and criminal acts. Proportionality between the crime and the punishment, in other words, is an essential tool for crime control. Jefferson writes, "and forasmuch the experience of all ages and countries hath shewn that cruel and sanguinary laws defeat their own purpose by engaging the benevolence of mankind to withhold prosecutions, to smother testimony, or to listen to it with bias, when, if the punishment were only proportioned to the injury, men would feel it their inclination as well as their duty to see the laws observed" (Jefferson, 1987b, p. 374).

Jefferson and Montesquieu were not the only eighteenth-century thinkers who believed in the retributive concept of proportionality. Yet they are representative of the general thought of the period. For many in the early days of the Republic, the retributive criminal justice system served two purposes – the first was moral, namely, that the responsibility of the state was to attend both to the common good and the individual offender. It is inappropriate, said Jefferson, for the state to inflict punishments that are too light, or not severe enough, when compared to the crime committed. Such action does not realign the political community to its previous state of balance. Similarly, it is equally problematic for a state to impose sentences that are too harsh. These sanctions ignore the moral duty owed to the individual.

The second purpose for a retributive system of justice, according to Jefferson, Montesquieu, and others, is more utilitarian. To be sure, there is a deterrent quality to public executions. Here, Jefferson says, the state is obliged to maintain a high degree of proportionality because of the need to demonstrate the capacity to achieve social and political order. Yet when he insists that punishment be "proportioned to the injury" so that "men would feel it their inclination as well as their duty to see the laws observed" he is announcing a more subtle point than one based simply on standard principles of deterrence. He is claiming that proportionality helps to establish the *credibility* of a government. It is an historical argument that is in many ways common to that time period. Pieter Spierenburg has argued that the link between public executions and state formation is clear in early modern Europe (Spierenburg, 1984). The formation of the modern nation state occurred at a time when public displays of punishment and violence were necessary for order maintenance.

Although not specifically linking capital punishment to the formation of the American state, Jefferson is implicitly arguing that a fledgling polity must attend to issues of proportionality for it to gain the legitimacy it needs to carry on its primary function of maintaining order. A criminal justice system, he says, cannot be properly realized – established, in the words of the constitutional Framers – if proportionality is ignored. Disproportionate sanctions, he claims, would "defeat their own purpose by engaging the benevolence of mankind to withhold prosecutions, [or] to smother testimony" (Jefferson, 1987a, p. 374). These disproportionate sentences inevitably create doubt in the minds of those who are looking to governmental institutions for evidence of security.

It is particularly unsurprising to hear these words from Jefferson at the moment in which they were written. In 1778 the American Revolution is in full swing and the newly independent government, under the still unratified Articles of Confederation, lacks the force and authority – indeed, the credibility – necessary to maintain a high degree of social and political order. America's experiment with independence cannot even be said to have begun yet. What is more, the fear of mob rule, revolution, social disruption, and so on, is in the air. Shays' Rebellion and other similar skirmishes are just a few years away. Even the state governments, which enjoyed a longer tradition of existence, were making the awkward transition from colonial rule to free and independent sovereignties. Consider the example of Rhode Island, which in the early 1780s witnessed an event so alarming – a mob-induced insurgency in the state legislature – that it eventually gave rise to the Constitutional Convention. The long and short of it was that the political situation in the United States before and after 1776 was precarious, and thus, leaders from all the states were looking for ways to improve institutional credibility among the American population and the international community.

One of the most effective methods of shoring up the credibility of a government is to publicly demonstrate a show of force, not against the population at large (that would be an expression of tyranny), but against those single individuals who, through their actions, choose to reject the community's established rules. Consequently, *public* executions in the late eighteenth century served multiple purposes. First, they were obviously meant to carry deterrent value, both insofar as the offender, once executed, would never repeat his crime and also in the hopes that those witnessing the execution would, if engaged in the same criminal activity, fear a similar fate. Second, executions assured the public that their government was attending to the common good, especially to the moral welfare that was damaged as a consequence of the original criminal act. Third, executions in the public square during the Founding period helped to solidify the entire community's belief in the capacity of a new government to protect the population. In Stuart Banner's words, "an execution was a dramatic portrayal of community at the moment when the fear of danger to the community was at its highest" (Banner, 2002, p. 31). Concerning the importance of the entire ritual of public hanging, Banner continues: "By setting the actual hanging apart from daily life, the ceremony demonstrated the separation of the legitimate violence inflicted by the state on this occasion from the illegitimate violence inflicted by anyone else .... By embedding the hanging within the ceremony, the state symbolically declared that the hanging was something very different from what one might see elsewhere. The sort of violence that *establishes* order was clearly marked off from the sort of violence that *disrupts* order" (Banner, 2002, p. 52; emphasis in original).

America at that time desperately needed "the sort of violence that *establishes* order." Gordon Wood describes the period surrounding America's independence as filled with episodes of "crisis," "instability," and "insecurity" (Wood, 1969, 2003). He is not alone in that assessment, of course. The newly independent states were barely managing to maintain public order, particularly when one thinks about the more remote and inaccessible territories on the western borders of some of these states. Announcing, advertising, and promoting public executions was one way state and federal officials could demonstrate the seriousness of the government's police powers. It was not the only way (there were appeals to reason, religion, etc.), but it was a particularly effective way. And what is more, it lent a certain degree of credibility to those governmental bodies that were not yet reputable.

Let us try to tackle this same point from an entirely different angle, one that is less historical and more theoretical. If we assume that one of the principal struggles of the Founding period was finding a way to construct a political design that would achieve the lofty aspirations identified in the Preamble to the United States Constitution, we might gain additional insight into one of the purposes for executions at the Founding. We begin, as do so many of the originalist interpreters of the Constitution, with the actual words of the constitutional charter. These words offer insight into the minds of the Framers, and, by implication, into their thoughts regarding the precarious state of an imagined system of criminal justice. Consider, first, that the constitutional text is self-referential: its introductory message is that "in order to form a more perfect union, we, the people, *do* ordain and establish this Constitution for the United States of America." The Constitution calls into being a new political order. If ratified, the Framers seem to be saying, this Constitution not only marks the birth of a new polity, but it also has an important hand in establishing where that polity will eventually go.

As the words above suggest, the Preamble announces the original creative moment, the beginning of sorts – the birth of a nation. With that said, it is interesting to note that the first substantive aspiration set out in the Preamble is to "*establish* justice." The word establish was presumably chosen carefully (it appears only six times in the entire 8,000 word original text), and its juxtaposition with justice in the opening sentence of the document is interesting. The Framers do not claim that the proposed constitution will "insure," "promote," or "secure" justice (all three would have implied that certain principles of justice were already established). Instead, the word suggests that a system of justice in the newly formed polity must be instituted or launched anew. Indeed, the particular use of the word strikes the reader as signifying a creative moment in the same way that the entire polity is "established," or created, by the constitutional text. In fact, the word "establish" appears as bookends, framing the entire Preamble's aspirational statement. At the end of the Constitution's introduction, we get a clear sense of the meaning of the word when the Founders note that the promise of a "more perfect union" can only be achieved through the act of "ordaining" and "establishing" this Constitution for the United States of America.

Turning back to the task at hand, all of this is to suggest that public executions at the Founding were part of a larger set of critical events that helped to secure the general power and authority of the state. Any comprehensive discussion about imposing death should consider not only the fact that it was an important component of early American criminal justice, but also that it played a critical role in building the credibility of the state and providing important legitimacy to undeveloped public institutions. The well-known pragmatism of the Founders suggests that it is reasonable to conclude that institutions like public executions, which were successful in displaying a show of government-sponsored force to a wide audience, served not only the purpose of deterrence but also the goal of anchoring the polity to a particular set of moral and religious values, and, perhaps most importantly, to a belief in the stability and security of the state. If we are to believe that retributive justice requires that the state take action to correct a moral harm, the public display of executions serves the additional purpose of lending moral legitimacy to governmental bodies at a time when they desperately needed them. The fear of disorder is a very real threat to a society not yet fully sure of itself.

THE CHANGING PURPOSES OF CAPITAL PUNISHMENT

For over two centuries now, America's state and federal officials have relied on a basic retributive philosophy to govern their individual criminal justice systems. As evidence, one need only look to decisions rendered by the current United States Supreme Court. In deciding whether capital punishment violates the Constitution's Eighth Amendment because it is deemed "excessive," contemporary justices have repeatedly referred to the authority of retributive principles as a guide to adjudication. Justice O'Connor writes in 1977, "the Eighth Amendment bars punishments that are excessive in relation to the crime committed" (*Coker v. Georgia*, at 592 (1977)). In 2002, O'Connor again insists (this time referring to the execution of the mentally retarded) that it must be clear that a death sentence "measurably contributes to the principal penological goals that capital punishment is intended to serve – retribution and deterrence" (*Atkins v. Virginia*, at 319 (2002)). She echoes that rule just three years later in *Roper v. Simmons*: "a sanction is therefore beyond the state's authority to inflict if it makes 'no measurable contribution' to accepted penal goals" (*Roper v. Simmons*, at 1206 (2005)).

Even though the conception of retribution has not changed much from the early days of the Republic, the *purposes* for which the state carries out retributive force have historically changed. In other words, the stated (and in some cases implied) reasons for carrying out particular punishments are significantly different now than they were at the Founding; we punish offenders in the same way we did at the birth of the nation, but our reasons for doing so have changed. This is particularly true when we consider the contemporary role capital punishment plays within the American penal landscape.

To uncover a few of these changing purposes, consider first the question of capital punishment's relation to public order. There should be little doubt that a general fear of disorder is still present and is every bit as forceful as it was at the Founding. Americans may not feel an identical type or degree of uneasiness, but particularly after September 11, 2001, a general fear of disorder is still with us. In other words, it cannot be denied that the American political experiment is still one that seeks to balance the twin principles of freedom and order. Toward the end of limiting or regulating that concern about disorder, many believe that even the prospect of state executions helps to ensure that peace is maximized and order is secured. As long as capital punishment is an option, these individuals say, its deterrent value contributes to crime control and general societal stability.

That, of course, may be true; one can easily locate studies that draw connections between capital punishment and deterrence. But insofar as the fundamental credibility of the American polity and its governmental institutions is no longer questioned, the implications for capital punishment are presumably less critical. In other words, the issue of establishing governmental credibility is no longer subject for debate, and thus one dimension of the equation regarding governmental stability and public order has disappeared. Finding evidence that the institutions of the American legal and political system have arrived, that they are no longer fully questioned, is obviously difficult. And yet consider the fact that in mainstream circles, there is very little talk of revamping the country's main institutional structure. To be sure, there are plenty of complaints about policies emanating from these political organizations or decisions handed down by judicial bodies, but rarely do those critiques rise to the level of asking for fundamental constitutional and legal restructuring. Our point here is simple: insofar as *establishing* order is different from *maintaining* order, the role of capital punishment in America has diminished. In the end, it must be admitted that one central purpose for embracing capital punishment during the late eighteenth and early nineteenth centuries – namely, to display the authority of the state at a time when the credibility of governmental institutions had not yet been established – cannot reasonably be said to still exist in contemporary America.

Let us consider the question of the loss of liberty as a second illustration of the changing purposes of capital punishment. The loss of liberty is one of the key philosophical justifications for the entire penal experiment. Owing in part to the revolutionary forces who gave rise to an independent nation based on the principle of liberty, Americans, it can be said, value freedom as much as any other philosophical belief. The revolution was fought for liberty; the Declaration of Independence was written to establish it, and the Constitution was drafted to "secure" its "blessings." It is, according to Publius in the *Federalist Papers*, the principal reason one constitutes a government in the first place.

But within the penal context, the loss of liberty is more guaranteed now, and that has implications for the use of capital punishment in the twenty-first century. In a recent nationwide study, a group of researchers found that out of an average daily prison population of 652,982, only 802 inmates escaped, and almost all of that number was eventually recaptured (Lillis, 1994). According to that data, the number of inmates who escaped represents 0.001% of the prison population. Why is this revealing? Because, once again, we suggest that the use of the death penalty in the period surrounding the Founding served purposes that are not necessarily still present. In this case, executing individuals was at least in part a response to the fact that the state could not guarantee security in its rudimentary prison systems. The idea of incarceration in formal facilities was still a relatively underdeveloped concept. Actual prisons in the late eighteenth century had only just been invented, and there were not many around. Even when facilities were available, convicted felons regularly escaped incarceration, and thus there were genuine concerns about the proportionality of a punishment that was not fully guaranteed to work. The finality of death was, during the late eighteenth century, compatible with a belief that other forms of punishment (namely incarceration) were not severe enough. Evidence suggests that they were not severe enough partly because of the tendency of inmates to escape prison at that time, and the comparative pain associated with a loss of liberty. At present, inmates do not escape prison at the same levels they did in the early period of the Republic.

Thus, if we compare the percentage of current escapees to the prevalence of prison escapes in the late eighteenth and early nineteenth centuries when prisons were not as sophisticated and not nearly as secure (one study, in 1882, found that over 1,100 inmates escaped prisons in 1880 *in just a few southern states*, McKelvey, 1977, p. 209), we can draw more speculative conclusions about the importance of capital punishment at the period of the Founding. As a number of historians have claimed, prison conditions were suspect in early America (McKelvey, 1977; Ignatieff, 1978). Those mechanisms that were in place to control the prison population were sketchy at best. Blake McKelvey's comprehensive history of American prisons in the eighteenth and nineteenth centuries concludes that altered designs, changing developments in structure, and general prison reform movements all came as a result of untold "outbreaks of disorder" in the prison communities of the time (McKelvey, 1977).

CONCLUSION

A society's primary values and beliefs evolve with political and historical changes. Similarly, the purposes of certain punishments will change according to how societies value that which they aim to harm. Perhaps, as Michael Ignatieff (1978) suggests, the real change in our penal perspectives came during the Industrial Revolution. The Industrial Revolution altered the nation's entire conception and value of time, labor, property, and independence. Coupled with this change was the growth of the degree to which people valued concepts which, quite frankly, they never had time to consider before, yet now seemed quotidian, and urgently so. James Reed describes this change, and its implication for punishment: "New methods of punishing crime seemed necessary during a period when cottage industries were in decline and being displaced by factories and when leaseholders were losing their places to day laborers. The casual attitudes toward time characteristic of pre-modern societies were giving way to the time-consciousness engendered by the intensified division of labor and the strangely anonymous social interdependence of an urban-industrial world" (Reed, 1983, p. 1199). A harsher world in eighteenth-century America provided for radically different penal standards than we are accustomed to today. Coupled with the changed way in which we value time and liberty, this fact implies that incarceration meant something very different. The loss of comfort associated with incarceration was probably not as severe as it is now.

We are not claiming that the beliefs and values of seventeenth, eighteenth, and early nineteenth-century Americans caused them to view execution as any less grave and immutable of acts than we do today. We are merely pointing out that execution and incarceration carry a different weight of proportionality than they do today, due in part to the nature of the historical context in which they were, and are, delivered. The technologies available, contemporary living standards, the priority of societal principles and values, the very philosophical movements defining how people conceive of themselves and their world – all of these contextualize the proportional weight of a particular mechanism of punishment.

This brings us back to arguments about the evolving standards of decency and the debate between originalists and those who see the Constitution as reflecting the maturing values of a modern society. Neither side is completely correct. Or, rather, both sides present powerful and deeply influential arguments. Our point is much simpler. Even if we cannot claim that contemporary jurists and practitioners should interpret the Constitution through contemporary lenses, it does make sense for all involved in the debate to consider how the purpose of state-sponsored execution has changed over the years. The words of the Fifth and Eighth Amendments may not have changed – their fixed meaning may even be perfectly clear to us – but certainly the reasons for executing individuals has changed in the past 200 years. At a minimum, the death penalty no longer serves the purpose of lending credibility to a fledgling state seeking to establish its authority, nor can it be said that its imposition is partially aimed at remedying the structural flaws of America's system of incarceration. To be sure, it is still exercised in the name of retribution, and there might even be additional reasons for its present use. But if we admit that, we must also be prepared to acknowledge that the continued justification of capital punishment because it was widely used at the time the Constitution was drafted is, at best, misleading.

REFERENCES

Banner, S. (2002). *The death penalty: An American history*. Cambridge, MA: Harvard University Press.

Durkheim, E. (1997). *The division of labor in society*. New York: Free Press.

Ignatieff, M. (1978). *A just measure of pain: The penitentiary in the industrial revolution* (pp. 1750–1850). New York: Columbia University Press.

Jefferson, T. (1987a). A bill for proportioning crimes and punishment. In: P. B. Kurland & R. Lerner (Eds), *The founder's constitution*. Indianapolis, IN: The Liberty Fund.

Jefferson, T. (1987b). Letter to Edmund Pendleton. In: P. B. Kurland & R. Lerner (Eds), *The founder's constitution*. Indianapolis, IN: The Liberty Fund.

Lillis, J. (1994). Prison escapes and violence remain down. *Corrections Compendium, 19*, 6–21.

McKelvey, B. (1977). *American prisons: A history of good intentions*. Montclair, NJ: Patterson Smith.

Montesquieu, B. de. (1987). The spirit of the laws. In: P. B. Kurland & R. Lerner (Eds), *The founder's constitution*. Indianapolis, IN: The Liberty Fund.

Reed, J. (1983). In: S. Kadish (Ed.), *The encyclopedia of crime and justice*. New York: Free Press.

Scalia, A. (1997). *A matter of interpretation: Federal courts and the law*. Princeton, NJ: Princeton University Press.

Scalia, A. (2004). God's justice and ours. In: A. Sarat (Ed.), *The social organization of law* (pp. 564–570). Los Angeles, CA: Roxbury Publishing Company.

Smith, A. (1976; originally published 1759). In: D. D. Raphael & A. L. Macfie (Eds), *The theory of moral sentiments*. Oxford: Clarendon Press.

Spierenburg, P. (1984). *The spectacle of suffering: Executions and the evolution of repression: From a preindustrial metropolis to the European experience*. Cambridge, MA: Cambridge University Press.

Sullivan, D. (2001). The death of capital punishment: A conversation with Jim Acker. *Contemporary Justice Review, 4*, 369–399.

Wood, G. (1969). *The creation of the American Republic: 1776–1787*. Chapel Hill, NC: The University of North Carolina Press.

Wood, G. (2003). *The American Revolution: A history*. New York: The Modern Library.

Worsnop, R. L. (1990). Death penalty debate centers on retribution. *Editorial Research Reports, 1* (July 13), 397–411.

CASES CITED

Atkins v. Virginia, 536 U.S. 304 (2002).

Coker v. Georgia, 433 U.S. 584 (1977).

Furman v. Georgia, 408 U.S. 238 (1972).

Gregg v. Georgia, 428 U.S. 153 (1976).

Roper v. Simmons, 125 S. Ct. 1183 (2005).

THE HEART HAS ITS REASONS: EXAMINING THE STRANGE PERSISTENCE OF THE AMERICAN DEATH PENALTY

Susan A. Bandes

ABSTRACT

The debate about the future of the death penalty often focuses on whether its supporters are animated by instrumental or expressive values, and if the latter, what values the penalty does in fact express, where those values originated and how deeply entrenched they are. In this chapter, I argue that a more explicit recognition of the emotional sources of support for and opposition to the death penalty will contribute to the clarity of the debate. The focus on emotional variables reveals that the boundary between instrumental and expressive values is porous; both types of values are informed (or uninformed) by fear, outrage, compassion, selective empathy and other emotional attitudes. More fundamentally, though history, culture and politics are essential aspects of the discussion, the resilience of the death penalty cannot be adequately understood when the affect is stripped from explanations for its support. Ultimately, the death penalty will not die without a societal change of heart.

Special Issue: Is the Death Penalty Dying?
Studies in Law, Politics, and Society, Volume 42, 21–52
Copyright © 2008 by Elsevier Ltd.
ISSN: 1059-4337/doi:10.1016/S1059-4337(07)00402-4

Before we can predict the fate of the death penalty, we need to understand why capital punishment has persisted for so long in the United States. Why have we continued to execute people into the twenty-first century, despite evidence of wrongful executions, a lack of hard evidence of the penalty's efficacy and the increasing isolation of our position in the industrialized world? The explanations for this persistence ought to provide insight into the question of whether the death penalty is dying. Unfortunately, the conventional discourse on this topic fails to adequately address one essential aspect of the death penalty's tenacity. As I will argue, the persistence of the death penalty is incomprehensible without addressing the role of emotion.

The conventional discourse about capital punishment proceeds along certain well-established, highly circumscribed paths. In general, it tracks the usual philosophical debate about the purposes of punishment. The traditional assumption is that capital punishment must serve an instrumental goal: deterrence, retribution or incapacitation. More recently, the notion that capital punishment might serve goals that are expressive in nature has gained currency. Questions about racial bias and systemic error are counterpoised against these basic rationales, so that the question becomes whether these problems with the system outweigh or detract from the penalty's penalogical goals. This is the shape of the legal and philosophical debate about whether the death penalty is justified. It is also the outward face of the public debate about the death penalty, since that debate is often framed and summarized by social scientists and pollsters whose questions track the traditional discourse (Ellsworth & Gross, 1994).[1]

The rather salient emotional content of the question of whether or when the state should kill is generally treated as a vexing and improper detour from the rigors of proper legal analysis or the scope of legitimate debate. This attitude toward emotion – a combination of denigration and denial – shapes both the debate about whether capital punishment should be maintained as a legitimate punishment and the debate about who should be executed. It creates a two-track discussion, in which one track is regarded as legally grounded, rigorous and acceptable and the other as illegitimate; not part of the accepted legal language or structure. The result is deleterious on two interrelated counts.

First, the "legally grounded" discussion, with its reference to time-honored but affectless concepts like "deterrence" and "incapacitation," fails to describe with any accuracy the way people actually arrive at decisions about the death penalty. The official "reasons" for the death penalty have only a tenuous connection to the real reasons why people support capital punishment. Researchers asking people why they support or oppose the death penalty repeatedly conclude that "most people's attitudes toward capital punishment are basically emotional. The 'reasons' are determined by the attitude, not the reverse" (Ellsworth & Gross, 1994, p. 95).

Second, the official discourse, as currently structured, perpetuates a misleading and problematic normative assumption: that the official reasons are devoid of emotion (except, perhaps, for a few carefully managed, "allowable" emotions). Capital punishment discourse too often operates on the assumption that rigorous, non-emotional reasons for or against the death penalty exist, but that the conversation keeps getting hijacked by unruly passion. I suggest that the reasons themselves, both the so-called instrumental reasons and the so-called expressive reasons, are imbued with emotional content. The boundary between instrumental and expressive values is porous, and at bottom, both types of values are informed (or uninformed) by fear, outrage, compassion, selective empathy and other emotional attitudes. Or to put it another way, the decision whether or not to maintain and implement our system of capital punishment is inherently an expressive decision; one which is both inescapably moral and inescapably emotional. The official discourse masks, sanitizes or denigrates much of this emotional content. The result is not to banish emotion from the system, but to drive discussion of it underground, to privilege certain emotions and to perpetuate a system that depends on moral and emotional distance and even disengagement.

The Court's approach in *California v. Brown* (1986), in which it upheld a jury instruction cautioning the jury that it "must not be swayed by mere sentiment, conjecture, sympathy, passion, prejudice, public opinion or public feeling" (p. 540), illustrates its misplaced faith in the existence of an emotionless realm and how it privileges certain emotions. The Court was confident that jurors would understand this instruction as a prohibition on the exercise of "mere" or "untethered" sympathy, and would understand that they were still permitted to exercise mercy or compassion. Justice O'Connor, in her concurrence, explained that the instruction properly recognized the jury's decision as "a moral inquiry into the culpability of the defendant, and not an emotional response to the mitigating evidence" (p. 545). Even apart from the question of how juries are to distinguish sympathy, mere sympathy, mercy and compassion, the larger point is that the Court mistakes the nature of moral decision making. Whether a juror votes to take or spare a life will depend in large part on empathy, distancing, anger, blame and other emotional variables, and these variables will constitute an essential component of his moral decision (Haney, 1997; Sundby, 2005). When the juror tries in good faith to fit these moral and emotional reactions into a legal framework, he will often conclude that he has been instructed to put his empathy for the defendant "aside." Because he has received no explicit instruction about anger, outrage, distancing and even disgust, and has usually received both explicit[2] and implicit messages that these states do not count as inappropriate or emotional, he is likely to conclude that they fit comfortably within the legal framework.[3]

Justice Blackmun's dissent in *Furman v. Georgia* (1974), in which he "ignored the advice" Chief Justice Burger had given him "not to wear his heart on his sleeve" (Greenhouse, 2005, p. 114), captures the determined struggle to "rise above" emotion in determining whether capital punishment is appropriate. Dissenting from the Court's holding that the death penalty as currently administered was unconstitutional, Blackmun said:

> Cases such as these provide for me an excruciating agony of the spirit. I yield to no one in the depth of my distaste, antipathy, and, indeed, abhorrence for the death penalty, with all its aspects of physical distress and fear and of moral judgment exercised by finite minds ... [A]lthough personally I may rejoice at the Court's result, I find it difficult to accept or to justify as a matter of history, of law, or of constitutional pronouncement. ([91]Furman V. Georgia, 1974: 414)

Ultimately, Justice Blackmun came to realize that the legal issues could not be neatly cabined in this way. In *Callins v. Collins* (1994, p.1145), he famously declined to continue to "tinker with the machinery of death." His passionate description of an execution[4] bespeaks a man who has long tried to grapple with capital punishment through the legal lens, but who can no longer distance himself from the fact that the death penalty involves the killing of a human being, and that the propriety of this state-sponsored killing is, at its crux, a moral and emotional question.

My contention is that the standard discussion about why we continue to execute – in the courts and the public forum – fails, to its great detriment, to engage the crucial role of emotion. It treats emotion as an optional and indeed unwelcome commodity – the heart on the sleeve. It assumes a division between the "proper" or "acceptable" reasons to support or oppose the death penalty, and the emotional reaction that is viewed as the abdication of reasoning.

I will argue, to the contrary, that emotion is deeply involved in legal and moral judgment, in ways that are not optional or severable. Emotion affects how we interpret facts, categorize, discern patterns, identify norms and deviations from norms and choose and prioritize among available options. It affects how we form our attitudes, values and beliefs, and how, once they are formed, we approach challenges to them. It affects what we find important, and what stirs us to action.

The standard discussion makes another important mistake about the nature of emotion: that it is private and internal. Emotion theory has become increasingly cognizant of the importance of understanding how emotions are affected by social interaction, and, in turn, how they affect societal notions of moral and ethical judgment (Haidt, 2001). When emotion is approached as interactional, rather than merely private and internal, its study sheds light on the nature of legal institutions: both on how institutions channel, encourage and even help shape our emotions, and on how the institutions in turn reflect the social and ethical value judgments those emotions help to shape.

This chapter will begin by recounting the traditional rationales for the death penalty and raising some questions about their content and limitations. It will then discuss the essential role of emotion in every aspect of the death penalty system – its formation, its definition, its maintenance and its persistence. Finally, it will explore the implications of emotion's role for the question at hand: whether the death penalty is dying.

THE TRADITIONAL RATIONALES REVISITED

The standard arguments for capital punishment, familiar to any first year law student, are first, that it will deter others from committing similar crimes, second, that it is retributive in nature, meting out just deserts for the crime committed and third, that it will permanently incapacitate the defendant so he cannot commit further crimes.[5] These penological theories are the subject of longstanding arguments which draw, implicitly and explicitly, from several types of authority. Deterrence arguments are viewed as utilitarian in nature (Carter & Kreitzberg, 2004), and thus based, at least implicitly, on empirical psychological assumptions about how people make decisions. Retributive theory, with its reference to what is morally right and deserved, is essentially non-empirical[6] (Radelet & Borg, 2000). It is philosophically, and even theologically, based – for example, in its use of the *lex talionis* as a proper yardstick (Owens & Elshtain, 2004, p. 4). However, retributive theory has undergone a shift, more recently drawing on psychologically based assumptions about the importance of punishment – and of participation in the sentencing process – to victims and, in capital cases, to their loved ones (Zimring, 2003; Sarat, 2001; Bandes, 1996a, 1996b). Incapacitation arguments are harder to characterize, particularly in the capital context: they sound utilitarian (some murderers must be executed to prevent them from killing again) but the calculus requires both a means of determining which murderers will be incapacitated only by execution and a moral standard for determining which lives should be taken in the face of recidivist impulses.[7] As to all three theories, what is noteworthy is the scope of the traditional debate about whether we should execute people. It is oddly devoid of reference to emotion.

RETRIBUTION

The omission is easiest to discern in the discourse on retributive theory. Retributivists "seek to punish an offender because she deserves to be punished in a manner commensurate to her legal wrongdoing and responsibility ... Not more, not less" (Markel, 2004, p. 1439). Retributivists struggle to explain *why* meting out "just deserts" is the proper role of the state, and *how* to determine what amount of punishment is just (Duff & Garland, 1995). Some retributivists define desert as simply legal guilt, and others have a broader view of guilt that incorporates moral blameworthiness (Murphy, 2006).[8] Volumes have been written about these questions, and I do not intend to rehearse those debates here. What is interesting about standard retributivist arguments is that they present the need to punish the offender, as well as the ability to determine what punishment the offender "deserves," as bloodless and abstract philosophical questions. Retributivism is often portrayed as a way to avoid or civilize emotional reactions to crime, a means of determining the fair and just punishment from the community's point of view, rather than acquiescing to the punishment that the victim or the community might desire out of anger and vengeful feeling (Markel, 2004; Sigler, 2000).

Indeed, retributivists tend to be especially eager to distance retribution from revenge. As Danielle Allen observes, "there is always ... the worry that retribution is too close to revenge and its ugliness in tone, purpose and effect" (Allen, 1999, p. 192). One defender of retributivism hastens to assure us that it "isn't just a fancy word for revenge[9] ... and is not the idea that it is good to have and satisfy {the emotion of vengefulness}" (Gerstein, 1974, p. 76). A similar aversion to the concept of revenge holds sway among jurors voting for death. Scott Sundby reports that a large proportion of jurors he interviewed identified the importance of their "desire to see justice done," though a very small proportion identified the importance of "feelings of revenge," and several were angered by the suggestion that revenge played a role in their decisions (Sundby, 2006, p. 127). He notes that similar results were found in a Gallup poll of the general population. As Frank Zimring succinctly observed: "Vengeance is an anachronism with a bad press" (Zimring, 2003, p. 58).

To what extent can retributivism, without reference to emotional affect, explain how societal or individual notions of fair and just punishment are shaped, particularly when the death penalty is at issue? What motivates a polity, or a community, to determine that the death penalty is the just desert for certain crimes? My contention here is not that the institution is fueled solely by the thirst for vengeance, or that jurors who vote for death are motivated solely by vengeful impulses. In fact, as I will argue, the emotional landscape is far more complex than that. Rather, I suggest that the traditional debate suffers for its insufficient attention to the emotional landscape in all its complexity. Without attention to emotion, retributive theory becomes circular, empty and indeterminate – we punish because it is the right thing to do, and we mete out the punishment that is right.

There are two separate but overlapping questions: first, why the United States – but no other Western country, and 38 of the states – but not the other 12, consider the death penalty the "just desert" for certain categories of murder. Retributive theory has no good answer to this question. "Modern notions of desert are ordinal rather than cardinal" (Robinson & Kurzban, 2006). That is, they address where on the continuum punishment should fall, but not what types of punishment should bracket the continuum.[10] Second, there is the question of why some jurors, in some cases, determine that a particular capital defendant deserves to die. Capital punishment in its "idealized" form has always assumed the existence of a group of heinous offenders, the worst of the worst, for whom there should be consensus that death is a just desert. Perhaps such a consensus could exist in theory – the "McVeigh Factor" has become a shorthand for the notion of crimes for which such a moral consensus might, hypothetically, come to exist (Sundby, 2006, p. 34; Sarat, 2001, p. 11). However, the idealized form bears little resemblance to the actual decision-making process engaged in by those faced with life or death decisions. In practice, the decision is – and always has been – heavily influenced by a host of variables unrelated to the nature and circumstances of the crime.

As Jeffrie Murphy recently observed (or, more accurately, characterized Nietzsche as observing) "our abstract theorizing – at least in moral theory – cannot fully be divorced from its social setting and from our own personal human psychology, a psychology that may affect us in ways of which we are not fully conscious" (Murphy, 2006). Murphy's own work, in which he unsparingly examines his evolving retributivist impulses, is instructive. He at one point admitted to – and indeed defended – an attitude of "retributive hatred," but later became wary of the hardness and arrogance of that attitude. He remains a "reluctant retributivist" (Murphy, 2006); the reluctance stemming from his awareness of the opacity of his own motives (Murphy, 1999). We should be similarly cautious when evaluating the fervent, frequent claim that retributivist philosophy in general, and retribution in sentencing in particular, are all about morality and justice, and not at all about emotion.

In contrast to standard retributivism, Robert Blecker has argued for what he terms emotive retributivism (Blecker, 2006). He argues that the death penalty is the just and even obligatory punishment for certain crimes, not as a matter of undifferentiated vengeance but as a means of giving voice to anger and rage toward the defendant and a way to show empathy for the victim's suffering. He argues that "moral desert can never be reduced strictly to reason, nor measured adequately by rational criteria: Forgiveness, love, anger, resentment are part of justice" (Blecker, 2003, p. 198). Once these emotional wellsprings of the legal and moral calculus are thus acknowledged, a more clear-eyed debate about retribution's proper role in our capital punishment system can take place.

Both the retributive philosophy and the retributive impulse are better understood with reference to the emotional dynamics that help shape our intuitions of justice. These intuitions are affected by social and political context, for example by societal views of crime and what needs to be done to keep us safe. The attitudes of the populace might be better understood with reference to the constellation of emotional factors that influence moral reasoning (Hauser, Young, & Cushman, 2006; Haidt, 2001), and specifically, those that influence our individual and collective experience of crime. Perceptions of crime level and the danger posed by crime are formed in light of pre-existing templates about how the world works.[11] The perceptions are also highly influenced by portrayals (e.g. media coverage or official pronouncements) that evoke strong emotions, including outrage, fear, the urge to blame and – too often – racial animus (Liebman et al., 2002; Baldus & Woodworth, 2004; Haney, 2005). Indeed, as Markus Dubber argues, it is difficult to assess the justice of a regime of punishment without considering its ability to promote empathy and "counteract the natural tendency of antipathy toward the offender" (Dubber, 2006, p. 117). The attitudes of individual capital jurors in particular might be better understood by examining all these same factors, as well as the anger, fear, compassion, empathy or prejudice elicited by capital defendants.

We might also gain a more dynamic understanding of how attitudes about what constitutes just punishment are communicated. Retributive theory is expressive: it assumes that punishment – via both its threat and its infliction – performs a signaling function (Markel, 2004), and thus is ostensibly concerned with the communication of norms and norm enforcement. Oddly, though, it pays little attention to how the signaling effect influences the measure of "just deserts." It fails to address how norms are communicated – both to the penal institutions and their actors, and to the populace.

It tends to assume a static model of top-down communication in which the signaling effect is achieved simply by the existence and enforcement of the law on the books (e.g. Markel, 2004, p. 1445). To put it another way, it tends to assume that the message is communicated in a vacuum, rather than in concert with other forces which might amplify or distort its meaning. It is doubtful that the dynamics of signaling are ever that simple, but we know that in the capital context, they are much more complex. Attitudes toward the appropriateness of the death penalty are not developed or passed along in a static, top-down manner. Positions on the death penalty both draw from and are aimed toward a broader, more unruly, more interactive pool of knowledge and misinformation.

The standard model fails to consider, for example, the "audience effect" on the punishment calculus: the notion that the presence of an audience increases the measure of moralistic punishment (Kurzban, DeScioli, & O'Brien, 2006). This effect has been documented in the death penalty context, for example in studies by Stephen Bright and Patrick Keenan (1995) and James Liebman (2000), which found that the prospect of running for re-election causes judges to render more – and more flawed – death sentences.[12]

The "just deserts" calculus, when the death penalty is at issue, is influenced by media coverage (Bandes, 2004), popular cultural representations of crime (Gross, 1998), elections and other political pressures (Robinson & Kurzban, 2006; Bright & Keenan, 1995; Liebman, 2000) and folk knowledge (Steiner, Bowers, & Sarat, 2001), all of which tend to traffic in fear, anger and prejudice (Lipschultz & Hilt, 2002; Bandes, 2004). The measure of just punishment, in the real world of capital litigation, is taken not in a vacuum, but in light of intense public pressure, raw emotion and political ambition.

Emile Durkheim may be correct that our attempts to redefine the emotions underlying our penalogical impulses are merely cosmetic (Durkheim, 1984, p. 46; Fisher & Chon, 1989, p. 4). At the very least, we mislead ourselves if we believe that the sanitized philosophical category of retribution does much work in explaining why we continue to execute.

DETERRENCE

The lack of attention to emotion's role in the debate about deterrence poses a different problem – how to account for the fact that those who rely on this rationale do not change positions when confronted with evidence that deterrence fails to work as advertised. Deterrence theory posits that capital punishment will dissuade others from committing similar crimes in the future, and that it will do so more effectively than alternative sentences like life imprisonment. (Carter & Kreitzberg, 2004). It is the most explicitly instrumental rationale for capital punishment, and the only one that makes what seems to be a testable empirical claim. Since capital punishment was held constitutional in the early 1970s, the deterrence rationale has been – until quite recently – the primary justification cited for support of the death penalty (Radelet & Borg, 2000). During the more than three decades of the modern death penalty era, as in earlier eras (Radelet & Borg, 2000), little support has emerged for the empirical claim on which deterrence theory is grounded. Studies have occasionally purported to find a deterrent effect (see e.g. Ehrlich, 1975, 1977 and Dezhbakhsh et al., 2003), though both the methodology of such studies and the uses made of their findings have been harshly criticized. See, for example, Fagan, Zimring and Geller (2006), collecting and summarizing critiques of Ehrlich; and Fagan et al. (2006), Berk (2005), critiquing the recent spate of studies purporting to find that the death penalty deters. The "empirical standoff" Justice Stewart identified in 1976 still exists. As John Donohue and Justin Wolfers sum up the current state of empirical knowledge:

> We are led to conclude that there exists profound uncertainty about the deterrent (or antideterrent) effect of the death penalty; the data tell us that capital punishment is not a major influence on homicide rates, but beyond this, they do not speak clearly. Further, we suspect that our conclusion that econometric studies are highly uncertain about the effects of the death penalty will persist for the foreseeable future.

Their bottom line: "Aggregating over all of our estimates, it is entirely unclear even whether the preponderance of evidence suggests that the death penalty causes more or less murder" (Donohue & Wolfers, 2005).[13]

In short, throughout the period during which deterrence was cited as the primary reason to execute, there was little if any reason to believe it worked.

By the late 1990s, the public was becoming disenchanted with the notion of deterrence: it saw rising rates of execution yet did not believe crime was decreasing. However, instead of withdrawing support for the death penalty, the populace simply shifted rationales. A decrease in support for the deterrence rationale began in the early 1990s, and has continued since (Gross, 1998). By 2004, only one-third of respondents to the Gallup Poll believed that the death penalty was a deterrent, compared to two-thirds in 1985 (Sundby, 2006, p. 29). Currently, "most Americans who favor the death penalty do so primarily for retributive reasons" (Gross, 1998, p. 453). As Sam Gross puts it, "changes in the level of belief in deterrence have had no obvious relationship to changes in support for the death penalty" (Gross, 1998, p. 454).

Put simply, in the capital context, the stated rationale is not very closely related to the depth or breadth of support. If we want to learn why people support capital punishment, and why, contrary to Justice Marshall's optimistic belief in the persuasive power of knowledge about the workings of the death penalty (*Furman v. Georgia*, 1972), they do not change their position in the face of information refuting the rationale for their support (Bohm, Clarke, & Aveni, 1990), we will have to look for less cognitively based explanations.[14] Or more accurately, we need to understand how beliefs which purport to be cognitively based are formed, and how, once formed, they are affected by additional information. As I will discuss later, such an understanding requires reckoning with the role of emotion.

INCAPACITATION

The incapacitation argument, when applied to the death penalty, holds that "we need to execute the most heinous killers in order to prevent them from killing again" (Radelet & Borg, 2000, p. 46). As one student guide puts it, "Obviously, a foolproof means of physically preventing a specific killer from ever killing again is to take his life" (Streib, 2005, p. 15). The label "incapacitation" has an almost scientific, clinical ring to it – it doesn't sound angry or uncivilized, the way the term "retribution" might. The emotional content of this justification operates below the radar. Yet the question posed is, inescapably, how we take the worth of a life. How do we decide a person is so irredeemable, and so threatening to our future safety, that he should be cast from the human community?[15] This question draws on deeply held attitudes that are not cognitively based, including perceptions and fears about crime, empathy or lack of empathy, and beliefs about mercy, forgiveness and adherence to rules (Tyler & Weber, 1982; Kahan & Braman, 2005).

In addition, as with the deterrence rationale, there is the question of whether these attitudes are open to reappraisal in the face of contrary evidence. Here the results are mixed, but the influence of emotion is clear. "Fear is one of the most prominent factors influencing jury decisions to impose capital sentences. Specifically, juries are fearful that even if they impose a sentence of life without parole, the defendant will be released and perhaps cause more harm" (Bandes, 2004, p. 595). This fear reflects both "erroneous folk knowledge about length of sentence" (Bandes, 2004, p. 595; Steiner, Bowers, & Sarat, 1999) and "pervasive media images of the world as a dangerous and violent place in which the criminal justice system has done too much for criminals and not enough to keep law-abiding citizens safe" (Bandes, 2004, pp. 595–596). On a hopeful note, once erroneous beliefs about length of sentence are acknowledged and addressed, they appear amenable to correction (Garvey, Johnson, & Marcus, 2000).

THE EXPRESSIVE RATIONALES COMPARED

The traditional theories of punishment have always generated unease and a sense that something essential about why we punish remains unexplained (Allen, 1999). When these theories are pressed into service to explain why we execute, their limitations are revealed to be particularly acute. The defects of the classical theories have motivated "expressive" theories[16] of punishment,

> under which punishment is inherently justified as a means of expressing symbolic defeats on wrong-doers, educating both criminals and law-abiding citizens, denouncing the criminal act and communicating the content of society's moral rules (Steele, 2001, p. 36).

David Garland recently observed that

> capital punishment is largely an expressive measure today, held in place chiefly by emotionally charged political considerations rather than by moral instrumental concerns such as deterrent crime control. (Garland, 2005, p. 349)

Assuming capital punishment is expressive, what does it express? Does it express a societal commitment to living by moral rules (Durkheim, 1984, p. 58); the strongest possible condemnation of those who break the rules (Feinberg, 1970); recognition of the moral worth of the victim (Murphy & Hampton, 1988); a desire to bring the victim's loved ones back into the community by giving voice to their anger and grief (Allen, 1999); the public enactment of revenge on the victim's behalf (Sarat, 2001); reassurance that the world is an orderly rather than a chaotic, unsafe place (Haney, 2005); a collective cry of outrage and pain (Durkheim, 1984), the desire to purge evil from the community (Lifton & Mitchell 2002, p. 251)? [17] The correct answer must be: all of the above, at least in some measure and at one time or another, and moreover, these expressive purposes are inextricably bound up with the instrumental concerns as well. The demarcation between traditional and expressive punishment leads us astray.

At the outset, I should note the confusion of the normative and descriptive that can muddy this debate. The traditional justifications for capital punishment are just that – arguments for the appropriateness of capital punishment. Expressive theories are sometimes billed as justifications for punishment, and sometimes as better, more accurate accounts of *why* we punish. Or at times, the very label "expressive" is used as a critique, counterpoising emotional and political concerns against instrumental, pragmatic concerns. As David Garland acutely observes, this way of dividing up penalogical purposes "implies a definite ranking" between an "instrumental part ... which gets things done" and a "symbolic part ... that is merely decorative or discursive and appears to have no substantive function" (Garland, 1990, p. 10).

The question of why the death penalty persists cannot be answered without reference to the expressive dimension of capital punishment. More accurately, the explanations are expressive all the way down. As I discussed above, retribution is explicitly expressive; all its benefits flow from the communication of the existence and implementation of punishment. Deterrence, though not often classified as such, is explicitly expressive as well. It is premised on the belief that would – be murderers will desist based on the advertised consequences to others before them. Punishment – and certainly capital punishment – is always a "deeply symbolic event" (Garland, 1990, p. 10) and we – as individuals and members of the polity – construct and understand that symbolism in a way that is not purely cognitive. Attitudes about whether the social order "requires" capital punishment, or about whether certain people "deserve" to die, or about which sorts of victims might be "owed" this punishment, are imbued with symbolic value. Moreover, they are premised on assumptions about how the world works and how it ought to work. There are no "moral instrumental" concerns or purely legal justifications that float free of emotional and political influence, or of communicative content. And just as our American death penalty is an expression of culture, politics, religion and other values, these values are themselves intricately tied to, and in many respects a product of, our emotional commitments.

THE ESSENTIAL ROLE OF EMOTION

The longstanding debate about the death penalty is intense, even polarized, despite (or perhaps, as I will discuss below, because of) the fact that the death penalty has little direct impact on most people (Ellsworth & Ross, 1983). To understand why our society continues to support the death penalty, and whether we are likely to abandon that support any time soon, we must first consider how people arrive at moral judgments and under what conditions they will reconsider these judgments. The standard assumption, and certainly the bedrock legal assumption, is that people encountering a moral dilemma engage in moral reasoning, that this reasoning leads to a judgment, and that "emotion may emerge from the judgment, but is not causally related to it" (Hauser et al., 2006). This assumption is noteworthy both for its chain of causality and for its treatment of moral reasoning as individual and internal. Although there is no unanimity about how moral reasoning works, it is fair to say that this standard model is under serious attack, particularly in light of recent findings in cognitive and social psychology calling its descriptive accuracy into question.

The phenomenon that perplexes those who study capital punishment, the stickiness of support for the death penalty even when the grounds for that support are shown to be spurious, is a nice illustration of what psychologist Jonathan Haidt calls "moral dumbfounding." He noted that groups interviewed about their attitudes toward hot button issues

were often "morally dumbfounded."; that is, they would stutter, laugh, and express surprise at their inability to find supporting reasons, yet they would not change their initial judgments ... (Haidt, 2001, p. 817)

This effect has been observed in numerous studies, many using neuro-imaging techniques like functional magnetic resonance imaging (fMRI) and positron emission tomography (PET) scans, whose results challenge the notion that moral reasoning is the cause, rather than the consequence, of moral judgment. These findings have generated alternative models of moral reasoning. For example, Haidt's social institutionalist model posits that emotion triggers judgment, and that reasoning occurs after judgment, offering a "post-hoc rationalization of an intuitively generated response" (Haidt, 2001). Another model, advanced by Antonio Damasio and others, posits that every moral judgment is the product of both emotion and reasoning (Damasio, 1994), or, alternatively, that emotion is triggered in moral dilemmas of a personal nature, whereas reason prevails in situations of a more impersonal nature (Greene, Sommerville, Nystrom, Darley, & Cohen, 2001; Hauser, 2006).

One problem with discussing and interpreting such theories, particularly across disciplines, is the lack of any agreed upon definition for the term *emotion*. To say, for example, that moral judgments are the product of both emotion and reason is to counterpoise the two terms and risk replicating an emotion/reason divide that should not be replicated (Bandes, 1999). This is not the proper place for an abstract discussion of this age-old problem, and as I argued earlier, a more complex understanding of the role of emotion renders the divide far less pronounced. For current purposes, an examination of the ways in which attitudes toward the death penalty are shaped will help illustrate both the malleability of the terms and the application of the moral reasoning debate to the question at hand.

If we categorize "deterrence," "retribution" and "incapacitation" as *reasons* for supporting the death penalty, and "fear" "forgiveness" and "outrage" as *emotions* that hijack the reasoning process, we will likely conclude, with the social scientists who have studied the matter, that "most people's attitudes toward capital punishment are basically emotional. The 'reasons' are determined by the attitude, not the reverse" (Ellsworth & Gross, 1994, p. 95). But if this conclusion implies that there is a realm of "pure reason" that could operate if only we could cordon off the emotions that continually interfere, then it should be approached with caution. Instead, social and emotional concerns are an inextricable part of the reasoning process itself.

Emotion affects our evaluation of capital punishment at the most basic level. Our pre-existing attitudes[18] about how the world works affect our beliefs about particular issues. Indeed, particularly when the attitudes are deeply held, they *protect* our beliefs from contradictory or threatening information. They affect the way we process and evaluate information. They affect *whether* we even consider new information, what category we assign it to, how much importance we give it and how much we care about it. Research on motivated reasoning has shown that when people become aroused – that is, motivated to arrive at a particular conclusion or to support a particular belief – they begin screening out contrary information at a very early stage. They search memory for beliefs, heuristics and rules that support their desired conclusion, but they do not realize that they are engaging in a biased process. They attempt to construct a persuasive rationale for their desired conclusion, so that it looks, even to them, as if they are engaging in an open-minded process of reasoning (Kunda, 1990, p. 495). Hence Haidt's "moral dumfoundedness effect": people are resistant to information that contradicts their pre-existing attitudes and often turn away such information at an early stage, but they are not conscious that they are doing this. (Kunda, 1990, p. 490; Bandes, 2006; Burke, 2006).

For example, how should the question of whether the death penalty is an effective deterrent be approached? It requires some notion of how people will behave when faced with the threat of draconian (and, in most cases uncertain) consequences. It also requires a sense of whether the draconian consequence of taking a life is called for. In order to answer these questions, people draw – intuitively or consciously – on their attitudes about how the world works. For example, some people see others as possessing fixed, unchanging moral traits; some see others' moral traits as malleable and dynamic (Dweck, Chiu, & Hong, 1995, p. 276). These assumptions about character and behavior will likely influence one's assessment of whether people can change their behavior in the face of threatened consequences (Blumenthal, 2006). Then there is the question of what sorts of people one might imagine when thinking about whether would-be murderers learn by example. What sorts of people are in the category of would-be murderers (Osofsky, Bandura, & Zimbardo, 2005)? Are they people for whom we might feel empathy or forgiveness, or evil, irredeemable people, or people from a different demographic world – one which may evoke hostility, fear or prejudice? Moreover, the question of whether the "ultimate" deterrent is necessary implicates emotion-laden attitudes about criminality, how it affects our safety, and how our safety might be best safeguarded. How fearful are we about the world around us? Does it feel chaotic and scary? Are we outraged by the government's failure to protect us and would we feel reassured if something visible and punitive were being done? What are our attitudes toward law enforcement – trusting and deferential or concerned about fallibility and corruption? Each of us shows up for the general debate with a worldview, and this worldview is emotional as well as cognitive.

Ellsworth and Ross found that attitudes toward the death penalty were emotionally based, and preceded, rather than stemmed from, reasoned beliefs, so that, for example, while "a belief in the relative deterrent efficacy of capital punishment is almost perfectly correlated with support for it ... this belief cannot be considered a major *reason* for this support" (Ellsworth & Ross, 1983, p. 162). Tom Tyler and Renee Weber, in a study seeking to measure whether support for the death penalty was instrumental or symbolic, concluded that "political and social attitudes are the major source of beliefs concerning the retributive value, deterrence value, and humanity of the death penalty" (Tyler & Weber, 1982, p. 41). They argued that the attitudes affecting death penalty support are basic, highly affective, pre-cognitive attitudes toward the world, such as liberalism, authoritarianism and dogmatism. These attitudes precede the formation of beliefs about particular issues, for example, beliefs about the value of retribution or deterrence, and the beliefs that develop will support the initially formed attitudes.

Tyler and Weber conclude that support for the death penalty is symbolic rather than instrumental. I draw a different lesson from these studies: that the distinction between the symbolic and the instrumental is not descriptively useful in this context. The way we view the world will affect both our notions of the efficacy of instrumental punishments and our sense of what punishment ought to express. In other words, those who support the death penalty will both think it works and agree with its symbolic message. For example, for those who see the world in terms of individual responsibility and deference to authority, the death penalty may seem to be a practical deterrent, and also a proper symbol; an expression of the strongest possible condemnation of deviant behavior. Those whose world-view encompasses concerns with racial inequality or societal causes of crime are likely to question the death penalty's ability to deter, and to disapprove of its symbolic repudiation of the possibility of forgiveness and redemption (Kahan & Braman, 2005, p. 157). The death penalty serves, always, as both a concrete policy and an abstract symbol – either of toughness, control and certainty or of inequality, vengeance and irreversible error. It projects a set of values, and to the extent those values are emotionally resonant, and consonant with the values of the population, it is viewed as legitimate (Baldus & Woodworth, 2004, p. 1427; Zimring, 2003, p. 127).

THE FEEDBACK LOOP

The emotional resonance that permits the death penalty to maintain its aura of legitimacy is a dynamic, interactional emotional state. The view of emotion as private and internal is a barrier to understanding a process that in fact takes shape in a social and cultural context[19] (Hochschild, 1983). Emotion exists in a complex feedback loop with institutions like the justice system. It has a role in shaping our institutions, and the institutions in turn have a role in shaping emotions – their expression, their display, and even, arguably, their inchoate nature. As Martha Nussbaum argues, we construct institutions that embody what we value (Nussbaum, 2001, p. 405). The continued existence of the death penalty is a societal declaration that death is the appropriate punishment for the most terrible crimes. This declaration rests on a complex and evolving legal/moral/emotional judgment about what we require in order to restore the sense of order and justice that are disturbed by a heinous crime. Thus, over the years, it has been possible to chart shifts, not only in public attitudes toward capital punishment, but in the emotional content and the emotional rhetoric of those attitudes.[20] For example, where once it was considered harsh and unenlightened to rely on retributive theory in support of the death penalty, in recent years it has become acceptable and common. As David Garland puts it,

> the background affect of policy is now more frequently a collective anger and a righteous demand for retribution than a commitment to a just, socially engineered solution. The emotional temperature of policymaking has shifted from cool to hot (Garland, 2001, pp. 10–11).

At the same time, the language of emotion and therapy has become welcome in the courtroom, as acknowledging the worth of victims and providing a forum for "closure" and healing to their survivors have become central goals of capital punishment (Zimring, 2003, pp. 57–63; Bandes, 1996a, 1996b, 2000a, 2000b). These institutional goals play a role in shaping emotions, by creating a set of emotional expectations that must be responded to. For example, the existence of the penalty has created an expectation that only capital punishment will truly honor the dignity and worth of the victim. This expectation has serious consequences. Despite the recommendations of numerous blue ribbon commissions to narrow the list of death eligible crimes, legislators come under pressure to expand the list in order to demonstrate the value of the lives of the victims in each category. As Scott Turow observed: "the fundamental equality of each survivor's loss creates an inevitable emotional momentum to expand the categories for death penalty eligibility" (Turow, 2003). Prosecutors routinely assure jurors that a death sentence is owed to the victim and the victim's survivors. Thus jurors are signaled that death is the default sentence, and that failure to impose it betrays the dead and the bereaved. Family members and other survivors of murder victims are encouraged to feel that they are entitled to a death sentence, and even that the failure to impose a death sentence is an additional infliction of pain they must bear.[21]

The trial court has been drafted into a therapeutic role, without much thought for whether it can or should serve that purpose (Henderson, 1985). Based on the questionable concept of closure, survivors[22] are assured that the execution will at last allow them to move on with their lives (Lithwick, 2006). Survivors have also been assured that only a death sentence can heal their wounds, and efforts to truncate the appellate process have been premised on the survivors' need to attain closure (Bandes, 2000a, 2000b; Zimring, 2003, pp. 57–63).

Thus the feedback loop perpetuates itself. We have the system we think we need, and it drives us to need the system we have. But the story is complicated. As Frank Zimring points out, the death penalty died in Western Europe despite broad popular support. It was abolished by those in leadership positions, and yet its abolition did not create an outcry from the populace (Zimring, 2003, pp. 22–24; Lifton & Mitchell, 2002, p. 247). It seems unlikely, at least in today's political climate, that U.S. leaders could (or would) play the same role,[23] and the reason is not so much the breadth of American support for the death penalty, but the intensity of the support. The differences between the European and American approaches to capital punishment raise complex historical, political and social questions which scholars like James Q. Whitman (2003), Garland, Lifton, Zimring and others have considered in depth, and which cannot be considered in detail here. My contention is that emotion theory, and particularly the role of salience, help illuminate the sources of that intensity, as well as a possible way to move the conversation forward.

SALIENCE

Salience is a term in technical use in psychology, neuroscience, semiotics and other disciplines. Although there are variations in meaning across and even within these disciplines, the term generally refers to the accessibility, intensity or attention-getting properties of an event or other entity, and so I will use it here (see e.g. Yen & Finkel, 2002). Salience is the key to understanding the role emotion plays in decision making. Emotion "acts as a great emphasizer and highlighter in the brain, an indicator of importance and urgency" (Goodenough & Prehn, 2004, p. 1717). It helps to determine what we will keep in the forefront of consciousness and what will drive us to act; for example what is salient. Salience helps explain, and may help change, both the societal and individual dynamics that have led to the persistence of capital punishment in the United States.

A unique aspect of the death penalty debate is the strange confluence between the broad intense public debate on the topic and the lack of personal exposure to the capital system. As Ellsworth and Gross observed:

> Capital punishment is an issue that is far removed from most people's direct experience.
> Few Americans have ever sat in the jury box or the dock in a capital case, or spent much

time with condemned prisoners, or known a victim well. And yet most people have opinions about capital punishment that are strong, definite, and difficult to change (Ellsworth & Gross, 1994, p. 161).

The intensity of public opinion on the topic is significant for a number of reasons. As we saw above, people often engage in motivated reasoning that leads them to ward off any information threatening to their beliefs. They go to great lengths to reaffirm what they "know," turning away conflicting specialized knowledge or subjecting it to different or higher standards of accuracy (Bohm, Clark, & Aveni, 1990, p. 181). As one researcher puts it, subjects would "twirl the emotional kaleidoscope until it gave them a picture that was comfortable" (Bedantam, 2006). People do not always reason this way, and in some cases they can be primed to strive for accuracy and therefore remain open to new information (O'Brien & Ellsworth, 2006). Motivated reasoning might be triggered by the need to feel good about, or reduce cognitive dissonance about, one's own actions and choices. Significantly, it might also arise from a desire to cling to strongly felt pre-existing beliefs about the world, even in situations that do not directly impinge upon one's life. It is not surprising that this effect has been observed in the capital punishment context (Lord, Ross, & Lepper, 1979; Baldus & Woodworth, 2004, p. 1431), a context in which Americans do not merely hold opinions, they "care a great deal" (Ellsworth & Gross, 1994, p. 161).

The intensity of belief contributes not only to the solidifying (or ossifying) of individual opinion, but to the polarization of group opinion. As Kahan and Braman observe, "the tendency of individuals to trust only those who share their orientation makes the belief-generative power of culture feed on itself" (Kahan & Braman, 2005, p. 154). Particularly with the sorts of symbolic, hot button issues that are "strongly connected to an individual's cultural identity" (Kahan & Braman, 2005, p. 164), the effect of additional information is often, perversely, to reinforce the chasm between opposing groups.

The deeply held feelings underlying the debate may be essential to understanding how the United States got left behind as most of the industrialized world moved toward abolition. As Zimring argues, although the top-down policy change in Western European countries did not much affect the breadth of support for the death penalty in those countries, it also did not provoke the backlash that would likely occur in the United States, in which the popular investment in the policy is much stronger (Zimring, 2003, p. 127; see also Whitman, 2003, p. 15).

The mix of intense emotional investment in the issue, polarization and lack of exposure to the facts on the ground is lethal. The conversation might begin couched in terms of deterrence or retribution, it might move to broader attitudinal claims about federalism, vigilantism and crime control, but it does not take long to get to the ultimate polarized place, in which one side is arguing for purging the society of evil and the other is calling the first side evil for advocating murder. At that level of high stakes abstraction, the prospects for nuanced conversation are bleak.

At this pass, salience is again relevant; indeed, it may offer the way out of the stalled conversation. At one level, the highly abstract conversation is peculiarly sensitive to high-profile events and trends. It has long been shaped by perceptions of violent crime, such as those driven by constant, sensationalized images of random, racialized violence (Haney, 2005; Bandes, 2004). It has been fueled by certain high visibility crimes, particularly the Oklahoma City bombings, which provided Timothy McVeigh, the poster boy for capital punishment. But it has also worked the other way, responding to the occasional high-profile execution of a sympathetic person, for example Karla Faye Tucker, and to high-profile exonerations like that of Rolando Cruz. These cases have elicited an accessible set of countervailing moral imperatives. The DNA exoneration cases in particular have been effective in part because they provide vivid, easy to grasp illustrations of the unfairness and immorality of executing someone who has been scientifically shown to be innocent.[24] Lifton and Mitchell argue that it was just this sort of moral outrage over individual miscarriages of justice that helped pave the way for abolition in some Western European countries (Lifton & Mitchell, 2002, p. 248).

But the exoneration cases illustrate a different, more nuanced point about salience. People are often able to pierce or move beyond abstractions when confronted with actual human lives in all their complex, messy concreteness. This is one well-known finding of the "trolley" experiments[25] examining the cognitive mechanisms that affect moral decision making. We approach a moral dilemma quite differently if we experience it as directly affecting us or those we care about (Greene et al., 2001). This difference has enormous significance for the death penalty on both the individual and societal levels.

One of the most important characteristics of the capital trial is the insistent message that the issue of whether the defendant should live or die is not an emotional issue. The very appearance of dispassionate process is an important part of the system's emotional landscape; a powerful implicit message to the jury as well as the other legal actors (Haney, 1997). The message is conveyed in many ways: *You are not making a profoundly disturbing ethical choice about the taking of a life. You are not directly responsible for the taking of a life; you are just one link in a complex chain.* That is, the conditions needed for moral disengagement are created, including the sanitizing of the decision to kill and the diffusion of responsibility for the decision (Haney, 1997; Osofsky et al., 2005). But jurors confronted with wrenching cases often find this dispassion and detachment impossible to attain. Scott Sundby quotes one such juror as saying, "You develop all these theories about the death penalty and the criminal justice system, but being in it is different. You come to grips with what you really think and feel" (Sundby, 2005, p. 171). Alex Kotlowitz described how a jury of men and women who strongly favored the death penalty as an abstract matter came to spare the life of Jeremy Gross, a capital defendant whom they had convicted of a brutal murder. He recounts how the jury, learning about Gross's own brutal childhood, gradually came to understand him and even to empathize with various aspects of his life. At first, jurors could not look him in the eye, and they adjudged him to be cold and indifferent. As they got to know more about him, they reread his demeanor, viewing what they initially thought was indifference to be shame. Their empathetic connection was crucial to their eventual decision to spare him (Kotlowitz, 2003).

Making the stakes concrete will not always work against the death penalty. Prosecutors use victim impact statements, for example, to make the victim's suffering salient and thereby encourage a death sentence.[26] Nevertheless, defense attorneys understand how crucial it is that juries hear the more elusive counter-narrative of the defendant's humanity; and that they do not distance themselves from the defendant's pain, the possibility of his redemption, and their own responsibility in determining his fate (Bandes, 1996a, 1996b).

As Scott Sundby recently observed, the death penalty might die because of a sea change, or because of a "death by a thousand cuts" (Sundby, 2006). Either scenario depends on piercing the veil of abstraction. There is ample evidence that the death penalty is at its most desirable when at its most abstract and symbolic. When people are confronted with concrete information about actual defendants,[27] the mechanics of lethal injection or other execution methods, or alternatives like life without parole, support for the death penalty lessens considerably (Haney, 2005, p. 90). As Lifton and Mitchell put it

> people embrace the principle as a psychological source of security – which turns out to be fragile because it is readily threatened by whatever reminds them that execution is a form of killing (Lifton & Mitchell, 2002, p. 252).

CONCLUDING THOUGHTS: CLAIMING THE EMOTIONAL TERRAIN

The debate about the death penalty is too often conducted in parallel rhetorical worlds. The traditional discussion about the purposes of punishment is based on assumptions about what count as legally and philosophically rigorous grounds for punishment. It divides up the world in a way that relegates certain concerns to the devalued realm of the decorative, the symbolic and the emotional, and views this realm as soft and illegitimate. When legal scholars, jurists and social scientists participate in the discussion on such terms, they become demoralized by the disconnect between "proper" reasons and the actual dynamics of the death penalty. I suggest that this disconnect is in part based on a misunderstanding about the role of emotion in the reasoning process. As I have often argued, the idea that emotion pervades the law poses a threat to law's most cherished self-conception. Unfortunately, to ward off that idea is simply to perpetuate and insulate the current emotional landscape; not to banish emotion from the legal process. In the conventional view, opposition to capital punishment is often denigrated as emotional and moral, and therefore lacking in the rationality and tough-mindedness the law requires. Yet those who support the death penalty tend to be driven by passion as well, a passion that is not fueled by legal, doctrinal concerns. The current system of capital punishment is rife with fear, anger, selective empathy, blame and the desire for revenge; all clothed or camouflaged in the language of rational legality. To avoid the discussion is simply to cede the ground.

We can allow ourselves to be borne along on waxing and waning emotional tides – fears, panics and sympathies – or we can address the emotional issues directly. Arguably, the direct approach proved quite successful for the pro-capital punishment camp; the emotional meaning of capital punishment evolved noticeably in the face of the victims' rights movement. When the deterrence rationale began to lose force, the new language of therapeutic healing and closure provided a way to maintain support without facing the ugly question of how much retribution resembles revenge.

The death penalty thrives under a set of rules, explicit and implicit, about what sorts of emotions can be displayed and even experienced in the legal arena. These rules encourage moral disengagement and discourage empathy. They keep the concrete reality of the death penalty at a safe remove. Many of those who support the death penalty do so in the abstract. Their support often wanes when they become viscerally aware of the fact that capital punishment involves the killing of human beings. Certain realities need to be made salient: the humanity and individuality of each capital defendant, the horror of the execution itself and the fact that each of us is implicated in and responsible for each execution and for the system that facilitates state-sponsored killing. These realities are at the moral and emotional center of the American system of capital punishment, and they should be at the center of the debate about its fate. They should incite passion and commitment. When that happens on a broad scale, the death penalty will die its well-deserved death.

NOTES

1. Moreover, the public opinion data is then cited in court opinions seeking to measure community attitudes (Haney, 2005, p. 78, discussing *Furman*, in which public opinion was discussed in five of the Justices' nine separate opinions).

2. For example, Justice Brennan's dissent in *Saffle v. Parks*, in which the jury had received an anti-sympathy instruction, quotes the prosecutor's language at length. At voir dire, in commenting on the instruction, the prosecutor told the jury, "And that's just as cold-blooded as you can put it ... You can be as sympathetic as you want to ... but you can't do it and sit on this jury." In his closing argument he said, among other similar comments, "You're not yourself putting Robyn Parks to death. You just have become a part of the criminal justice system that says when anyone does this, that he *must* suffer death. So all you are doing is you're just following the law ... it's not on your conscience ... God's law is the very same ... So don't let it bother your conscience, you know." (494 U.S. 1257, 1272–1273 n13, 1990).

3. See generally Craig Haney's book, *Death by Design*, for discussion of the many ways in which the capital punishment system is structured to create distance from the moral and emotional dimensions of the decision. As Scott Sundby observed, aggravating factors like "especially heinous" or "vile" give the jurors arguing for a death sentence a "legal" factor that they can point to and say "see the law requires this – it is right here on the verdict form." Letter from Scott Sundby to Susan Bandes, August 8, 2006.

4. "The witnesses ... will behold Callins *v.* Collins (1994) no longer a defendant, an appellant, or a petitioner, but a man, strapped to a gurney, and seconds away from extinction" (510 U.S. 1141, 1143, 1994).

5. This is the theory of general deterrence. The theory of specific deterrence differs: it refers to the ability of punishment to deter the particular defendant from committing other crimes. There is some ambiguity in the literature as to the use of the terms "specific deterrence" and "incapacitation." Execution seems better described as incapacitating, in that it makes it impossible for the defendant to commit more crimes, rather than deterring the defendant, which implies that it will convince him not to repeat the conduct (see Victor L. Streib, Death Penalty in a Nutshell, 15, 2005).

6. Although Paul Robinson argues for the category of "empirical desert." See Note 8. Robinson and Robert Kurzban, for example, have conducted empirical

studies attempting to measure moral intuitions about punishment (see Robinson and Kurzban, 2006).

7. Of course, all the aforementioned categorizations are highly oversimplified and indeed problematic. For example, retributive theory is sometimes characterized as utilitarian – it reaffirms the value of observing the law, thus creating a safer society. See e.g. Jeffrie Murphy, Legal Moralism and Retribution Revisited (Presidential Address to the American Philosophical Association, Pacific Division, March 24, 2006).

8. In a recent article, Paul Robinson argued that the term encompasses three separate concepts which are used without sufficient distinction: vengeful desert (which focuses on the harm to the victim), deontological desert (which focuses on the blameworthiness of the wrongdoer) and empirical desert (which focuses on measuring the punishment commensurate with the community's intuitions of justice) (see Robinson, 2006).

9. Mary Sigler critiques Martha Nussbuam for collapsing retribution, retributivism and retributive anger. Sigler distinguishes retribution (a compensating reaction designed to restore the balance upset by an initial action) and retributivism (a theory of punishment based on the moral blameworthiness of wrongdoers, predicated on the assumption that the blameworthy are deserving of punishment) from retributive anger, which assumes anger and cruel excess (see Mary Sigler, 2000).

10. See Hugo A. Bedau, Retributivism and the Theory of Punishment, 75, Journal of Philosophy, 601, 613 (1978):

Although there may be little difficulty in making uniform judgments of ordinal culpability ... or of ordinal harmfulness, there is no unique non-arbitrary way to combine these judgments into one judgment of ordinal seriousness. ... Even if that problem is solved, and even if a plausible penalty scale can be constructed in terms of ordinal severity ... there is no unique non-arbitrary way to identify the severity of the appropriate punishment, given only the severity of the crime ...

11. For an interesting treatment of the acute challenges pre-existing and preconscious assumptions (and the courts' unwillingness to address them) pose in a context other than capital punishment. See Andrew E. Taslitz (2005).

12. See also Justice O'Connor's concurring opinion in *Republican Party of Minnesota v. White*, 536 U.S. 765, 788 (2002), raising concerns about whether judges subject to reelection can decide controversial cases without violating the due process clause, and citing Bright and Keenan's findings (see also Freedman & Smith, 2004, p. 248–249, discussing the due process issue).

13. But see Paul H. Rubin, Reply to Donohue and Wolfers on the Death Penalty and Deterrence, The Economist's Voice 3. Available at http://www.bepress.com/ev/vol13/iss5/art4 (last visited June 11, 2006).

14. Nor does the efficacy of deterrence explain why people oppose the death penalty. As Ellsworth and Gross note, there are not nearly so many polls tracking the attitudes of death penalty opponents. The polls suggest that most opponents would continue to oppose the death penalty even if it were an effective deterrent. Their opposition tends to be based on the moral conviction that capital punishment is wrong, rather than on utilitarian considerations (Ellsworth & Gross, 1994, p. 19).

15. There is a sense in which one might approach this as an empirical question, or rather two closely related empirical questions. The first is whether there is a class of murderers who are so dangerous, such committed recidivists, that if they were freed

they would kill again. The second is whether execution is the only way, or the best way, to prevent such people from killing again. Both questions have been approached empirically. On the issue of recidivism, for example, a study was done to determine how many of those whose death sentences were commuted after *Furman* went on to kill again (Marquart & Sorensen, 1989; reprinted in Bedau, 1997), and it determined that only about one percent went on to kill again, about the same as the number later found to be innocent (Radelet & Borg, 2000, p. 46). On the issue of whether execution is necessary to incapacitate for life, there is empirical evidence that, under modern penal conditions and in light of the availability of life imprisonment without parole, prison is equally effective. (Radelet & Borg, 2000, p. 46).

16. There is a rich literature about the expressive functions law serves, not only in the punishment context, but more generally (see e.g. Cass R. Sunstein, 1996: On the Expressive Function of Law).

17. Another fascinating point for debate is whether these expressions are political and fluid, as David Garland suggests, (Garland, 2005) or cultural and more deeply rooted, as Frank Zimring suggests (Zimring, 2003).

18. Attitude is sometimes defined as "the psychological predisposition or tendency to respond to an entity with a positive or negative evaluation" (Herek, 2004, p. 17). Dan Kahan refers to what he calls "cultural commitments," (Kahan & Braman 2005, p. 148) and others refer to "implicit theories" (Dweck et al., 1995, p. 276). These terms generally refer to the same concept: templates about how the world works and how people behave, not necessarily consciously held.

19. Recently, albeit more than two decades after the publication of her landmark work. The *Managed Heart*, the field of sociology has taken up Arlie Hochschild's challenge to consider emotion in dynamic, institutional contexts, as exciting new work addresses the sociology of emotions (see e.g. Turner & Stets, 2005).

20. See, for example, V.A.C. Gatrell's The Hanging Tree: Execution and the English People, 1770–1868 (Oxford: Oxford University Press, 1994), and Randall McGowen, A Powerful Sympathy: Terror, the Prison, and Humanitarian Reform in Early Nineteenth-Century Britain, The Journal of British Studies, 25, 312–334, (1986) discussing the shifts in the emotional meaning of public execution – and in the evolution in "public emotion" generally, in eighteenth and nineteenth century Britain.

21. For more extensive discussion of the role of victims and the concept of closure in capital cases, see Bandes, 1996a, 1996b, 2000a, 2000b.

22. The question of who should be treated as a survivor for this purpose is sometimes complex, and never more so than in prosecutions for mass murder. See, for example, Wayne Logan's discussion of the use of victim impact testimony in the sentencing hearing of Zacharias Moussaoui for his role in the September 11 attacks. As Logan recounts, the court permitted former mayor Rudolph Guliani and others to testify to the impact of the murders on institutional victims like the New York Police Department and the City of New York, a decision which greatly upset some of those who lost close relatives in the attack (Logan, 2008).

23. Taking a strong position against the death penalty is generally a surefire recipe for political suicide. See e.g. Alan Berlow, The Wrong Man at 80, The Atlantic Monthly, November 1999, ("it is highly implausible that a candidate who refused to

take a strong position in favor of the death penalty {in a judicial election race} could be elected" (see also Bandes, 2004, pp. 595–596; Kropf, 2006 (quoting William W. Wilkins, chief judge of the U.S. Court of Appeals, Fourth Circuit, as saying "No one {in South Carolina} can be elected to statewide office who is opposed to the death penalty.")

24. However, the Supreme Court has been highly reluctant to recognize claims of actual innocence, or to ease the procedural barriers to their recognition. See e.g. *Schlup v. Delo*, 513 U.S. 298 (1995) (creating high bar for habeas petitioners seeking to avoid procedural default through claim of actual innocence) and *Herrara v. Collins*, 506 U.S. 390 (1993) (creating extraordinarily high bar for habeas petitioners seeking to raise freestanding claims of actual innocence). Most recently, in *Bell v. House*, 539 U.S. 937 (2003), the Court appeared to suggest that the lower courts had been a bit too demanding in their application of the *Schlup* standard. Yet the Court declined to find the *Herrara* standard met in that case, despite recognizing that it was more likely than not that no reasonable juror would have lacked a reasonable doubt of the suspect's guilt had the juror been privy to the now-available DNA evidence. See also Susan Bandes, Simple Murder: A Comment on the Legality of Executing the Innocent, 44, Buffalo Law Review, 537 (1996). See also Shaw (2006), Wrong on Wrongful Executions, contradicting Justice Scalia's recent claim in his concurrence in *Kansas v. Marsh* that there has not been "a single case – not one – in which it is clear that a person was executed for a crime he did not commit." *Kansas v. Marsh*, 126 S. Ct. 2516, 2533 (2006).

25. These are artificial dilemmas, whose parameters can be manipulated, which are designed to test the dynamics of moral judgment. One well-known study concluded that those dilemmas experienced as personal affected different areas of the brain and led to different moral reasoning processes from those experienced as impersonal. Greene, Joshua D., Sommerville, R. Brian, Nystrom, Leigh E., Darley, John M. and Cohen, Jonathan D., An fMRI Investigation of Emotional Engagement in Moral Judgment. Science 293, 2105 (2001). But see Hauser (2006) (questioning whether the impersonal/personal dichotomy explains results of studies).

26. The Moussaoui verdict was interesting in this regard. Moussaoui is the only person yet to be tried in a U.S. courtroom for the September 11 attacks. More than three dozen family members of those killed in the attacks gave victim impact testimony. The jury (which was reportedly quite divided on the issue) did not sentence Moussaoui to death, partly because of lingering doubt about his role in the plot. As the *New York Times* put it, "The Moussaoui jury acted as capital juries typically do. It accepted the government's argument in the abstract, but when push came to shove, it stopped short of sending the defendant to his death" (Adam Liptak, Moussaoui Verdict Highlights Where Juries Fear to Tread, The New York Times as A21, May 5, 2006).

27. Or, for that matter, actual victims and survivors, some of whom do not want the death penalty. Bandes (1996a, 1996b, 2000a, 2000b). The voices of victims are sometimes suppressed in capital sentencing hearings when they do not advance the prosecution agenda. For example, in the sentencing hearing of Timothy McVeigh, the prosecution barred testimony by the mother of a child killed in the Oklahoma City bombing because she opposed the death penalty (Bandes, 1999, p. 341).

ACKNOWLEDGMENTS

I wish to thank Austin Sarat for inviting me to write this chapter, and Joe Rollins and Scott Sundby for valuable comments on earlier drafts. I am also grateful to the faculty of New York Law School, and particularly Robert Blecker, the faculty of Temple Law School, and particularly Peter Huang, Eleanor Myers, Muriel Morisey and Mark Rahdert, for their collegiality and their incisive comments on this chapter . Finally, I am grateful to the anonymous reviewer for very helpful comments.

REFERENCES

Allen, D. S. (1999). Democratic disease: Of anger and the troubling nature of punishment. In: S. Bandes (Ed.), *The passions of law* (pp. 191–216). New York: New York University Press.

Baldus, D. C., & Woodworth, G. (2004). Race discrimination and the legitimacy of capital punishment: Reflections on the interaction of fact and perception. *DePaul Law Review, 53*, 1411–1496.

Bandes, S. (1996a). Empathy, narrative, and victim impact statements. *University of Chicago Law Review, 63*, 361–412.

Bandes, S. (1996b). Simple murder: A comment on the legality of executing the innocent. *Buffalo Law Review, 44*, 501–525.

Bandes, S. (1999). Victim standing. *Utah Law Review*, 331–347.

Bandes, S. (2000a). When victims seek closure: Forgiveness, vengeance and the role of government. *Fordham Urban Law Journal, 27*, 1599–1606.

Bandes, S. (2000b). *The passions of law.* New York: New York University Press.

Bandes, S. (2004). Fear factor: The role of media in covering and shaping the death penalty. *Ohio State Journal of Criminal Law, 1*, 585–597.

Bandes, S. (2006). Loyalty to one's convictions: The prosecutor and tunnel vision. *Howard Law Journal, 49*, 475–494.

Bedantam, S. (2006). How the brain helps partisans admit no gray. *Washington Post*, July 31.

Berk, R. (2005). New claims about executions and general deterrence: Déjà vu all over again? *Journal of Empirical Legal Studies, 2*, 303–330.

Blecker, R. (2003). Roots: Resolving the death penalty: Wisdom from the ancients. In: J. Acker, R. Bohn & C. Lanier (Eds), *America's experiment with capital punishment: Reflections on the past, present, and future of the ultimate penal sanction* (2nd ed., pp. 169–231). Durham, NC: Carolina Academic Press.

Blecker R. (2006) The encyclopedia of American civil liberties. In: P. Finkleman (Ed.), *Entry on retribution* (p.1329). Oxford: Routledge.

Blumenthal, J. (2006). *Implicit theories and capital sentencing: An experimental study.* Available on SSRN at http://ssrn.com/abstract = 909603

Bohm, R. M., Clarke, L. J., & Aveni, A. F. (1990). The influence of knowledge on reasons for death penalty opinions: An experimental test. *Justice Quarterly, 7*, 175–188.

Bright, S. B., & Keenan, P. J. (1995). Judges and the politics of death: Deciding between the bill of rights and the next election in capital cases. *Boston University Law Review, 75,* 759–835.

Burke, A. S. (2006). Improving prosecutorial decision making: Some lessons of cognitive science. *William and Mary Law Review, 47,* 1587–1633.

Carter, L. E., & Kreitzberg, E. (2004). *Understanding capital punishment law.* Newark, NJ: LexisNexis.

Damasio, A. (1994). *Descartes' error.* Boston, MA: Norton.

Dezhbakhsh, H., Rubin, P., & Shepherd, J. (2003). Does Capital punishment have a deterrent effect? New evidence from postmoratorium panel data. *American Law and Economics Review, 5,* 344–376.

Donohue, J., & Wolfers, J. (2005). Uses and abuses of statistical evidence in the death penalty debate. *Stanford Law Review, 58,* 791–846.

Dubber, M. D. (2006). *The sense of justice: Empathy in law and punishment.* New York: New York University Press.

Duff, R. A. & Garland, D. (Eds). (1995). *A reader on punishment (Oxford readings in socio-legal studies).* New York: Oxford University Press.

Durkheim, E. (1984). In: W. D. Halls (Ed.), *The division of labor in society.* New York: Free Press.

Dweck, C. S., Chiu, C. C., & Hong, Y. Y. (1995). Implicit theories and their role in judgments and reactions: A world from two perspectives. *Psychological Inquiry, 6,* 267–285.

Ehrlich, I. (1975). The deterrent effect of capital punishment: A question of life and death. *American Economic Review, 65,* 347–417.

Ehrlich, I. (1977). Capital punishment and deterrence: Some further thoughts and additional evidence. *Journal of Political Economy, 85,* 741–788.

Ellsworth, P. C., & Gross, S. R. (1994). Hardening of the attitudes: Americans' views on the death penalty. *Journal of Social Issues, 50,* 19–52.

Ellsworth, P. C., & Ross, L. (1983). Public opinion and capital punishment: A close examination of the views of abolitionists and retentionists. *Crime and Delinquency, 29,* 116–169.

Fagan, J., Zimring, F. E., & Geller, A. (2006). Capital punishment and capital murder: Market share and the deterrent effects of the death penalty. *Texas Law Review, 84,* 1803–1807.

Feinberg, J. J. (1970). *'The expressive function of punishment.' Doing and deserving.* Princeton, NJ: Princeton University Press.

Fisher, G. A., & Chon, K. K. (1989). Durkheim and the social construction of emotions. *Social Psychology Quarterly, 52,* 1–9.

Freedman, M. H., & Smith, A. (2004). *Understanding lawyers' ethics* (3rd ed.). Newark, NJ: LexisNexis.

Garland, D. (1990). Frameworks of inquiry in the sociology of punishment. *The British Journal of Sociology, 41,* 1–15.

Garland, D. (2001). *The culture of control: Crime and social order in contemporary society.* Chicago, IL: The University of Chicago Press.

Garland, D. (2005). Capital punishment and American culture. *Punishment and Society, 7,* 347–376.

Garvey, S. P., Johnson, S. L., & Marcus, P. (2000). Correcting deadly confusion: Responding to jury inquiries in capital cases. *Cornell Law Review, 85,* 627–655.

Gerstein, R. S. (1974). Capital punishment – "cruel and unusual?": A retributivist response. *Ethics, 85*, 75–79.

Goodenough, O. R., & Prehn, K. (2004). A neuroscientific approach to normative judgment in law and justice. *Philosophical Transactions of the Royal Society of London Series B, 359*, 1709–1726.

Greene, J. D., Sommerville, R. B., Nystrom, L. E., Darley, J. M., & Cohen, J. D. (2001). An fMRI investigation of emotional engagement in moral judgment. *Science, 293*, 2105–2108.

Greenhouse, L. (2005). *Becoming justice Blackmun: Harry Blackmun's Supreme Court journey.* New York: Times Books.

Gross, S. R. (1998). Update: American public opinion on the death penalty – it's getting personal. *Cornell Law Review, 83*, 1448–1462.

Haidt, J. (2001). The emotional dog and its rational tail: A social intuitionist approach to moral judgment. *Psychological Review, 108*, 814–834.

Haney, C. (1997). Violence and the capital jury: Mechanisms of moral disengagement and the impulse to condemn to death. *Stanford Law Review, 49*, 1447–1486.

Haney, C. (2005). *Death by design: Capital punishment as a social psychological system.* New York: Oxford University Press.

Hauser, M., Young, L., & Cushman, F. (2006). Reviving rawls' linguistic analogy: Operative principles and the causal structure of moral actions. In: W. Sinnott-Armstrong (Ed.), *Moral psychology and biology.* New York: Oxford University Press.

Henderson, L. N. (1985). The wrongs of victims' rights. *Stanford Law Review, 37*, 937.

Hochschild, A. (1983). *The managed heart: Commercialization of human feeling.* Berkeley: University of California Press.

Kahan, D. M., & Braman, D. (2005). Cultural cognition and public policy. *Yale Law & Policy Review, 24*, 147–169.

Kotlowitz, A. (2003). In the face of death. *The New York Times Magazine*, July 6.

Kropf, S. (2006). Judge discusses death penalty. *The Charleston post and courier*, September 15.

Kunda, Z. (1990). The case for motivated reasoning. *Psychological Bulletin, 108*, 480–498.

Kurzban, R., DeScioli, P., & O'Brien, E. (2006). Audience effects on moralistic punishment. Available at http://www.psych.upenn.edu/PLEEP/pdfs/in press Kurzban DeScioli Obrien.pdf

Liebman, J. S. (2000). The overproduction of death. *Columbia Law Review, 100*, 2030–2156.

Liebman, J. S., Gelman, A., Davies, G., Fagan, J., West, V., & Kiss, A. (2002). A broken system: Part II: Why there is so much error in capital cases, and what can be done about it. Available at http://www.law.columbia.edu/brokensystem2/report.pdf

Lifton, R. J., & Mitchell, G. (2002). *Who owns death?: Capital punishment, the American conscience, and the end of executions.* New York: HarperCollins.

Lipschultz, J. H., & Hilt, M. L. (2002). *Crime and local television news: Dramatic, breaking, and live from the scene.* Mahwah, NJ: Lawrence Erlbaum Associates, Inc.

Lithwick, D. (2006). Does Killing really give closure? *Washington Post*, March 26.

Logan, W. (2008). Confronting evil: Victims' rights in an age of terror. *Georgetown Law Journal, 96*.

Lord, C. G., Ross, L., & Lepper, M. R. (1979). Biased assimilation and attitude polarization: The effects of prior theories on subsequently considered evidence. *Journal of Personality and Social Psychology, 47*, 2098–2109.

Markel, D. (2004). Against mercy. *Minnesota Law Review, 88*, 1421–1480.

Murphy, J. (1999). Moral epistemology, the retributive emotions, and the "clumsy moral philosophy" of Jesus Christ. In: S. Bandes (Ed.), *The passions of law* (pp. 149–167). New York: New York University Press.

Murphy, J. (2006). *Legal moralism and retribution revisited*. Presidential Address, American Philosophical Association, Pacific Division, delivered on March 24, 2006.

Murphy, J., & Hampton, J. (1988). *Forgiveness and mercy*. Cambridge, MA: Cambridge University Press.

Nussbaum, M. C. (2001). *Upheavals of thought: The intelligence of emotions*. Cambridge, MA: Cambridge University Press.

O'Brien, B., & Ellsworth, P. C. (2006). Confirmation bias in criminal investigations, September 19. Available at SSRN: http://ssrn.com/abstract=913357

Osofsky, M. J., Bandura, A., & Zimbardo, P. G. (2005). The role of moral disengagement in the execution process. *Law and Human Behavior, 29*, 371–393.

Owens, E. C., & Elshtain, E. P. (2004). Religion and capital punishment: An introduction. In: E. C. Owens, J. D. Carlson & E. P. Elshtain (Eds), *Religion and the death penalty: A call for reckoning* (pp. 1–22). Grand Rapids, MI: Wm B. Eerdsmans Publishing Co.

Radelet, M. L., & Borg, M. J. (2000). The changing nature of death penalty debates. *Annual Review of Sociology, 26*, 43–61.

Robinson, P. H. (2006). *Competing conceptions of modern desert: Vengeful, deontological, and empirical*. University of Pennsylvania Law School, Public Law Working Paper No. 06-32. Available at SSRN: http://ssrn.com/abstract=924917

Robinson, P., & Kurzban, R. (2006). *Intuitions of justice*. University of Pennsylvania. Law School, Public Law Working Paper No. 06-20. Available at http://ssrn.com/abstract= 887958

Sarat, A. (2001). *When the state kills: Capital punishment and the American condition*. Princeton: Princeton University Press.

Shaw, T. M. (2006). Wrong on wrongful executions, *The Washington Post*, July 2.

Sigler, M. (2000). The story of justice: Retribution, mercy, and the role of emotions in the capital sentencing process. *Law and Philosophy, 19*, 339–367.

Steele, J. (2001). A seal pressed in the hot wax of vengeance: A Girardian understanding of expressive punishment. *Journal of Law and Religion, 16*, 35–68.

Steiner, B. D., Bowers, W. J., & Sarat, A. (1999). Folk knowledge as legal action: Death penalty judgments and the tenet of early release in a culture of mistrust and punitiveness. *Law and Society Review, 33*, 461–505.

Streib, V. L. (2005). *Death penalty in a nutshell*. St. Paul, MN.: Thomson/West.

Sundby, S. E. (2005). *A life and death decision: A jury weighs the death penalty*. New York: Palgrave MacMillan.

Sundby, S. E. (2006). The death penalty's future: Charting the crosscurrents of declining death sentences and the McVeigh factor. *Texas Law Review, 84*, 1929–1972. Available at http://ssrn.com/abstract=909176

Sunstein, C. R. (1996). On the expressive function of law. *University of Pennsylvania Law Review, 144*, 2021–2053.

Taslitz, A. E. (2005). Willfully blinded: On date rape and self-deception. *Harvard Journal Law and Gender, 28*, 381–446.

Turner, J., & Stets, J. E. (2005). *The sociology of emotions*. New York: Cambridge University Press.

Turow, S. (2003). To kill or not to kill: Coming to terms with capital punishment. *The New Yorker*, January 6.

Tyler, T., & Weber, R. (1982). Support for the death penalty: Instrumental response to crime, or symbolic attitude? *Law and Society Review, 17*, 21–44.

Whitman, J. Q. (2003). *Harsh justice: Criminal punishment and the widening divide between America and Europe*. New York: Oxford University Press.

Yen, S.-C., & Finkel, L. H. (2002). *Encyclopedia of the human brain* (Vol. 4). Holland: Elsevier Science.

Zimring, F. E. (2003). *The contradictions of American capital punishment*. New York: Oxford University Press.

CASES CITED

California v. Brown, 479 U.S. 538 (1986).

Callins v. Collins, 510 U.S. 1141 (1994) (cert. denied) (Blackmun, J., dissenting).

Furman v. Georgia, 408 U.S. 238 (1972).

Herrara v. Collins, 506 U.S. 390 (1993).

Schlup v. Delo, 513 U.S. 298 (1995).

Bell v. House, 539 U.S. 937 (2003).

Republican Party of Minnesota v. White, 536 U.S. 765 (2002).

RULE OF LAW ABOLITIONISM

Benjamin S. Yost

ABSTRACT

In the dark days of the 1980s and 1990s, the abolition of capital punishment was virtually unthinkable. However, a new form of abolitionism – which I call Rule of Law abolitionism – has raised the hopes of death penalty opponents. In this chapter, I elucidate the logic of the Rule of Law abolitionist argument, distinguishing it from its more familiar doctrinal and moral variants. I then assess its strengths and weaknesses. On the basis of this critique, I indicate the route Rule of Law abolitionism must travel to bring about the demise of the death penalty.

The 1980s and 1990s were dark days for death penalty abolitionists. Rabid public support for capital punishment combined with the Supreme Court's attacks on federal habeas corpus made abolition virtually unthinkable. However, the emergence of a new form of abolitionism, coupled with the growing power of the moratorium movement, has occasioned a remarkable improvement in the abolitionist mood. I call this abolitionism "Rule of Law abolitionism."

While certain versions of Rule of Law abolitionism, most notably the "new abolitionism" or "legally conservative abolitionism" championed by Austin Sarat, have been discussed in the literature; there has been insufficient analysis of its conceptual claims. This chapter will remedy this oversight by illuminating the structure, logic, and specific content shared by

Special Issue: Is the Death Penalty Dying?
Studies in Law, Politics, and Society, Volume 42, 53–89
ISSN: 1059-4337/doi:10.1016/S1059-4337(07)00403-6

different versions of Rule of Law abolitionism. Doing so will enable us to understand better the strengths and weaknesses of Rule of Law abolitionism, which is crucial if we are to evaluate how, and to what degree, it might contribute to the demise of capital punishment. This investigation is especially important given the organizing premise of this volume: the abolitionist movement is at a rare moment of opportunity, as the death penalty has come under attack from unusual political, cultural, and religious quarters.

Rule of Law abolitionism eschews controversial moral theory and futile disagreement with the Supreme Court's recent Eighth Amendment jurisprudence. Instead, it stands on intuitive, non-polemical assertions about the value of legal institutions. In the first part of the chapter, I compare Rule of Law abolitionism to more familiar types of abolitionism: (a) moral abolitionism, which argues that the death penalty violates substantive moral values; and more importantly (b) doctrinal abolitionism, which argues that the death penalty violates the U.S. Constitution. I then detail the conceptual contours of Rule of Law abolitionism, with frequent reference to the essays of Austin Sarat, Justice Harry Blackmun's *Callins* dissent, and seminal cases in the Supreme Court's capital jurisprudence. (As the reader will see, my conception of Rule of Law abolitionism is heavily indebted to Austin Sarat's "new abolitionism.") I show that Rule of Law abolitionism begins with the intuition, honored in *Furman* and *Gregg*, that legal violence must be more rational than extra-legal violence. Law's violence must be rational, rule-bound, and consistent. Rule of Law abolitionists argue that capital sentencing *cannot* be rationalized, and conclude that we must no longer "tinker with the machinery of death." Indeed, Rule of Law abolitionism concludes, we have a duty to oppose capital punishment. Along the way, I show that what distinguishes this argument from doctrinal or moral ones is the claim that rationality is a condition of legal legitimacy. Rule of Law abolitionists argue that by continuing to execute, capital jurisdictions reduce law to a species of mere coercion.

In the second part of the chapter, I submit Rule of Law abolitionism to critical scrutiny. I first identify its important rhetorical advantages, showing how Rule of Law abolitionism enables debates about capital punishment to occur outside the moralistic vocabulary that so often hampers the abolitionist cause. These benefits should not, however, obscure the weaknesses of Rule of Law abolitionism. I argue that Rule of Law abolitionism typically proves too much – its claim that sentencing procedures cannot be rational and rule-bound bleeds into an unpalatable argument against punishment as such. And some versions prove too little – their procedural criticisms function as a roadmap for the reform, and strengthening, of the capital punishment regime. Although these problems complicate the promise of Rule of Law abolitionism, I conclude by gesturing toward some conceptual modifications that will hopefully help Rule of Law abolitionism realize its full potential.

THE DISTINCTIVENESS OF RULE OF LAW ABOLITIONISM

Three types of abolitionist arguments have been made in the United States in the past 50 years. I call them doctrinal abolitionism, Rule of Law abolitionism, and moral abolitionism. Doctrinal abolitionists argue that capital punishment is unconstitutional, and that the Supreme Court's capital jurisprudence since *Gregg* is wrong. Rule of Law abolitionists claim that the death penalty violates Rule of Law values. Doctrinal abolitionism and Rule of Law abolitionism are easily confused because they both invoke the procedural values of rationality, consistency, and fairness. Both argue that these values should trump other legal values (e.g., finality) whenever there are conflicts in capital cases. The difference is that Rule of Law abolitionism claims that Rule of Law values must prevail because they legitimate legal violence, not because the Constitution says so. Rule of Law abolitionism claims that Rule of Law values *legitimate* law, and therefore cannot be given up in favor of other legal values. Rule of Law abolitionism's contrast with moral abolitionism is much sharper. Moral abolitionist arguments proceed from premises found in moral philosophy and theology. Moral abolitionists typically claim that capital punishment contravenes substantive moral values such as human dignity.

To clarify the argument of Rule of Law abolitionism, I will first set it off from doctrinal abolitionism. This discussion must begin with a caveat: pure doctrinal abolitionists might not exist. I assume that most, if not all, of the judges and lawyers who have a doctrinal disagreement with *Gregg* have other reasons for opposing the death penalty.[1] This presents no problem because I use terms such as "doctrinal abolitionism" (or "Rule of Law abolitionism" or "moral abolitionism") to refer to certain types of arguments, not to characterize people's actual beliefs.

There are two types of doctrinal abolitionism. One contends that the death penalty violates the Eighth Amendment's cruel and unusual punishment clause. A variety of arguments have been proposed along these lines: the death penalty is excessive, which means both that it "serve[s] no valid legislative purpose,"[2] and that it is excessively painful, both physically and emotionally[3]; death is an unusually severe punishment, insofar as it is final and irrevocable[4]; the death penalty violates human dignity.[5]

The most influential Eighth Amendment abolitionist arguments attack the foundation of the Supreme Court's post-*Furman* capital jurisprudence, the "death is different" doctrine.[6] The Court first gave precedential weight to the distinction between capital and non-capital forms of punishment in *Furman*:

> Death is a unique punishment in the United States. In a society that so strongly affirms the sanctity of life, not surprisingly the common view is that death is the ultimate sanction. This natural human feeling appears all about us. There has been no national debate about punishment, in general or by imprisonment, comparable to the debate about the punishment of death. ... This Court, too, almost always treats death cases as a class apart. ... Death is today an unusually severe punishment, unusual in its pain, in its finality, and in its enormity. No other existing punishment is comparable to death in terms of physical and mental suffering. (*Furman v. Georgia*, 1972, pp. 286–287, 306)

Because of this qualitative difference, "there is a corresponding difference in the need for reliability in the determination that death is the appropriate punishment in a specific case" (*Woodson v. North Carolina*, 1976, p. 305). The "death is different" doctrine says that since capital punishment is the ultimate sanction, capital punishment statutes must (a) establish special procedural safeguards to ensure that the death penalty is not imposed in an arbitrary and capricious manner (*Gregg v. Georgia*, 1976, p. 188) and (b) allow for "individualized" sentencing procedures (procedures that consider all relevant mitigating evidence such as the defendant's character, the circumstances of the offense, etc.) (*Woodson*, 1976; *Lockett v. Ohio*, 1978). The "death is different" requirements reflect the Court's view "heightened reliability" requires a heightened emphasis on the values of consistency and individuality.

Doctrinal abolitionists contend that the constitutional conditions specified by the "death is different" doctrine cannot be met. The basic strategy is to stress the constitutional indispensability of the value of rationality and consistency, and then to argue that capital punishment regimes cannot respect those values. For example, Zimring and Hawkins (1986) argue that basic facts about human psychology render capital sentencing a necessarily arbitrary and capricious process (p. 77–84).

The second set of arguments claim that capital punishment violates the Fourteenth Amendment's due process and equal protection guarantees.

Most of these arguments point to the ingrained racism of capital punishment, and most base their claims on what is known as the Baldus study. In this study, David Baldus, George Woodworth, and Charles Pulaski (1983) analyzed over 2,000 murder cases in Georgia.[7] Baldus and his colleagues make a persuasive showing that the race of the murder victim significantly influences sentencing decisions: when a victim is white, the murderer is 11 times more likely to receive a death sentence. The dissent in the landmark *McCleskey v. Klemp* (1987) argues that such bias clearly violate African American's right to equal protection under the law,[8] and the American Bar Association (ABA) (1997) called for a moratorium on the death penalty partially on these grounds.

Although I will not evaluate doctrinal abolitionism in detail, I will note that it has recently produced important substantive constraints on capital punishment. In 2002, *Atkins v. Virginia* barred execution of the mentally retarded. And in 2005, *Roper v. Simmons* barred execution of minors. Both decisions comment on how certain characteristics – mental retardation and youth – create intractable problems for capital sentencing. The Court concludes that neither minors nor mentally retarded capital defendants will receive reliable and adequate mitigating consideration from sentencers, and therefore cannot be considered constitutionally death eligible (see, e.g., *Atkins v. Virginia* (2002) 536 U.S. 304, 320; *Roper v. Simmons* (2005) 543 U.S. 551, 572–573). In both cases, the Court weighs the value of mitigation against the value of stare decisis, and finds mitigation more important. (Of course, both decisions rest on a particular interpretation of "evolving standards of decency," as I will discuss below.)

But as a tool for the *abolition* rather than the curbing of capital punishment, the doctrinal approach is dead. To most legal observers, *McCleskey* sounded the death knell for any type of Fourteenth Amendment abolitionist argument.[9] And Eighth Amendment arguments appear just as bloodless. The Court's capital jurisprudence from the 1980s onward has moved away from ensuring the procedural safeguards promised by the "death is different" doctrine.[10] In fact, these decisions have produced a cruel irony: in some cases, a prosecutor's decision to seek the death penalty triggers *fewer* safeguards than do other forms of punishment (Denno, 2002, p. 437). So barring a miraculous ideological shift, the Court's early 21st century capital jurisprudence will enable, rather than inhibit, the death penalty.

This point is best captured by the Court's ruling in *Herrera*, where, as part of a sustained attack on habeas corpus, the Court rejected consideration of Herrera's newly discovered evidence of innocence on the grounds that "the

State's interest in finality must outweigh the prisoner's interest in yet another round of litigation."[11] As Chief Justice Rehnquist writes:

> The central purpose of any system of criminal justice is to convict the guilty and free the innocent ... [but] due process does not require that every conceivable step be taken, at whatever cost, to eliminate the possibility of convicting an innocent person. To conclude otherwise would all but paralyze our system for enforcement of the criminal law. (*Herrera v. Collins*, 1993, p. 399)

Herrera illustrates the Court's willingness to uphold state sentencing schemes with minimal procedural protections. Concerned to protect states' "right" to minimal delay between sentencing and execution, *Herrera* indicates the Court's willingness to trump the values of fairness, rationality, and consistency with the value of finality. This calculus will never result in an abolition of capital punishment.

THE LOGIC OF RULE OF LAW ABOLITIONISM

The apparent death of doctrinal abolitionism, and the sociolegal research conducted in support of it, have spurred a search for new types of arguments against capital punishment.[12] While Rule of Law abolitionism grows out of this failure, it is not a radical departure from doctrinal abolitionism – in fact, the two look quite alike. For this reason, my first goal is to establish the difference between them. After doing so, I will lay out the logic and structure of the Rule of Law abolitionist argument, paying particular attention to why I call it "Rule of Law" abolitionism. Throughout this section, I will make liberal reference to the two most prominent Rule of Law abolitionist thinkers, Austin Sarat and Justice Harry Blackmun.

Doctrinal abolitionism employs *legal* arguments, whose form and content is dictated by U.S. legal conventions. These arguments occur in court opinions and law review articles; are made by judges, lawyers, and legal scholars; and are aimed at other lawyers, judges, legal scholars, and sometimes policymakers. The premises of these arguments are legal premises – previous holdings as well as "legal principles ... applied by the courts" (*Furman v. Georgia*, 1972, p. 269) – and their evidence consists of court opinions and psychological or sociological research. Of course, doctrinal arguments sometimes invoke what look like moral concepts: "cruelty" is a prevalent, and salient, example. But in the writings of the Court, the word "cruelty" refers to what the Court says cruelty is; the ordinary moral meaning of cruelty is bracketed. Justice Brennan's analysis of the meaning of "cruelty" in terms of the Court's evolving interpretation of the cruel and unusual punishments clause is an instructive example of this substitution (pp. 258ff.).

Rule of Law abolitionist arguments are found in similar publications, appeal to similar premises and types of evidence, and employ a similar vocabulary. But Rule of Law abolitionism makes use of an important "porousness" in the operation of law: the Supreme Court sometimes appeals to *explicitly extra-legal* constraints on legal punishment. Most importantly, the Eighth Amendment says that legal punishments must not be excessive, or disproportionate to the crime. Modern Eighth Amendment jurisprudence, Justice Scalia notwithstanding, holds that standards for determining proportionality and excessiveness are set, in part, by the "evolving standards of decency" of society (*Weems v. United States*, p. 1910; *Trop v. Dulles*, 1958). That is, the Eighth Amendment envisions law as necessarily responsive to external norms of justice.[13]

Sarat contends – and I agree – that this responsiveness reveals that law must engage in practices of legitimation. He argues that these practices are fundamental to the smooth operation of legal institutions, insofar as those institutions regulate our lives through violence or the threat of violence.[14] For Sarat, the people who carry out law's violence are legal officials, juries, or private actors whose violent acts are statutorily required (in the case of police officers) or permitted (as in acts of self-defense) (Sarat & Kearns, 1991, p. 210). The violence they impose is of two sorts. The first is physical (incarceration, execution) and material (welfare cutbacks, "cleansing" of homeless camps, etc.). The second is metaphorical or interpretive violence; this violence "is inflicted wherever legal will is imposed on the world, whenever a legal edict, a judicial decision, or a legislative act cuts, wrenches, or excises life from its social context" (*ibid.*). This is a pretty capacious definition, and indeed, Sarat admits that under such a conception, it is difficult to identify any legal practice that is non-violent (*ibid.*). It is also somewhat reductive. Since law is part of our "social context" – as legal consciousness research demonstrates[15] – it seems mistaken to say that the legal process tears people out of their social context. Sarat makes this claim somewhat more specific when he says that interpretive violence consists (a) in legal institutions enforcing the illusion that legal rules are impartial rules, and are discovered rather than created (Sarat & Kearns, 1991, pp. 210, 217–218); and (b) in legal institutions claiming that judicial-interpretive acts (such as sentencing someone to death) do not differ in kind from the violence of punishment (actually executing someone) (Sarat & Kearns, 1991, p. 211). For now I will focus on his claims about how law's material violence

– the most important being acts of punishment – do not differ in kind from acts of violence the law is meant to forestall or avenge.

Legal institutions and legal actors, Sarat (1997) argues, are aware of their violence, indeed "the proximity of law to, and its dependence on, violence raises a nagging question and a persistent doubt about whether law can ever be more than violence or whether law's violence is truly different from, and superior to, what lurks beyond its boundaries". This nagging worry can be answered only through practices justifying and legitimating that violence. Legitimacy, he claims, is "the minimal answer to skeptical questions about the ways that state violence differs from the turmoil and disorder the state is allegedly brought into being to conquer" (Sarat, 2001, p. 19). (Although he does not say so, his view seems to be that the force at law's disposal is intrusive enough for us to object to it, but not powerful enough to compel assent and obedience – hence the need for justification and legitimation.)

On this point, Sarat finds support in everyday intuition, as well as a host of literature in legal and political philosophy.[16] Sarat goes on to argue that practices of legal legitimation take a particular form. Law legitimates its violence by drawing attention to ways in which its violence differs from, and is preferable to, extra-legal violence – the private violence of muggings, revenge killings, domestic abuse, etc. The law produces narratives that try to answer doubts about the law's violence by contrasting it to the allegedly worse violence of a lawless society (Sarat & Kearns, 1991, p. 221). Such narratives originate not only with lawyers or judges, I would add, but also with Hobbes' *Leviathan* and subsequent accounts of the anarchy of the state of nature. These narratives portray the law's own violence as superior insofar as it is rational and rule-bound (Sarat, 2001, pp. 38–39; 252). Indeed, one might add, it is *only* by rationalizing violence that the violence of the state of nature can be tamed. To be legitimate, Sarat concludes, a legal institution must impose – or appear to impose – violence in a rule-bound way.[17]

Rule of Law abolitionism must, of course, show that capital punishment cannot be imposed in a rule-bound way. But due to its focus on legitimating practices, Rule of Law abolitionism need not limit itself to strict doctrinal interpretations of rule-boundedness. For example, in the second chapter of *When the State Kills*, "The Return of Revenge: Hearing the Voice of the Victim in Capital Trials," Sarat argues that the use of victim impact statements – statements that detail the harm undergone by the family of the murder victim – during capital sentencing encourages a passionate identification with the family of the victim rather than a rule-bound consideration of the defendant's legislatively defined blameworthiness.

Although he touches on Eighth and Fourteenth Amendment issues, Sarat focuses on the way that the law's legitimation story depends on a philosophical distinction between revenge and retribution that is undermined by the use of victim impact statements. And in the fifth chapter, "The Role of the Jury in the Killing State," he employs a more sociological analysis to show how juror's folk beliefs influence capital sentencing in ways that are at odds with the law's idealized picture of itself.

Sarat's work is a sustained effort to show that capital punishment violates "central legal values and the legitimacy of the *law itself*" (Sarat, 2001, p. 253, emphasis mine). All Rule of Law abolitionism is about the "law itself." At this point, I must tackle the ambiguities in the term "law," since my explication of Rule of Law abolitionism depends on the meaning of this word. I find Alan Gewirth's view helpful that there are three primary senses of law (Gewirth, 1970). First, "law" can refer to the collection of characteristics that underlie all minimal legal systems (e.g., they guide human conduct). In this sense, "law" can refer to a conceptual unity or to a set of cultural practices. Second, "law" can refer to a particular legal system (e.g., U.S. law as opposed to French law). Finally, "law" can refer to a legal rule (e.g., Florida's attempted felony-murder rule), or, I would add, a systematic group of legal rules ("the law of capital punishment"). I take Rule of Law abolitionism to be arguing that the distinction between legal violence and extra-legal violence characterizes "law" in a sense that sits between Gewirth's first and second senses. "Law" refers to something more historical than law in the first sense and more basic than law in the second sense. Law refers to a set of practices that we can call "modern law" or "post-Enlightenment law." Doctrinal abolitionism, on the other hand, restricts its claims to law in the second sense, and can be agnostic about the existence of the first sense.

So according to the Rule of Law argument, law is partially constituted by the attempt to draw distinctions between rule-bound violence and extra-legal violence. The insistence on this constitutive feature of law differentiates doctrinal and Rule of Law abolitionism. On the latter view, as we can see in Sarat's essays mentioned above, the problem with the death penalty is not that it violates the Constitution "correctly understood" (although most Rule of Law abolitionists would say that it does), but that it is incongruent with the "nature" of law. It threatens to undermine the difference between legal violence and extra-legal violence. It threatens to reduce law to a species of coercion.

Now that we have gotten clearer on the conceptual boundaries of Rule of Law abolitionism, we can see why it is both interesting and important. Rule of Law abolitionism derives its *normative* claims from the conception of law found in a rich set of legal *practices*. The argument begins with the idea that legal institutions must impose violence in a rule-bound way. This "must" refers to the fact that practices of legitimation constitute legal institutions as legal institutions. The second step is to show that capital punishment does not allow for such ruliness, and thereby renders legal institutions illegitimate. One must then conclude that since the death penalty destroys law, it ought to be purged from the law.[18] This "ought" is a normative one: we have a duty to abolish the death penalty. (This argument is actually an enthymeme, and requires a further premise: "it is desirable to have legal institutions.") In this way, Rule of Law abolitionism exerts a pull on our practical deliberation that is not available to doctrinal abolitionism. In short, Rule of Law abolitionism can make stronger normative claims than doctrinal abolitionism, yet need not rely on moral authority to ground these claims.

RULES, RATIONALITY, AND LEGITIMACY

Having examined the structure of Rule of Law abolitionism, I will turn to its basic content, analyzing the particular narrative of legitimation found in the U.S. Supreme Court. The Supreme Court's contemporary capital jurisprudence does indeed draw a distinction between legal violence and extra-legal violence, and uses that distinction to justify legal violence. This analysis will reveal why I call Rule of Law abolitionism "Rule of Law" abolitionism.

In his *Furman* opinion, Justice Stewart writes:

> The instinct for retribution is part of the nature of man, and channeling that instinct in the administration of criminal justice serves an important purpose in promoting the stability of a society governed by law. When people begin to believe that organized society is unwilling or unable to impose upon criminal offenders the punishment they "deserve," then there are sown the seeds of anarchy – of self-help, vigilante justice, and lynch law. (*Furman v. Georgia*, 1972, p. 308)[19]

This discussion of extra- or pre-legal violence becomes part of Stewart's majority opinion in *Gregg v. Georgia*: "In part, capital punishment is an expression of society's moral outrage at particularly offensive conduct. This function may be unappealing to many, but it is essential in an ordered society that asks its citizens to rely on legal processes rather than self-help to vindicate their wrongs" (*Gregg v. Georgia*, 1976, p. 83, footnote omitted). Stewart's bold assertion requires careful interpretation. Marshall's dissent understands these passages as claiming that a society lacking legal institutions empowered to mete out the death penalty would descend into a state of nature. "It simply defies belief," Marshall responds, "to suggest that the death penalty is necessary to prevent the American people from taking the law into their own hands" (*Gregg v. Georgia*, 1976, p. 238). But Marshall misreads Stewart. Stewart is not justifying the *death penalty*; rather, he is justifying legal violence, indeed legal *institutions*, more generally. He thinks that legal institutions, and the violence they inflict, are legitimate because they have provided a way out of the chaos of the state of nature, because they have ensured a society ruled by law. He is not claiming that if the law were not violent, people would not obey it, but rather that if the law were not violent, it would not serve the purposes it is supposed to serve. He is saying that since citizens have transferred their power to forcefully right wrongs to the law, legal institutions must not fail to exercise this violence. He writes:

> [Capital punishment's] precise origins are difficult to perceive, but there is some evidence that its roots lie in violent retaliation by members of a tribe or group, or by the tribe or group itself, against persons committing hostile acts toward group members. Thus, infliction of death as a penalty for objectionable conduct appears to have its beginnings in private vengeance. As individuals gradually ceded their personal prerogatives to a sovereign power, the sovereign accepted the authority to punish wrongdoing as part of its "divine right" to rule. Individual vengeance gave way to the vengeance of the state, and capital punishment became a public function. (*Furman*, 1972, p. 333, citations omitted)

By claiming that the law's violence is a violence "essential" to the formation and preservation of civil society, the Court defuses objections to legal violence. But while this line of reasoning is meant to legitimate the law and legitimate the law's imposition of violence, it clearly does not legitimate *any* violence the law imposes. Insofar as law preserves the difference between civil society and the state of nature, its violence must be different from the violence it channels and forestalls. The Court establishes this difference in one way through Eighth Amendment limits on the kinds of violence that may be imposed. States are prohibited from drawing and quartering criminals, or making use of thumbscrews. But Stewart's remarks about law's debased copies – "vigilante justice" and "lynch law" – suggest that what is *more* important in marking this difference is restricting the procedures that determine how law decides who is to be punished and how they are to be punished. Both lynch law and official law put people to death (and hanging has never been declared unconstitutionally cruel) but lynch law employs inappropriate procedures.

What characterizes this foreclosed way of doing "justice" from which legitimate law is distinguished? Passion and emotion, especially hateful or vengeful passions or emotions (*Gregg*, 1976, p 154). Subjectiveness – violence that is "different in different men ... [dependent] upon constitution, temper" (*McGautha v. California*, 1970, p. 285). Whimsy and caprice (*Gregg*, 1976, p. 200). In other words, violence should not be an expression of our "baser selves" (*Furman*, 1972, p. 345), the "vice, folly, and passion to which human nature is liable" (*McGautha*, 1970, p. 285).

These matters are vague, if not obscure. Even a careful reader is precluded from delineating precisely the Court's conception of human fallibility, given its brief, scattered, and inchoate remarks. Furthermore, the Court has never been a forum for the production of penetrating analyses of human nature. But what is more important is the Court's characterization of legitimate punishing procedures. *Legitimate* legal punishment is imposed in a rule-bound way. Through rules, the law escapes the passion and prejudice that afflict human decision-making, and through rules, ours becomes a "government of laws, and not of men."[20]

This view of rules emerged almost whole cloth in *Furman*. Before *Furman* was handed down, almost every state with the death penalty gave its sentencers, be they juries or judges, absolute discretion to dispense death or mercy (Steiker & Steiker, 1995, p. 364). One year before *Furman*, *McGautha v. California* held that standardless jury sentencing did not violate the due process clause of the Fourteenth Amendment. Justice Harlan, writing for the *McGautha* majority, argued that introducing capital sentencing standards would be futile. He derided the attempts of the *Model Penal Code* authors to produce adequate sentencing criteria,[21] claiming that the rules provide no more than the most minimal control over the sentencing authority's discretion: "they do not purport to give an exhaustive list of the relevant considerations or the way in which they may be affected by the presence or absence of other circumstances" (*McGautha v. California*, 1970, p. 207). Nor do they even try to exclude constitutionally impermissible considerations, such as the race or sex of the offender. In short, Harlan claimed, these standards provide no protection against a jury deciding on the basis of "whimsy or caprice." The proposed standards "do no more than suggest some subjects for the jury to consider during its deliberations, and they bear witness to the intractable nature of the problem of 'standards' which the history of capital punishment has from the beginning reflected" (*ibid.*). Indeed, Harlan thought, there is no reason to expect any effort in this regard to succeed, and certainly no reason to say that the Constitution requires a jury's sentencing decision to be rule-governed.[22]

A year later, the Court abruptly changed its mind (in a manner of speaking – see footnote 23). *Furman* held that standardless sentencing rendered the death penalty unconstitutional (although two justices claimed that it was per se unconstitutional). Actually, it is hard to say what *Furman* said, because each justice issued a separate opinion. For this reason, I will follow most legal scholarship in reading *Furman* through *Gregg* and subsequent capital cases. According to *Gregg*'s plurality opinion, *Furman* stands mainly for the proposition that "where discretion is afforded a sentencing body on a matter so grave as the determination of whether a human life should be taken or spared, that discretion must be suitably directed and limited so as to minimize the risk of wholly arbitrary and capricious action" (*Gregg*, 1976, p. 189).[23] The *Gregg* plurality agrees that the statutes examined in *Furman* are cruel and unusual, but, citing Justice Stewart, says that they are "cruel and unusual in the same way that being struck by lightning is cruel and unusual" (*Gregg*, 1976, p. 188). That is, statutes that give juries unfettered discretion encourage random sentencing decision. Or, as Justice White argues, the statutory schemes analyzed in *Furman* provided "no meaningful basis for distinguishing the few cases in which [the death penalty] is imposed from the many cases in which it is not" (*Gregg*, 1976, p. 188). No agreement about the "worst" class of murderers could be induced from sentences handed down by juries.

But while the *Gregg* plurality agrees with this strand of *Furman*, they do not think that it is impossible to render capital sentencing more rule-bound, less arbitrary, and capricious. With a nod to Harlan, *Gregg* says that "while some have suggested that standards to guide a capital jury's sentencing deliberation are impossible to formulate, the fact is that such standards have been developed" (p. 193, citation omitted). To back up this claim, the plurality trots out the very same *Model Penal Code* sentencing standards excoriated by Harlan. *Gregg* then finds that Georgia's sentencing scheme provides similar guidance through its requirement that a jury find one of several statutory aggravating circumstances beyond a reasonable doubt before imposing a death sentence.[24]

Gregg's conception of rule-bound violence has two main components. First, *Gregg* characterizes the ruliness of violence in terms of consistency; when similar punishment is meted out for similar crimes, those punishments are administered in rule-bound way (p. 222). That is, lawful violence will be governed by the like cases principle ("treat like cases alike").[25] This leads to the second point. Legal violence cannot be lawful unless individual sentencing judgments are made in a "rational" way (pp. 189–194). So

Gregg says that capital sentencing standards must control and constrain the *way* the jury decides.

Clearly, "rationality" means many things, and while the word appears all over the Court's opinions, the Court takes no pains to define it. The Court's basic position seems to be that judges or juror sentences rationally when they base sentences on good reasons. To sentence properly, or rationally, is to sentence on the basis of *legal* reasons, reasons specified by legislatures and approved by the Court. In capital sentencing, good reasons for sentencing someone to death are statutory aggravators. Bad reasons are reasons that are "wholly unrelated to the blameworthiness of a particular defendant," or unrelated to the "character of the individual and the circumstances of the crime" (*Booth v. Maryland*, 1987, pp. 496, 502). Bad reasons are either irrelevant reasons, like whether one's breakfast is digesting well, or repugnant reasons, such as the race, class, or gender of the accused.[26]

Furthermore, to sentence rationally, sentences must make decisions on the basis of proper motivations. Take, for example, a sentencer who employs a "good" reason – a statutory aggravator such as "the murder was committed for pecuniary gain" – yet uses this reason as a cover for his or her racist view of the defendant. This is not an instance of proper sentencing. Proper sentencing requires a judge or juror to make a disinterested or impersonal sentencing decision (*Payne v. Tennessee*, 1991, p. 844).

Negatively speaking, this means that a sentencer should ignore his or her emotional response to the crime or the victim (*Booth v. Maryland*, 1987, pp. 508–509).[27] More specifically, sentencers should not make their decision out of a sense of sympathy with the victims of the defendant's crime or antipathy toward the defendant; sentencing should not be an exercise of passionate identification, or vengeance (*California v. Brown*, 1987). Positively speaking, a sentencer must endorse the law's "objective" standards (*Gregg*, 1976, p. 198; *Callins v. Collins*, 1994, p. 144). This entails a certain self-understanding or self-identification on the part of the sentencer. Sentencers should understand themselves (at least implicitly) to be agents of the state or of the legal institutions of the state, rather than private actors (*Furman*, 1972, p. 333).[28] This means that sentencers should make the law's reasons their own. The law specifies aggravating circumstances – "the murder was committed for pecuniary gain" – not to enable juries to eliminate one more poor black man from society, but to pick out the worst of the worst murderers as defined by the state. Of course, one's preferences *can* come into play, as long as these are statutorily permissible, and as long as they hold the weight the law says they should hold. But then they are not private reasons, they are legal ones.

It should now be clear why I call it "Rule of Law" abolitionism. Rule of Law abolitionism makes heavy use of this narrative of legitimation. Again, the idea is that law's violence should differ from extra-legal violence, and that this difference is the difference between rule-bound and "unruly" violence.[29] Rule of Law abolitionism is a claim that law must operate according to *rules*, that its sentencing decisions be rational and consistent.[30] It is at the same time a claim about the necessity of law's *rule*, the necessity that the law's reasons be authoritative in practical decisions about the imposition of law's violence. Sentencing is rule-bound when it proceeds on the basis of the reasons the Court endorses and for the reasons the Court specifies. Finally, Rule of Law *abolitionism* is the claim that the death penalty *cannot* be imposed according to rules, and therefore, legal systems that employ it are illegitimate.[31]

There is one more conceptual component of Rule of Law abolitionism. Rule of Law asserts a *duty* to oppose capital punishment, a duty to help legal institutions live up to the "core legal values" that constitute the definition of law. It asserts that we – judges, jurors, laypeople – have a duty to help the law in its attempt to distinguish its violence from extra-legal violence. For abolitionists, this general duty can be put in more specific terms: jurors have a duty to refuse to sentence to death, appellate judges have a duty to overturn lower court verdicts, citizens have a duty to campaign against capital punishment, or vote against politicians who support it. If abolitionism does not assert a duty – if it merely draws our attention to some inconsistency in the law – it is less an argument against capital punishment than a collection of information about legal practices of legitimation. If it is the latter, it cannot say that there is anything *wrong* with the death penalty.

This abolitionist duty must have two important characteristics. First, heeding this duty is not necessarily reducible to complying with federal or state statutes. To realize the core values of law, to prevent a law-killing violence, one might have to disobey the statutes that undermine or contravene those values. Law itself demands that a juror enter into capital sentencing with a firm conviction that he or she will not impose the death penalty; and perhaps even lie about these convictions during voir dire. Put more generally, the obligatoriness of law is not reducible to the command "obey valid rules." As a result, an investigation into the obligatoriness of law should not proceed on the terms found in the debate about the "prima facie obligation to law" that pre-occupies so many philosophers of law.[32]

Second, the duty to improve the law has a *legal* rather than a moral ground. Indeed, it is on this basis that I distinguish Rule of Law abolitionism from moral abolitionism. This emphasis on legal grounds also illuminates a conception of legal duty that differs from that which prevails in the Anglo-American philosophical world. Most philosophers of law argue that if we have duties to law, we have them only when these duties are *morally* justified. (Rawls might be an exception.[33]) This means either that the particular rule, and the duty it imposes is just, or that the legal institution as a whole is *morally* just.[34]

STRONG AND WEAK RULE OF LAW ABOLITIONISM

I said above that Rule of Law abolitionism claims that the death penalty cannot be imposed according to rules. There seems to be some confusion about this claim in the Rule of Law abolitionist literature. This confusion leads to the existence of two general types of Rule of Law abolitionism, a weak and a strong one. Rule of Law abolitionism wants to argue that capital sentencing procedures cannot impose a sufficient amount of rationality, and that therefore, the death penalty must be given up. But by focusing on deficient death penalty procedures, abolitionists risk arguing only that the law has *not yet* devised adequate sentencing procedures. Rule of Law abolitionism would then be arguing only that the death penalty, *as currently administered*, is illegitimate. This would be a valuable critique of contemporary death penalty procedures, but not an argument against capital punishment.[35] Indeed, the focus on procedure has the rather awkward consequence of implying that the death penalty is redeemable, that the death penalty could be legitimately in principle.

On this weak interpretation, Rule of Law abolitionism can do little more than support calls for a moratorium on capital punishment. To be sure, it is quite good at *that*: justifications for moratoria are often couched in Rule of Law abolitionist terms. In Nebraska, for example, one of the co-authors of a moratorium bill was an ardent supporter of the death penalty, yet convinced his colleagues that a moratorium was required to respect "equal protection ... and due process."[36] This was not a doctrinal claim, as the constitutionality of the state's capital punishment regime was not the topic of discussion. Rather it was about the legitimacy, or as most senators put it, the "justice" of the legal system. Former Governor Paris Glendening justified Maryland's moratorium by citing the necessity of having "complete confidence that the legal process involved in capital cases is fair and impartial" (cited in American Bar Association, 2003). Finally, in the words of former Illinois Governor George Ryan, once a staunch supporter of capital punishment:

> I started with this issue concerned about innocence. But once I studied, once I pondered what had become of our justice system, I came to care above all about fairness. Fairness is fundamental to the American system of justice and our way of life. The facts I have seen in reviewing each and every one of these cases raised questions not only about the innocence of people on death row, but about the fairness of the death penalty system as a whole. If the system was making so many errors in determining whether someone was guilty in the first place, how fairly and accurately was it determining which guilty defendants deserved to live and which deserved to die? What effect was race having? What effect was poverty having?[37]

It is important to understand the connections of Rule of Law abolitionism and the moratorium movement, because many abolitionists – especially Sarat (1997) – have placed heavy expectations on the moratorium movement. And not without cause: the movement seems to be a powerful one. In 1999, the ABA passed a resolution exhorting every capital punishment jurisdiction to institute a moratorium. By 2001, legislation to address the ABA's concerns had been introduced in 37 of the 38 states with the death penalty (Kirchmeier, 2002, p. 45). As of 2003, moratorium legislation had been introduced in 21 states as well as Congress. Former Governors Ryan and Glendening instituted moratoriums through executive order (Glendening's moratorium was overturned by Governor Robert Erlich). In January 2006, the New Jersey State Senate became the first legislature to institute a moratorium. Nationwide polls show that over 60 percent of U.S. citizens support a moratorium on capital punishment; this is a significant number, given that support for capital punishment has often been above 75 percent.[38] Add the support from conservatives such as George Will and Pat Robertson, and the idea of putting Rule of Law abolitionism in the service of the moratorium movement seems like a good one.

But it is not. Much of the anxiety behind the moratorium movement centers on the fallibility of capital procedures, the risk of error, the possibility of states taking innocent lives. Although this is a worry about the damage capital punishment does to legal legitimacy, it can be resolved by improving capital punishment procedures. It is a worry about getting the wrong man, not a man getting the wrong punishment. The moratorium movement is an exercise in *reform*, not abolition.[39] As Gross and Ellsworth have pointed out, "there is no inconsistency in the fact that sixty-four percent of the population favors a moratorium (at least when DNA is mentioned), and about the same number favors the death penalty" (cited in Kaufman-Osborn, 2001, p. 684).

And while abolitionists should certainly welcome any reform of capital punishment, reform can impede, rather than further, the goals of abolitionism. I agree with Mona Lynch's claim that reformist gestures *enable* capital punishment by telling the courts, and the public, what must be done for the death penalty to gain full legal legitimacy (Lynch, 2002, pp. 918–919). Put in the service of reform, the invocation of Rule of Law values enables the law to assure us that its ultimate violence is bound by rational procedures. An illustration is the Report of the Illinois Governor's Commission on Capital Punishment. Governor Ryan appointed the Commission in 2000, following the release of the 13th person sentenced to death by Illinois which raised, in his eyes, "serious concerns with respect to the process by which the death penalty is imposed."[40] Ryan's concerns, as we have seen above, are about the fairness, or ruliness of legal violence. Moved by these concerns, Ryan charged the Commission with studying the state's system of capital punishment, and making suggestions for improvement. The Commission returned an impressive 200-page report with 85 recommendations for improvements to a broad range of issues including police investigation, forensic testing, prosecutorial discretion, trial lawyering, statutory aggravators and mitigators, post-conviction hearings, and more.[41]

While many of these recommendations are worthy ones, the very quality of the Report is a double-edged sword. The Report is a tool for reform, and, at the same time, a tool for achieving the appearance of legal legitimacy. It is easy to imagine retentionists happily agreeing to such studies, and even agreeing to implement many of their recommendations, because of the effect this would have on the seeming legitimacy of execution.[42] In fact, while few of the Report's recommendations have been acted on by the Illinois Legislature, its existence seems to have ameliorated concerns about the death penalty. Illinois courts have restarted the capital punishment machine, and nine people currently sit on death row.

For Rule of Law abolitionism to be a vigorous abolitionism, it must hew to a more robust argument. Abolitionism cannot ask only for "*more* rationality"; it cannot demand only that the majority, or some percentage, of legal events be characterized by reason rather than passion. Unless more rationality is impossible to attain, the demand for more rationality will be a *reformist* demand.[43] Enter strong Rule of Law abolitionism. Strong Rule of Law abolitionism claims that legitimacy can *never* be achieved in the context of capital sentencing; it claims that reform is impossible. Since the project of establishing rational capital sentencing procedures is doomed to fail, the argument goes, we must give up execution for good.

Clearly, irrationality is a crucial component of this argument. Unfortunately, strong Rule of Law abolitionists spend little time explaining what they mean by it. To remedy this oversight, I will present the conception I see to be most congruent with the strong Rule of Law argument. This conception might not be faithful to the letter of Sarat and Blackmun's texts, but I think it puts their claims in the strongest light.

To say that capital sentencing is always irrational is to say that every legal actor's actions are always partly motivated by idiosyncratic, or subjective, reasons. It is to say that personal reasons always interfere with legal reasons. If only *some* people's actions were motivated by passion and prejudice, the state could give the task of devising sentencing guidelines, sitting on juries, appointing judges, etc., to those able to think impersonally and objectively. If everyone's actions were *sometimes* irrationally motivated, we could, in our better moments, devise tests that determine the rationality of a policy, sentencing guideline, or sentencing decision. In either of these cases, there would be enough rationality to legitimate the death penalty.

But strong Rule of Law abolitionism need not adopt the controversial view that *human beings* are inherently irrational (although Sarat and Blackmun sometimes suggest as much). It requires only that *legal* judgments be irrational. As I pointed out above, legal judgments are irrational when personal reasons interfere with legal reasons. And, according to a popular view in contemporary moral philosophy, this interference is an inevitable fact of practical life. We *always* deliberate on the basis of reasons that are peculiar to us; as Bernard Williams would say, we always deliberate on the basis of reasons contained in our specific "motivational set" (Williams, 1982, pp. 101–113). When a jury member decides to sentence on the basis of a statutory aggravator, she does so *only* because she so desires.

(Notice that an act that is irrational from a legal perspective can be perfectly rational from a general practical perspective. Acting in accordance with our "personal" interests is often the most rational thing to do. For example, one can imagine situations in which an African-American juror is right to refuse to convict an African-American defendant of possession of cocaine with the intent to distribute.)

We find this strong Rule of Law argument in what Sarat calls "new abolitionism" or "legally conservative abolitionism." Sarat's abolitionism asserts the necessity of rationalizing capital sentencing, while also asserting its impossibility. Legal rules, he argues, cannot check our personal desires. The reason is that law is an inherently violent enterprise.[44] Even the most legitimate legal institution imposes legitimate violence, law is, at some level, always an instrument of coercion. And when we are confronted with threats of violence, Sarat suggests, we no longer deliberate in a disinterested fashion. At work here is a quasi-Hobbesian account of human psychology, where the drive for security and self-preservation overrides all other motivations. "Force," Sarat contends, "is disdainful of reason; it pushes it aside; it takes over completely" (Sarat & Kearns, 1991, p. 240). In short, the operation of law inevitably calls up passions that "short-circuit" our ability to make decisions in accordance with legal rules.

This conception of irrationality focuses on the experience of laypeople negotiating legal rules in their daily lives; it captures my situation when I deliberate about downloading music I have not purchased. This does not get the abolitionist very far, since judges, lawyers, and juries are not typically confronted by such threats of force. But in "A Journey through Forgetting," Sarat and Kearns (1991) identify three additional sources of legal irrationality: the indeterminacy of legal rules, ideological indoctrination, and the inherent subjectivity of practical deliberation.[45] This third source is just what the abolitionist needs, especially if "subjectivity" means that we can never escape self-interest. From here, Sarat can easily move to an abolitionist conclusion. *Gregg* states that capital punishment is legitimate only when rational and rule-bound. Since capital sentencing procedures are *necessarily* irrational, we must reject the death penalty if we want to preserve the distinction between law and violence (Sarat, 1997, 2001, 2002).

We find another example of strong Rule of Law abolitionism in Justice Blackmun's *Callins* dissent. Blackmun, too, argues that rules can never channel passion or prejudice. Blackmun says that *Furman* and *Gregg* mandate that "the death penalty must be imposed fairly, and with reasonable consistency, or not at all" (*Callins v. Collins*, 1994, pp. 1144, 1147). Surveying 30 years of the Court's capital jurisprudence, Blackmun notes that despite the wealth and diversity of capital sentencing schemes, and despite the Court's review of, and intervention into, these schemes, "the problems that were pursued down one hole with procedural rules and verbal formulas have come to the surface somewhere else" (p. 1144). The cases that come before the Court show that capital punishment remains fraught with "arbitrariness, discrimination, caprice, and mistake" (p. 1144).[46]

Although Blackmun's explanation of this irrationality is even leaner than Sarat's, he concurs with Sarat in important respects.[47] Blackmun grudgingly accepts Harlan's view that capital sentencing guidelines cannot control arbitrariness, calling Harlan's *McGautha* opinion "partly prophetic" (p. 1146). The reason for this, Blackmun claims, is that the "decision

whether a human being should live or die is ... inherently subjective"
(p. 1153). He attributes this subjectivity to the fact that deliberation is
steeped in "all of life's understandings, experiences, prejudices, and
passions" (p. 1153). And this claim can be cashed out in the same fashion
as Sarat's. "Life's understandings" inevitably undermine the act of making
law's reasons our own. Since arbitrariness and irrationality is an inherent quality of capital sentencing, Blackmun concludes, we must "no
longer ... tinker with the machinery of death" (p. 1145).

RULE OF LAW ABOLITIONISM – PROMISE AND PERIL

If doctrinal abolitionism is dead, what are the prospects for Rule of Law
abolitionism? (From here on out, I will use "Rule of Law abolitionism" to
refer to strong Rule of Law abolitionism, since weak Rule of Law
abolitionism is not really abolitionism.) I think the persuasive possibilities of
this argument are interesting and compelling. Since one need appeal only to
traditional legal values, one can employ this argument without occupying
the position of a bleeding-heart liberal. One can champion it without
refusing to be "tough on crime," or without defending the life of figures such
as Timothy McVeigh. On the other hand, Sarat writes, traditional
abolitionism

> has been associated with, and is an expression of, humanist liberalism, political
> radicalism, or religious doctrine. Each represents a frontal assault on the simple and
> appealing retributivist rationale for capital punishment. Each puts opponents of the
> death penalty on the side of society's most despised and notorious criminals. (Sarat,
> 2001, p. 249)

Although Sarat (2001, p. 11) makes rather heavy weather of the rhetorical
difficulties posed by McVeigh – calling him "the ultimate trump card, the
living, breathing embodiment of the necessity and justice of the death
penalty" – his general point is basically sound. When I try to explain my
abolitionist views to skeptics, they almost invariably ask if I would object to
the death penalty for McVeigh, Hitler, etc. As I understand it, this question
expresses the intuition that there are *some* crimes that are so heinous, death
is the only warranted punishment. And this intuition is not unreasonable.
But Rule of Law abolitionism allows abolitionists to sidestep this problem.
Rule of Law abolitionists can *agree* with moral, religious, or philosophical
justifications of the death penalty while renouncing capital punishment.

Rule of Law abolitionism suggests that we reject the death penalty for the harm it does to "us," and "our" prized legal institutions, rather than for the harm it does to convicted murderers.

Although Sarat calls his abolitionism "legally conservative abolitionism," I am not suggesting that a Rule of Law abolitionist must take (or feign) a conservative position on crime. My point is that he or she need not take any position whatsoever. One of the great merits of Rule of Law abolitionism is that it operates outside stale ethical and political categories. Rule of Law abolitionism does not attack law in the "politically radical" fashion of Critical Legal Studies; it does not portray reigning legal values as legitimating tools of oppressive socioeconomic hierarchies. Nor does it attempt to re-evaluate, undo, or undermine these values.[48] And it does not, in the way of a particularly aggressive version of natural law theory, foist a moral code on the law. Rather, it comprises an "embrace" of law's central values and an attempt to uphold and strengthen these values. If Rawls is right that certain legal values can be endorsed regardless of one's substantive moral or political views, Rule of Law abolitionism seems to be one of them. (The co-authors of a Nebraska moratorium bill, a liberal and a conservative, described their differences as greater than those between "God and Satan," yet could agree that the death penalty was broken (Tysver, 1999).)

This feature is especially important in light of the death penalty's role in our broader "culture wars." This role has been explored at length elsewhere, and I will not pursue it here.[49] Needless to say, in a society where simplistic narratives of guilt and responsibility are encouraged and accepted, moral discourse, with its emphasis on will and responsibility, seems too heavily weighted in favor of the prosecution. Insofar as Rule of Law abolitionism avoids moral terminology, it enables debate about capital punishment to occur outside the conceptual confines of the culture wars. As Sarat (2001, p. 253) writes, Rule of Law abolitionism allows one to say that "the most important issue in the debate about capital punishment is one of fairness, not one of sympathy for murderers; concern for the law abiding, not for the criminal."

My claims about the rhetorical power of Rule of Law abolitionism are not idle speculation. In 2000, the New Hampshire state legislature voted to abolish capital punishment. Sarat conducted a series of interviews with state legislators and analyzed the reasons they gave for their votes. Sarat (2002, p. 361) presents evidence that the logic of Rule of Law abolitionism played a significant role in the debate. One senator's remarks indicated that he or she (the article does not include identifying information) had been converted by Rule of Law abolitionist arguments:

> You know, when they blow up a building in Oklahoma, it is pretty hard to stick with mercy and forgiveness. ... But when you think about all the injustice that is done in figuring out who gets the death penalty, it doesn't seem right. We aren't infallible, so who gets to choose who lives and who dies? That's why I decided to vote to get rid of the whole thing. (cited in Sarat, 2002, p. 363)

Another said that Rule of Law abolitionist arguments would enable her to sell her vote to her constituents:

> It ain't right to kill, and it doesn't matter who does the killing. ... But that is just what I think and I'm not sure that I could convince anyone else who thought differently. But when it comes to issues having to do with the fairness of the way people get treated, then that's different. Everyone can relate to that. I can go out and explain that I'm against this state having the death penalty because of the real problems in the way it works. ... I don't mind giving speeches about that. (cited in Sarat, 2002, p. 364)

While I cannot evaluate Sarat's evidence here, I think these citations make a prima facie case for the empirical effectiveness of Rule of Law abolitionism.

That said, there are some serious problems with Rule of Law abolitionism. First, strong Rule of Law abolitionism proves too much. While it imagines itself to be aimed at the abolition of capital punishment, it targets punishment as such. Neither Blackmun nor Sarat want to argue for the illegitimacy of every type of legal sanction. Blackmun writes, "the decision whether a human being *should live or die* is so inherently subjective – rife with all of life's understandings, experiences, prejudices, and passions – that it inevitably defies the rationality and consistency required by the Constitution" (*Callins*, 1994, p. 1153, emphasis added). Sarat adds: "when formality fails, when the forms of legal procedure cannot contain and control any particular form of legal violence, *that particular violence* must be rejected to that law itself can survive" (Sarat, 1997, emphasis added). But if we accept strong Rule of Law abolitionists' account of legal deliberation, if practical reason functions in the way Rule of Law abolitionists must say it does, judges, lawyers, and juries cannot impose punishment legitimately. As Sarat and Kearns (1991, p. 240) write, the modern criterion for legal legitimacy is that "rules, not personal will and desire ... really determine law's actions. If human beings cannot adopt the legal reasons enshrined in the justification of law as their own, personal will determines legal actions, and legal violence is indistinguishable from extra-legal violence. Unruliness cannot be limited to capital sentencing, and law's legitimating narrative is irredeemable. In this way, the attempt to mark one particular punishment as illegitimate slips into a wholesale indictment of the legitimacy of punishment, and Rule of Law abolitionism becomes a doctrine of "total abolitionism." [50]

Second, if lawfulness is unachievable – if people are incapable of acting in accordance with legal reasons – legal institutions can only be *coercive*. And if legal institutions are only coercive, they cannot generate duties or obligations. Recall H.LA. Hart's famous distinction between "obligation" and "being obliged" (Hart, 1994, pp. 84–85). We might say that someone faced with the barrel of an Uzi is "obliged" to hand over their money to a mugger, but they have no "obligation" to do so. Obligations are, in some sense, not optional. "Obligation" refers to actions that we must perform or must refrain from doing. But obligations are *also* non-coercive. (For the purposes of this chapter, I will bracket the question of what makes obligations non-coercive.) So if law is simply an exercise of coercion, we can never have a duty to abolish capital punishment. Indeed, if law is an exercise of coercion, the duty to make that law accord with its legitimating principles, the duty to make the law's violence distinct from extra-legal violence, is really a type of violence. The problem, then, is a serious one: Rule of Law abolitionism forecloses the possibility of a duty to improve the law, and, as I have argued above, *that duty is precisely what a theory of abolitionism must defend.*[51]

And for those unimpressed by these conceptual issues, a deep rhetorical problem remains. Strong Rule of Law abolitionism violates the practical principle of "ought implies can," i.e., the principle that we have duties only when we are capable of doing what the duty commands us to do. For this reason, strong Rule of Law abolitionism lends itself to a fatalism at odds with the duty to improve the law. If rule-bound punishment is impossible, legal institutions can never be lawful. If lawfulness is unachievable, if legal institutions can only be coercive, this must cast doubt on the value of the Rule of Law abolitionist claim itself. It would be difficult to refute the obvious objection: If nothing can be done to make the law better, why should we try? Why should we eliminate one punishment, only to see others destroy law just as easily?

It might seem that Blackmun provides a version of strong Rule of Law abolitionism that escapes these problems. This would not be grounded in his views on the "inherent subjectivism" of judgment, but in his identification of an irresolvable conflict between the values of fairness and individuality. Fairness dictates that a capital sentencing scheme treat those convicted of murder with the "degree of respect due the uniqueness of the individual" (*Lockett v. Ohio*, 1978, p. 605).[52] To treat like cases alike, the sentencer must consider information about the defendant that enables an educated judgment about relevant similarities to, or differences from, other capital defendants.[53] Indeed, *Lockett* requires sentencers to consider any relevant mitigating evidence, i.e., evidence that would justify a sentence less than death. The upshot is that sentencers have broad discretion to withhold capital punishment. In his *Callins* (1994), dissent, Blackmun argues that states cannot eliminate this discretion without also eliminating fairness: "a step toward consistency," he writes, "is a step away from fairness" (p. 1149). So the death penalty, as a sort of legal tragedy, provokes a contradiction in the due process values of consistency and individualization.[54] The "irreconcilability" of these values means that if the death penalty is administered, it will violate one value or the other; "the consistency and rationality promised in *Furman* are *inversely related* to the fairness owed to the individual when considering a sentence of death" (pp. 1155, 1149, emphasis mine). And since both values are of equal weight, and respect for both values is constitutionally necessary, capital punishment must be given up.

Since this "unique level of fairness" is applicable only to capital contexts, this argument does not undermine the very possibility of legal legitimacy. But it has its own weakness: there *is* no contradiction between consistency and fairness. Indeed, consistency *requires* sentencers to engage in individualized consideration.[55] While consistency requires that sentencing admit of rational patterns (or rules), consistency also requires those patterns to reflect the particularities of the defendants who come before the courts. If consistency is found only at the vague levels specified in most statutory aggravators, it is a false consistency. To produce a meaningful consistency, to really treat like cases alike, sentencers must know all the relevant facts about a defendant and the circumstances of his or her crime. So Blackmun can maintain the existence of a contradiction between consistency and fairness only by adopting an artificial, abstract, and simplistic interpretation of the concepts involved, by massaging the concepts of rationality and individualized consideration into an unrecognizable form, or by smuggling abolitionist content into the conceptualization of these values. Such an argument cannot adopt the morally neutral stance that befits Rule of Law abolitionism.

CONCLUSION

On my account, Rule of Law abolitionism floats between Scylla and Charybdis. Weak Rule of Law abolitionism fails as an argument against capital punishment, while strong Rule of Law abolitionism proves too much. However, I think it is possible to improve and strengthen strong Rule of Law abolitionism. Although a detailed discussion is beyond the scope of this chapter, I will conclude by indicating the path I think Rule of Law abolitionism ought to take.[56]

I would begin by softening the requirements of legal legitimacy. Legal systems can be legitimate even when legal judgments are not made solely on the basis of "desire-independent" reasons. But this softening does not mean we must endorse the status quo. It means we must add another component to legal legitimacy: legitimate law must acknowledge the frailty and limitations of legal actors, and incorporate procedures that correct those limitations. Legal institutions must engage in an ongoing effort to improve legal procedures, and to fix the mistakes that result from imperfect procedural mechanisms. As Emmanuel Levinas argues, legitimate legal institutions must act on the principle that justice should always be "more just," that justice is "not yet just enough" (Levinas, 2001, pp. 51–52). Although this aspect of legitimacy might sound unfamiliar,[57] it is expressed, however ambivalently, in contemporary U.S. legal practices such as appellate review, habeas corpus, executive clemency, and the Eighth Amendment's evolving standards of decency clause.

This conception of legitimacy strengthens, rather than weakens, abolitionism. Postconviction review, clemency, and the evolving standards of decency clause all express the important legal value of, for lack of a better word, *revisability*. Revision is the law's answer to our imperfect rationality, and is a crucial component of legal legitimacy: to be legitimate, the law must revisit and revise its mistakes. Now, if mechanisms for revision are a condition of legal legitimacy, it is easy to see how an abolitionist argument would be made. *Any* punishment can be revised except the punishment of death. Death really is different, "unusual in its pain, finality, and enormity" (*Furman*, 1972, pp. 286–287). Since the death penalty cannot be revised, it undermines the legitimacy of law in a unique and troubling way. And as Sarat (1997) writes, "those who love the law ... must hate the death penalty for the damage it does to the object of that love."

This new argument has the advantages of existing versions of Rule of Law abolitionism, while enjoying two additional benefits. First, its compatibility with a more nuanced picture of legal deliberation is likely to find more assent than the accounts provided by current forms of Rule of Law abolitionism. Second, it does not generate a wholesale attack on legal legitimacy: the value of revisability cashes out in a rejection of capital punishment, not a rejection of punishment as such. This modesty enables the mainstream political appeal that abolitionists avidly seek. As such, this argument from revisability adds an important new layer to Rule of Law abolitionism, strengthening its role in the struggle against capital punishment.

NOTES

1. There have been doctrinal retentionists. In *Furman*, Justice Blackmun dissents from the plurality opinion holding that the death penalty violates the cruel and unusual clause of the Constitution. However, he writes, "I yield to no one in the depth of my distaste, antipathy, and, indeed, abhorrence, for the death penalty, with all its aspects of physical distress and fear and of moral judgment exercised by finite minds" (p. 405). As we will see, Blackmun later changed his mind.

2. *Furman v. Georgia* (1972, p. 331). According to Justice Marshall, the Supreme Court's capital jurisprudence holds that only considerations of deterrence and retribution would make the death penalty non-excessive; neither, Marshall adds, does so (*Gregg v. Georgia*, 1976, pp. 233ff.)

3. *Gregg v. Georgia* (1976, p. 230; Justice Brennan, dissenting), Denno (2002), Bedau (1987).

4. *Furman v. Georgia* (1972, pp. 287ff.; Justice Brennan, concurring).

5. *Gregg v. Georgia* (1976, p. 241; Justice Marshall, dissenting), *Gregg v. Georgia* (1976, pp. 228–232; Justice Brennan, dissenting), Bedau (1997). This argument is typically the basis of international abolitionist movements. See, for example, the *Second Optional Protocol to the International Covenant on Civil and Political Rights*, Office of the United Nations High Commissioner for Human Rights. http://www.ohchr.org/english/law/ccpr-death.htm (accessed July 20, 2006).

6. The best brief conceptual, doctrinal, and historical introduction to the Supreme Court's post-*Furman* capital jurisprudence is Carol and Jordan Steiker's "Sober Second Thoughts: Reflections on Two Decades of Constitutional Regulation of Capital Punishment" (Steiker & Steiker, 1995).

7. See also Baldus, Woodworth, and Pulaski (1990) and Gross and Mauro (1989).

8. The *McCleskey* majority did not disagree with Baldus' methods or results, and did not disagree that the victim's race is one of the most important factors determining a murderer's sentence, but did not consider this sufficient to demonstrate "a constitutionally significant risk of racial bias affecting the Georgia capital sentencing process."

9. See, for example, Lynch (2002, pp. 903–908).

10. This is not limited to Eighth Amendment issues: in *Lockhart v. McCree* (1986), the Court upheld the constitutionality of death-qualified juries even though such juries are more likely to convict than juries selected for much less heinous crimes. There is a vast literature on this regrettable turn (see generally White, 1991; Denno, 1992; Harris, 1991). See also Justice Brennan's dissent in *Butler v. McKellar* (1990).

According to many legal scholars, the most significant aspect of this turn is the Court's restrictions on federal habeas corpus petitions (see Goldstein, 1990–1991; Weisberg, 1990). In 1996, Congress further limited federal habeas corpus protections by passing Title I of the Anti-Terrorism and Effective Death Penalty Act.

However, in "Sober Second Thoughts," Steiker and Steiker make a strong case, this turn is not really a turn, i.e., that the regulatory promises of *Furman* and *Gregg* were never met, and that the institution of capital punishment is hardly different today than it was before *Furman*, when sentences had unlimited discretion.

11. *Herrera v. Collins* (1993, p. 426). Although *Herrera* holds that a claim of actual innocence does not entitle a prisoner to a federal habeas hearing, in some ways, the holding is not as mind-boggling as it appears (see Berger, 1994).

12. See Lynch (2002) and Zimring (1993).

13. These extra-legal standards are meant to serve as "objective indicia" (Gregg, 1976) of these norms, rather than express the subjective opinion of the courts. However, the tests for the existence of these standards can get very complicated; they are much more than a matter of reading public opinion surveys or counting up bills passed by state legislatures. In *Atkins v. Virginia* (2002), the Court takes aspects of the wider cultural context, such as the fact that "anticrime legislation is far more popular than legislation providing protections for persons guilty of violent crime" as evidence for a consensus against execution of the mentally retarded (p. 315).

14. See Sarat and Kearns (1991).

15. Ewick and Silbey (1998) and Merry (1990).

16. See Reiman (1986) and Michelman (1986). Even legal positivists such as Alexander and Sherwin (2001, p. 189) agree. Raz (1983) does as well, although he does not immediately equate the distinction in violence with legitimacy (p. 30).

17. Sarat does not consider this to be a sufficient conception of law. He claims that law uneasily incorporates both a demand for rules and a demand for mercy (see Sarat & Hussein, 2004).

18. One can find many expressions of the intuition underlying Rule of Law abolitionism. Take, for example, Senator Russ Feingold's remarks during the introduction of the Federal Death Penalty Abolition Act of 1999: "The continued use of the death penalty demeans us. The death penalty is at odds with our best traditions .... And it's not just a matter of morality ... the continued viability of our justice system as a truly just system requires that we do so" (cited in Sarat, 2001, p. 260). See also Chapter 3 of Zimring and Hawkins' *Capital Punishment and the American Agenda* and Radin (1980).

19. Note that Stewart calls revenge "retribution." Supreme Court justices always equate retribution with revenge: Marshall does so (*Furman*, 1972, p. 343), although his remarks in *Gregg* are somewhat ambiguous (*Gregg*, 1976, pp. 237, 239–240); White does so (*Roberts v. Louisiana*, 1976, p. 355); and so does Brennan (*Furman*, 1972, p. 296). Their descriptions of "retribution" are almost completely equivalent to Nozick's description of revenge. I am not sure what is behind this conflation, but precision demands distinguishing them. There is a sea of legal and philosophical literature on this distinction and the meaning of retribution more generally. Other than Nozick's influential account, see Benn (1985), and Rawls (1985). One of the more thoughtful works is Robert Solomon's "Justice v. Vengeance: On Law and the Satisfaction of Emotion" (Solomon, 1999).

20. This phrase originates in the revolutionary *Marbury v. Madison*, and is cited in countless opinions, including Brennan's *McGautha* dissent.

21. The *Model Penal Code* 210.6 (Proposed Official Draft, 1962, and changes of July 30, 1962) is a famous attempt to subject sentencing to rules. The *Code* suggests

that a murder be found death eligible only if a sentencer finds one of the following proposed aggravating circumstances:

(a) The murder was committed by a convict under sentence of imprisonment.

(b) The defendant was previously convicted of another murder or of a felony involving the use or threat of violence to the person.

(c) At the time the murder was committed the defendant also committed another murder.

(d) The defendant knowingly created a great risk of death to many persons.

(e) The murder was committed while the defendant was engaged or was an accomplice in the commission of, or an attempt to commit, or flight after committing or attempting to commit robbery, rape or deviate sexual intercourse by force or threat of force, arson, burglary or kidnapping.

(f) The murder was committed for the purpose of avoiding or preventing a lawful arrest or effecting an escape from lawful custody.

(g) The murder was committed for pecuniary gain.

(h) The murder was especially heinous, atrocious, or cruel, manifesting exceptional depravity.

22. Harlan writes, "To identify before the fact those characteristics of criminal homicides and their perpetrators which call for the death penalty, and to express these characteristics in language which can be fairly understood and applied by the sentencing authority, appear to be tasks which are beyond present human ability" (*McGautha*, 1970, p. 204). Harlan argues that sentencing guidelines would be either so general as to constitute "meaningless boiler-plate" or so transparent and commonsensical ("a statement of the obvious") that they not be written into law (p. 208). General rules are not rules because they are too broad to eliminate discretion (even statutory aggravators such as "the murder was committed with an utter disregard for human life" pass constitutional muster (*Arave v. Creech*, 1993)); and since they will be understood differently by different juries they will not provide predictability and consistency. Rules specific enough to guide judgments (and lead to predictability and consistency) would be so specific as to be redundant or not wide enough to apply to more than a handful of cases; in either case, they, too, lose their function as rules. One could, of course, develop a complex hierarchical system of rules that allowed one to know which primary rules were to be followed in which circumstances. But, Harlan argues, solving the logical problem of rule-creation would only strengthen the practical problem of rule-application, as juries would be incapable of understanding such a system.

23. In a rather odd move, *Furman* and *Gregg* read arbitrariness and capriciousness in the language of the Eighth Amendment's cruel and unusual punishments clause, rather than the Fourteenth Amendment's guarantee of procedural due process. More than likely, this was to avoid overturning *McGautha* – which held that current capital punishment systems did not violate procedural due process – after only one year. This can get confusing, because *Furman* held that the death penalty violates the Eighth and Fourteenth Amendment (*Furman*, 1972, p. 240). To keep things straight

one must keep in mind that the Fourteenth Amendment guarantee of "due process" contains a procedural and a substantive due process clause. The substantive due process clause binds states to Eighth Amendment prohibitions against cruel and unusual punishment (see *Furman*, 1972, p. 241; also *Robinson v. California*, 1962). It is this part of the Fourteenth Amendment that *Furman* held was violated by capital punishment.

But Brennan traced the prohibition of arbitrariness and capriciousness to the Eighth Amendment's concern for human dignity (*Furman*, 1972, p. 274).

24. *Gregg* also holds that capital punishment schemes should have a separate guilt and sentencing phase, must provide for appellate review, and must insure that sentencing juries receive clear, accurate, and relevant sentencing information (pp. 189ff.).

25. Or at least a broad version of the like cases principle. The like cases principle is here understood to govern cases *within* a specific capital jurisdiction. But these can define the "worst" in different ways.

McCleskey suggests that the Court no longer cares much about consistent sentencing outcomes, or at least thinks that rational sentencing decisions can exist even when sentencing outcomes are inconsistent. Faced with the compelling evidence of the Baldus study, the *McCleskey* Court said that prejudice in McCleskey's *individual* case could not be inferred from evidence of systematic racial disparities in sentencing (pp. 292–297).

26. Many of the Court's concerns with arbitrary sentences are based in the fear of unchecked power in the hands of government officials or government offices that is also at the basis of the Court's due process jurisprudence, but I will not follow up these discussions.

27. The "Juror's Creed," printed in the handbook given to prospective jurors in Massachusetts, reads: "I am a JUROR. I am a seeker of truth …. I must lay aside all bias and prejudice. I must be led by my intelligence and not by my emotions" (cited in Nussbaum, 1995, p. 182, n. 86).

28. Technically, a crime is not committed against a person, but against the state. A typical bill of indictment for murder announces "John Doe did feloniously and unlawfully murder Jane Smith on or about____, in the City and County of____, all of which is against the peace and dignity of the State" (cited in Forer, 1980, p. 29).

29. And my account of the Court's legitimating distinctions – which perhaps imposes too much order on the imprecise logic of the Court's opinions – shows that Sarat's use of Nozick is not unhappy. Many of the Court's distinctions are contiguous with Nozick's. For Nozick, retribution is done for an officially specified wrong that requires some element of blameworthiness, rather than a harm (which is measured by the pain it causes to the victim). Retribution is carried out by a person or institution with no personal connection to the victim, while revenge is personal. Retributive punishments are meted out dispassionately, while revenge implies a particular "emotional tone," such as Schadenfreude. Retribution is based on general principles, which mandate like punishments for like crimes, while being vengeful in one case does not commit one to being so in others.

30. In *McGautha* (1972) Brennan argues that effective sentencing standards are necessary for the "rule of law" to prevail over the unfettered power of states to kill (p. 249). Sarat mentions the Rule of Law a number of times throughout his text,

although he gives it a very broad definition. He comes close to what I have argued when he writes that to "appear impartial and principled rather than personal and particularistic ... [is] crucial to the premises of what is called the 'rule of law' in liberal political thought" (1991, p. 218 n34) and that "all that is required to generate opposition to execution is a commitment to ... the rule of law" (2001, p. 254).

31. While the phrase "Rule of Law" is usually thrown around with abandon, it is the object of focused debate among some legal theorists and philosophers. Robust interpretations re-state in various ways Aristotle's view that "law is reason unaffected by desire" (*Politics*, iii, 16, 1287). Weak interpretations argue that the Rule of Law is reducible to the principle nulla poena sine lege, no punishment without law. This principle is often understood to correspond with the constraint that laws cannot demand the impossible and that laws must be understandable to a "rational" person.

For a comprehensive discussion of the distinction between robust and weak versions of the Rule of Law, see Neumann (2002, pp. 1–19). For robust interpretations of the Rule of Law, see Allen (1996) and Weinrib (1987). For weak interpretations of the Rule of Law, see Neumann (2002) and Lovett (2002). Raz and Fuller's interpretation of the Rule of Law occupies a position between these two extremes.

The Rule of Law theory that Rule of Law abolitionism endorses sits on the robust side of the continuum, but is weaker than that of Aristotle, Allen, or Weinrib.

32. Wellman and Simmons (2005), Alexander and Sherwin (2001), Wolff (1999), Wasserstrom (1999), Smith (1999), Raz (1999), Lyons (1984), Ladd (1970), and Gewirth (1970).

33. He argues for the existence of a "natural duty of justice" that "requires us to support and to comply with just institutions that exist and apply to us. It also constrains us to further just arrangements not yet established, at least when this can be done without too much cost to ourselves" (Rawls, 1999, p. 99). However, this mention of a duty to "further just arrangements not yet established" is only a suggestion, and is not taken up in the rest of the book. Nor has it received any critical notice. Simmons announces agreement with it without defending it (Simmons, 1981, p. 147). Gewirth mentions a duty on the part of citizens to influence the content of laws according to their beliefs (Gewirth, 1970, p. 80). This type of duty, he says, applies to everyone in a constitutional democracy, but is especially weighty in unjust legal systems (Gewirth does not, I assume, bar the possibility that constitutional democracies can be unjust). However, Gewirth says this is a "political" duty rather than a legal one. I will not tackle the problem of the political here!

34. See Reiman (1986, p. 178), Michelman (1986, p. 71), and Flathman (1970).

35. This point is by no means original. See Garland (2002, p. 480) and Kaufman-Osborn (2001, p. 684).

36. O'Hanlon (1999). Governor Mike Johanns vetoed the bill.

37. The text comes from "I Must Act," Governor Ryan's speech at Northwestern University College of Law announcing a blanket commutation of Illinois death sentences. Ryan emphasized that he tried multiple times to get the Illinois state legislature to reform capital sentencing procedures. The full text can be found in *The New York Times*, January 11, 2003.

38. A comprehensive collection of poll data, with links to original sources, can be found at ;http://www.religioustolerance.org/execut2.htm (accessed July 20, 2006).

39. It should be noted that Zimring and Hawkins (1986) argue that moratoria were an important factor in the gradual abolition of capital punishment in Western Europe (p. 22).

40. Executive Order No. 4 Creating the Commission on Capital Punishment. http://www.idoc.state.il.us/ccp/ccp/executive_order.html (accessed July 20, 2006).

41. The full text of the report can be found at the homepage of the Illinois Committee on Capital Punishment: http://www.idoc.state.il.us/ccp/ (accessed July 20, 2006).

42. A recent bill allocating one billion dollars to provide state and federal inmates with DNA testing won bipartisan support. "Bipartisan Deal Reached on DNA Tests for Inmates," *Washington Post*, Thursday, October 2, 2003, A2. As one of the sponsors of the bill said, "I'm a believer in the death penalty, but there has to be 100 percent certainty. What we do in this bill is fix a flawed system."

43. The *McCleskey* majority recognizes this strategy, and rejects it: "Given [the] safeguards already inherent in the imposition and review of capital sentences, the dissent's call for greater rationality [in capital sentencing] is no less than a claim that a capital punishment system cannot be administered in accord with the Constitution" (*McCleskey*, 1987, pp. 314–315, n. 37).

44. This argument is the focus of "A Journey through Forgetting," which is itself inspired by the work of Robert Cover. It is perplexing to read this essay in light of Sarat's Rule of Law abolitionism. Sarat and Kearns argue that Rule of Law theory's very attempt to portray law as "impartial and principled" is a form of what they call interpretive violence (Sarat & Kearns, 1991, p. 217–218). As far as I can tell, interpretive violence occurs when legal institutions hide the fact that they traffic in physical violence (p. 221). If this is what Sarat thinks, there is a real tension between this essay and his more abolitionist ones. It seems to me that Sarat's abolitionist work endorses a de jure conception of legitimacy, while his other work endorses a de facto conception.

45. Sarat also makes this point by reference to empirical examples – the Baldus study, Sarat's own investigation of victim impact statements, and so on (Sarat, 2001).

46. While Blackmun employs an almost exclusively constitutional vocabulary – he is, after all, writing for the U.S. Supreme Court – his abolitionism is not merely doctrinal. Indeed, he maintains that the Constitution permits the imposition of capital punishment (p. 1147). His argument rests on the value of individualized sentencing consideration, which derives from "standards of decency that have evolved over time" (p. 1151). As I argued above, this invocation of evolving standards is a response to law's need to legitimate its violence. Blackmun's real concern is that absent legitimating constraints on capital punishment, execution comes "perilously close to simple murder" (*Herrera*, 1993, p. 446).

47. Sarat often refers to Blackmun's *Callins* dissent as a paradigm of "legally conservative" abolitionism.

48. For an introduction to the wide range of arguments advanced by critical legal scholars, see Kairys (1982). For a sensitive and sympathetic critique of Critical Legal Studies, see Kennedy (1997).

49. Connolly argues that debates about capital punishment restage debates between those liberal pluralists and those who consider pluralism to be moral nihilism (Connolly, 1999). Abolitionists should counter these charges of nihilism, he argues, by exposing the instability of the categories of guilt and responsibility.

Like Connolly, Sarat contends that the death penalty affects not only actors involved in capital trials, but also the culture at large. *When the State Kills* argues that capital punishment encourages American society to adopt simplistic solutions to difficult problems of achieving reconciliation, inflames the legal battle between victims of crime and criminals to achieve the status of "real" victims, and endorses "flattened narratives" of personal responsibility that are meant to restore a chaotic society to some sort of moral order. In my view, Sarat's most persuasive defense of this claim is his careful analysis of rhetoric of guilt and responsibility in the capital trial of William Brooks (2001).

Simon and Spaulding argue that most statutory aggravators are symbols of cultural narratives of evil (Simon & Spaulding, 1999).

50. For a defense of total abolitionism, see Scheerer (1986) and Steinert (1986).

51. Anyone who argues that law is reducible to coercive violence must agree to a dubious phenomenological position. If we cannot make legal reasons (the justifying reasons given by a specific legal institution) our own reasons, law is senseless. This does not mean that legal subjects cannot make sense of law, that if someone asks me "what is law?" I will have to say "I don't have the slightest idea." One can always have thoughts about law and even write books about it. The senselessness is not theoretical, but practical. What it means is that law will have authority not only in the sense that it can, through the threat of violence, get people to do what it says they should do, but in the sense that legal rules will have authority in our practical life even though that authority is not recognized or even *capable of being* recognized. When I drive, I must stop at a stop sign. It is open to me to step on the brakes or press the gas pedal, and I will probably step on the brakes because I do not want to pay a fine. But regardless of my deliberations, the "must," the brute authority of the stop sign, remains. This brute authority will be a coercive one: the law imposes "norms" on me that I must live with, but have no control over. Since they are not receptive to any claims I might make on my behalf, I cannot ward them off or even negotiate their influence. The sheer authority of legal rules, not just the threat of their violent enforcement, would, in Nietzsche's words, confront us like as "something unforeseen, a dreadful natural event, a plunging, crushing rock" (*On the Genealogy of Morals* II, §14). Of course, it would be hard to imagine a legal system where *no* rules are experienced in this way. But in the picture of law that Rule of Law abolitionists provide, it is constitutive of our relation to law that every legal rule is coercive at the level of our practical life.

52. *Woodson* reads, "in capital cases the fundamental respect for humanity underlying the Eighth Amendment ... requires consideration of the character and record of the individual offender and the circumstances of the particular offense" (*Woodson*, 1976, p. 304).

53. Steiker and Steiker (1995) trace the odd development of individualization doctrine from the Court's concern with fairness and desert. The Steikers' analysis suggests that the conceptual and doctrinal issues surrounding fairness are even more complicated than I have let on, but that need not detain us here.

54. Scalia and Thomas both agree with Blackmun that individualized sentencing entails arbitrariness and irrationality (*Graham v. Collins*, 1993, p. 494). But Scalia draws a drastically different conclusion, arguing that the *Woodson/Lockett* line of cases should be overturned, and that he will not longer enforce them (*Walton v. Arizona*, 1990).

55. Steiker and Steiker (1995) make a related point in "Sober Second Thoughts," arguing that the values of consistency and individualized consideration are subsumed under the more general value of fairness.

56. I defend these claims in detail in *Thou Shalt Not Kill?: Legal Normativity and the Problem with Capital Punishment* (Yost, 2007).

57. Unger's discussion of "internal development" has important similarities (Unger, 1986, pp. 15–25).

ACKNOWLEDGMENTS

I would like to thank Jonathan Simon and Christopher Kutz for their helpful comments on an early version of this paper.

REFERENCES

Alexander, L., & Sherwin, E. (2001). *The rule of rules: Morality, rules, and the dilemmas of law*. Durham, NC: Duke University Press.

Allen, F. A. (1996). *The habits of legality: Criminal justice and the rule of law*. Oxford: Oxford University Press.

American Bar Association (1997). *Section of Individual Rights and Responsibilities*. Recommendation 107.

American Bar Association. (2003). *Building momentum: The American Bar Association call for a moratorium on executions takes hold*. Report of the ABA's Death Penalty Moratorium Implementation Project. http://www.abanet.org/moratorium/4thReport/4thAnnualReport.doc (accessed July 20, 2006).

Baldus, D., Woodworth, G., & Pulaski, C. (1983). Comparative review of death sentences: An empirical study of the Georgia experience. *Journal of Criminal Law and Criminology, 74*, 661–753.

Baldus, D., Woodworth, G., & Pulaski, C. (1990). *Equal justice and the death penalty: A legal and empirical analysis*. Boston, MA: Northeastern University Press.

Bedau, H. A. (1987). *Death is different: Studies in the morality, law and politics of capital punishment*. Boston, MA: Northeastern University Press.

Bedau, H. A. (1997). *The case against the death penalty*. Washington, D.C.: ACLU Publications.

Benn, S. I. (1985). Punishment. In: J. Murphy (Ed.), *Punishment and rehabilitation* (2nd ed.). Belmont, CA: Wadsworth.

Berger, V. (1994). *Herrera v. Collins*: The gateway for death-sentenced prisoners leads nowhere. *William and Mary Law Review, 35*, 943–1023.

Connolly, W. E. (1999). The will, capital punishment, and cultural war. In: A. Sarat (Ed.), *The killing state*. Oxford: Oxford University Press.

Denno, D. W. (1992). 'Death is different' and other twists of fate. *Journal of Criminal Law and Criminology, 83*, 437–467.

Denno, D. W. (2002). When legislatures delegate death: The troubling paradox behind state uses of electrocution and lethal injection and what it says about us. *Ohio State Law Journal, 63*, 631–260.

Ewick, P., & Silbey, S. (1998). *The common place of law: Stories from everyday life*. Chicago, IL: Chicago University Press.

Flathman, R. E. (1970). Obligation, ideals, and ability. In: J. R. Pennock & J. W. Chapman (Eds), *Nomos XII: Political and legal obligation*. New York: Atherton.

Forer, L. (1980). *Criminals and victims*. New York: W.W. Norton.

Garland, D. (2002). The cultural uses of capital punishment. *Punishment and Society, 4*, 459–488.

Gewirth, A. (1970). Obligation: Political, legal, moral. In: J. R. Pennock & J. W. Chapman (Eds), *Nomos XII: Political and legal obligation*. New York: Atherton.

Goldstein, S. (1990–1991). Chipping away at the great writ: Will death sentenced federal habeas corpus petitioners be able to seek and utilize changes in the law? *New York University Review of Law and Social Change, 18*, 357–414.

Gross, S., & Mauro, R. (1989). *Death and discrimination: Racial disparities in capital sentences*. Boston, MA: Northeastern University Press.

Harris, D. R. (1991). Note: Capital sentencing after *Walton v. Arizona*: A retreat from the 'Death Is Different' doctrine. *American University Law Review, 50*, 1389–1429.

Hart, H. L. A. (1994). *The concept of law* (2nd ed.). Oxford: Oxford University Press.

Kairys, D. (Ed.) (1982). *The politics of law*. New York: Pantheon.

Kaufman-Osborn, T. (2001). Regulating death: Capital punishment and the late liberal state. *Yale Law Journal, 111*, 681–735.

Kennedy, D. (1997). *A critique of adjudication*. Cambridge, MA: Harvard University Press.

Kirchmeier, J. (2002). Another place beyond here: The death penalty moratorium movement in the United States. *University of Colorado Law Review, 73*, 1–116.

Ladd, J. (1970). Legal and moral obligation. In: J. R. Pennock & J. W. Chapman (Eds), *Nomos XII: Political and legal obligation*. New York: Atherton.

Levinas, E. (2001). In: J. Robbins (Ed.), *Is it righteous to be?: Interviews with Emmanuel Levinas*. Stanford, CA: Stanford University Press.

Lovett, F. (2002). A positivist account of the rule of law. *Law and Social Inquiry, 27*, 41–78.

Lynch, M. (2002). Sarat's *when the state kills* and the transformation of death penalty scholarship. *Law and Social Inquiry, 27*, 903–922.

Lyons, D. (1984). *Ethics and the rule of law*. Cambridge, MA: Cambridge University Press.

Merry, S. E. (1990). *Getting justice and getting even: Legal consciousness among working-class Americans*. Chicago, IL: Chicago University Press.

Michelman, F. I. (1986). Justification (and justifiability) of law in a contradictory world. In: J. R. Pennock & J. W. Chapman (Eds), *Justification: Nomos XXVIII*. New York: New York University Press.

Neumann, M. (2002). *The rule of law: Politicizing ethics*. Burlington, VT: Ashgate.

Nussbaum, M. (1995). Equity and mercy. In: A. J. Simmons, M. Cohen, J. Cohen & C. Beitz (Eds), *Punishment*. Princeton, NJ: Princeton University Press.

O'Hanlon, K. (1999). *Debate looming on death penalty moratorium*. Associated Press.

Radin, M. J. (1980). Cruel punishment and respect for persons: Super due process for death. *Southern California Law Review, 55*, 1143–1185.

Rawls, J. (1985). Punishment as a practice. In: J. Murphy (Ed.), *Punishment and rehabilitation* (2nd ed.). Belmont, CA: Wadsworth.

Rawls, J. (1999). *A theory of justice* (Revised Ed.). Cambridge, MA: Harvard University Press.

Raz, J. (1983). *The authority of law: Essays on law and morality*. Oxford: Oxford University Press.

Raz, J. (1999). The obligation to obey: Revision and tradition. In: W. A. Edmundson (Ed.), *The duty to obey the law: Selected philosophical readings*. New York: Rowman & Littlefield.

Reiman, J. (1986). Law, rights, community and the structure of liberal legal justification. In: J. R. Pennock & J. W. Chapman (Eds), *Justification: Nomos XXVIII*. New York: New York University Press.

Sarat, A. (1997). Abolitionism as legal conservatism: The American Bar Association, the death penalty and the continuing anxiety about law's violence. *Theory and Event, 1*. http://muse.jhu.edu/journals/theory_and_event/v001/1.2sarat.html

Sarat, A. (2001). *When the state kills*. Princeton, NJ: Princeton University Press.

Sarat, A. (2002). The "new abolitionism" and the possibilities of legislative action: The new Hampshire experience. *Ohio State Law Journal, 63*, 343–369.

Sarat, A., & Hussein, N. (2004). On lawful lawlessness: George Ryan, executive clemency, and the rhetoric of sparing life. *Stanford Law Review, 56*, 1307–1344.

Sarat, A., & Kearns, T. (1991). A journey through forgetting: Toward a jurisprudence of violence. In: A. Sarat & T. Kearns (Eds), *The fate of law*. Ann Arbor, MI: Michigan University Press.

Scheerer, S. (1986). Towards abolitionism. *Contemporary Crises: Law, Crime and Social Policy, 10*, 5–20.

Simmons, A. J. (1981). *Moral principles and political obligations*. Princeton, NJ: Princeton University Press.

Simon, J., & Spaulding, C. (1999). Tokens of our esteem: Aggravating factors in the era of deregulated death penalties. In: A. Sarat (Ed.), *The killing state: Capital punishment in law, politics, and culture*. Oxford: Oxford University Press.

Smith, M. B. E. (1999). Is there a prima facie obligation to obey the law? In: W. A. Edmundson (Ed.), *The duty to obey the law: Selected philosophical readings*. New York: Rowman & Littlefield.

Solomon, R. (1999). Justice v. vengeance: On law and the satisfaction of emotion. In: S. Bandes (Ed.), *The passions of law*. New York: New York University Press.

Steiker, C., & Steiker, J. (1995). Sober second thoughts: Reflections on two decades of constitutional regulation of capital punishment. *Harvard Law Review, 109*, 355–438.

Steinert, H. (1986). Beyond crime and punishment. *Contemporary Crises: Law, Crime and Social Policy, 10*, 21–38.

Tysver, R. (1999). Strange bedfellows pushed execution moratorium. *Omaha World-Herald*, May 23.

Unger, R. M. (1986). *The critical legal studies movement*. Cambridge, MA: Harvard University Press.

Wasserstrom, R. A. (1999). The obligation to obey the law. In: W. A. Edmundson (Ed.), *The duty to obey the law: Selected philosophical readings*. New York: Rowman & Littlefield.

Weinrib, E. J. (1987). The intelligibility of the rule of law. In: A. Hutchinson & P. Monahan (Eds), *The rule of law: Ideal or ideology*. Toronto: Carswell.

Weisberg, R. (1990). A great writ while it lasted. *Journal of Criminal Law and Criminology, 81,* 9–36.

Wellman, C., & Simmons, A. J. (2005). *Is there a duty to obey the law?* Cambridge, MA: Cambridge University Press.

White, W. S. (1991). *The death penalty in the nineties: An examination of the modern system of capital punishment.* Ann Arbor, MI: Michigan University Press.

Williams, B. (1982). *Moral luck.* Cambridge, MA: Cambridge University Press.

Wolff, R. P. (1999). The conflict between authority and autonomy. In: W. A. Edmundson (Ed.), *The duty to obey the law: Selected philosophical readings.* New York: Rowman & Littlefield.

Yost, B. S. (2007). *Thou shalt not kill?: Legal normativity and the problem with capital punishment.* Ph.D. dissertation, Department of Rhetoric, University of California, Berkeley.

Zimring, F. (1993). On the liberating virtues of irrelevance. *Law & Society Review, 27,* 9–18.

Zimring, F., & Hawkins, G. (1986). *Capital punishment and the American agenda.* Cambridge: Cambridge University Press.

CASES CITED

Arave v. Creech. 507 U.S. 463. (1993).

Atkins v. Virginia. 536 U.S. 304. (2002).

Booth v. Maryland. 482 US 496. (1987).

Butler v. McKellar. 494 U.S. 407. (1990).

California v. Brown. 479 U.S. 538. (1987).

Callins v. Collins. 510 U.S. 1141. (1994).

Furman v. Georgia. 408 U.S. 238. (1972).

Graham v. Collins. 506 U.S. 461. (1993).

Gregg v. Georgia. 428 U.S. 153. (1976).

Herrera v. Collins. 506 U.S. 390. (1993).

Lockett v. Ohio. 438 U.S. 586. (1978).

Lockhart v. McCree. 476 U.S. 162. (1986).

McCleskey v. Kemp. 481 U.S. 279. (1987).

McGautha v. California. 398 U.S. 936. (1970).

Payne v. Tennessee. 501 U.S. 808. (1991).

Roberts v. Louisiana. 428 U.S. 325. (1976).

Robinson v. California. 370 U.S. 660. (1962).

Roper v. Simmons. 543 U.S. 551. (2005).

Trop v. Dulles. 356 U.S. 86. (1958).

Walton v. Arizona. 497 U.S. 639. (1990).

Woodson v. North Carolina. 428 U.S. 280. (1976).

Weems v. United States. 217 U.S. 349. (1910).

NOT WISER AFTER 35 YEARS OF CONTEMPLATING THE DEATH PENALTY

Leigh B. Bienen

ABSTRACT

Is the death penalty dying? This autobiographical essay offers observations on the application of capital punishment in three very different legal jurisdictions at three different time periods when – partially by happenstance and partially by design – she was a homicide researcher, a participant and an observer of profound changes in the jurisdiction's application of the death penalty.

The first illustrative case is Nigeria in the early 1970s when the federal government's authority and credibility had been badly damaged by a recent civil war. In Nigeria the military government created a parallel legal system to the ordinary criminal justice system. That parallel legal system could and did order especially harsh and summary penalties, including public executions. Public executions were a visible and highly symbolic way for the State to announce it had established civil rule. There was no public debate and little or no public dissent expressed or allowed.

The second example is New Jersey in the 1980s when capital punishment was reenacted by the legislature in 1982 after decades of its absence. The Supreme

Special Issue: Is the Death Penalty Dying?
Studies in Law, Politics, and Society, Volume 42, 91–133
ISSN: 1059-4337/doi:10.1016/S1059-4337(07)00404-8

Court of New Jersey responded to the legislative reimposition of capital punishment by establishing new, highly detailed and technically complex due process procedures, the result of which was: no executions have occurred in New Jersey as of November 2006, and few persons have been sentenced to death or have had their death sentences upheld by the state high court.

The third illustrative example is the extraordinary commutation of 167 death sentences and four pardons, the emptying of the Illinois death row, by departing Governor George Ryan in January 2003. That dramatic and unprecedented commutation did not happen in a political vacuum. Prior to the commutations, a set of unpredictable cases, some long in preparation and others not, revealed in a relatively compressed time period that 13 men on death row in Illinois were innocent, or wrongfully convicted, or both.

And finally these illustrative cases are compared with the surprisingly successful, recent, live challenges to the entire system for implementing capital punishment in the United States: the lethal injection cases. This procedural challenge crosses federal and state jurisdictional lines and threatens to bring to a halt all executions in the United States without raising any legal challenges to the death penalty itself with regard to the manner or constitutionality of its imposition.

INTRODUCTION

This is an autobiographical essay provoked by the question – Is the death penalty dying? Four illustrative case studies from my experience as a researcher on homicide and capital punishment over the past 35 years are an occasion to reflect upon my experience with capital punishment in very different circumstances over what seems like a long period of time. One theme is common to all these examples: that is, how inextricable the law, both decisional law and statutory law, is from the larger, surrounding politics of time and place. If the death penalty is dying in the United States, individuals will play a decisive and pivotal role, but there must be a political moment, an opportunity, a confluence of forces, which may be fleeting, for that to happen.

In the description of the death penalty case studies that follows, the pattern which emerges, if there is one, is a pattern of particularity and individuality. New Jersey and Illinois have never had similar legal institutions. It would be hard to imagine a New Jersey Governor acting as George Ryan did when he emptied death row in Illinois, and equally impossible to imagine the Supreme Court of Illinois taking the course chosen by the Supreme Court of New Jersey in the 1980s. Nigeria is offered as an example of a regime using capital punishment as a tool for different objectives. The lethal injection cases, popping up all over the country after 2002, are an example of the unpredictability of legal outcomes in a system with thousands of actors and adjudicators when the political climate changes every moment and then momentum is established.

ILLUSTRATIVE CASE NO. 1 – NIGERIA AND THE ARMED ROBBERY TRIBUNAL IN 1972–1973

My first experience with capital punishment was in the Western State of Nigeria in 1971 when I was looking for a research project to earn six academic credits while on leave of absence after my first year of law school. The truth was I had found the first year of legal education so devoid of intellectual and personal rewards that I had no commitment to continue. I had always loved research, and I was looking for a project to while away the time. This research on capital punishment in Nigeria, now so distant in time and place, and its methodology, so simple, continues to resonate with my present work on capital punishment 35 years later. Perhaps the commonality is the interplay between the law's overarching, studied formality, its seeming objectivity, and the deep human irrationality of its application in the particular. This juxtaposition, so striking in the many manifestations of capital punishment, makes the study of the death penalty endlessly seductive. Just when understanding seems imminent, a new conundrum, a fresh contradiction presents itself.

While reading through all of the books in English on African Law in the University of Ibadan Library in 1970, I came across Paul Bohannan's *African Homicide and Suicide* (1960), a series of commissioned essays from the 1950s, mostly by British colonial officers who later became anthropologists, about patterns in homicide and suicide in their colonial districts. These anthropologists were careful observers, and this was the beginning of the academic study of homicide, coming into its own with the publication of Marvin Wolfgang's *Patterns in Criminal Homicide* (Wolfgang, 1958), just as quantitative sociology was transforming the discipline. One droll aspect of doing research on homicide in Nigeria in the 1970s was the repeated, solemn observation by British and American academics that the expected rates and patterns of homicide in Nigeria would resemble those of blacks in Philadelphia, because Wolfgang's study differentiated between blacks and whites. While this suggestion was absurd, the association of the study of homicide with issues of race, as well as class and gender, is long standing and persistent (Bienen, Weiner, Denno, Allison, & Mills, 1988, p. 27).[1]

I designed a research project replicating the simple model suggested in *African Homicide and Suicide* (Bohannan, 1960). After many inquiries, and many people telling me no records existed, I came upon all the handwritten opinions of the Western State Supreme Court since they had started keeping written records of their opinions. These opinions were similar to records from the eighteenth or nineteenth century in Britain or America. The court first summarized the facts and the evidence presented, and then issued a brief legal ruling. There was an appellate avenue to the federal Supreme Court, but few cases were taken there. These case files, a few pages for each case, carefully written in dipped ink on slick British copying paper, included 114 homicides, a new and fresh set of data on Nigerian homicide cases from the late 1960s, which I addressed following the guidelines given by Paul Bohannan to his anthropologists in the 1950s. What little I knew of criminal law was based upon one semester of a textbook and lecture course in the first year of law school.

This seemed like a worthwhile and manageable project: a straightforward account of homicides in Western Nigeria, a state which then had a population about the size of my home state, New Jersey. The law was simple enough. Homicide was a crime, defined in the same way as it was defined in New Jersey: as the unlawful killing of another without justification. The penalty was life imprisonment, or death. The source of the law, including the law supporting the imposition of the death penalty, was British common law and some statutory law, just like in New Jersey. I counted the homicides, identified patterns, such as in the kind of weapon used, the relationship between victim and defendant, and the circumstances of the homicide, such as whether it occurred in the home or on the road, or during the commission of another felony such as robbery.[2] There was a new wrinkle, however.

The military government had come to power in January 1966, and there had been a second military coup in July 1966 when Yakubu Gowon assumed power on August 1, 1966.[3] In 1970 the regime in power was the military government with Gowon as Chair of the Supreme Military Council. The military government had suspended certain provisions of the federal constitution regarding the rights of criminal defendants. The criminal courts and the rules governing trials and procedures in the Western State of Nigeria, however, were basically unaffected by the fact of a military government with one important exception.

A legal body called the Armed Robbery Tribunal was created after the Nigerian Civil War under the authority of the military tribunal by a Decree

(Laws of the Federation of Nigeria, 1984).[4] The Nigerian Civil War (1967–1970) had resulted in civilian and military deaths between two and three million, involved the secession of the Republic of Biafra in the Southeastern region, which was primarily Ibo, the subsequent blockade and siege of the region by the Federal army with many hundreds of thousands of deaths of soldiers, civilians, and children.

At the end of the war there was vast civil and economic disruption, with large numbers of weapons and arms in the hands of people who had no prospect of integration into the society or economy. Civilians in places such as Ibadan, where I was living and which was not part of the former Republic of Biafra, were fearful of going out in cars at night, and there were daily reports of armed holdups, burglaries, and murders. Whether this was a crime wave, or hysteria promoted by the press or the government, was unknown. Evidence of the destruction of the civil war was everywhere, as was the sense of disorder and the lack of governmental control. Everyone had weapons, the government officers, the police, and the criminals.[5]

Meanwhile, in this time before the internet, when international telephone calls and telegrams were expensive, sporadic, and unreliable, I had two sources of information about homicide in Western Nigeria: some very dated books in the library, my collection of handwritten cases from the Western State Supreme Court Library, and the Nigerian newspapers and tabloids, which sold copies by reporting murders, the sexual escapades of prominent people, acts of violence, and the corruption and hypocrisy of politicians.[6] These same tabloids periodically featured gruesome reports, complete with photographs, of public executions on the Bar Beach in the national capital, Lagos, under the authority of the Armed Robbery Tribunal. Ten to twenty at a time would be executed by firing squad, their bodies then thrown to the sharks swimming in the Bay while crowds numbered in the thousands watched.

So in the heat and dust and confusion of Western Nigeria in 1971–1972 – there was little or no air conditioning – I pursued two parallel tracks of inquiry, a pattern I have continued to this day: the first, an academic, formal, quantitative, seemingly objective annotation of patterns in homicide, and the second, a narrative description of the unstructured chaos that I observed around me. This is not to imply that one form of inquiry is superior to the other, but rather that the two approaches complement one another; indeed each is deficient without the other. The seemingly objective approach of measuring the attributes of killers and victims and the circumstances of murder is also deeply irrational, in spite of its being couched in scientific rhetoric. And the observation of the irrational turns to the law, or science, to impose order.

There was the formal law, the cases and statutes, the rules of evidence – impeccable and impenetrable, and not very different from what I had read in my casebook in New Jersey – and the circus surrounding the public executions reported in the tabloids. The stories included pictures of those about to be executed, and, after execution, reports of last rites and the last words of penitence, or curses, by those being executed, as well as stern admonishments by judges from the Tribunal and law enforcement officials.

Western Nigerians were at that time justifiably proud of their completely Africanized criminal justice system. True, there were cracks in the formal system – such as the rule that the standard for insanity for the law in Western Nigeria was what would be considered acceptable to the average man on the street in an English provincial city, such as Leeds or Manchester – but the consensus on the part of both professionals and the public was that this was a functioning legal system. The trial court judges assigned counsel to indigents in every murder case, protected the due process rights of defendants, and followed the British rules of evidence even when such legal protections were no longer required under the federal constitution.

While the formal criminal law was the British common law, including a provision for the death penalty, in fact, under the ordinary criminal system in the Western State of Nigeria, the death sentence was rarely imposed and only upheld after lengthy appeals. When executions under the ordinary criminal law did take place – perhaps three or four in a decade – there was no publicity or notoriety or sensationalism surrounding them. The next of kin were simply informed that the convicted murderer who had languished without publicity in prison during a series of British type of appeals based upon legal precedent had been executed.

Then there was this other legal system, the one which was tying the condemned to posts, shooting them and throwing their bodies to the sharks in the Bay. That legal system took its authority from the 1970 Decree of the military government, not from a statute passed by a legislature, not from the common law traditions of the British legal system, and not from traditional African legal norms.

The Decree of 1970 had created a new quasi-judicial body called the Armed Robbery Tribunal, consisting of a trial court judge, a military officer, and a police officer. This Tribunal had one function, to decide whether a defendant was guilty under the provisions of the Decree (Development Policy Centre Nigeria, 2000).[7] Those eligible to be convicted were not just murderers and armed robbers, but also those 'in the company of' those committing an armed robbery. If a person was found guilty, the sentence was an automatic death sentence.[8] There were no appeals to the ordinary State criminal justice system or to the federal courts from decisions of this Tribunal, although the military Governor did have the authority to grant clemency.[9] And the executions were public.

As this research proceeded, I decided to observe every level of adjudication in the criminal justice system.[10] I discovered when I went to my first murder trial – my journalistic instincts told me I should see what was actually happening in trials before writing anything – that the proceedings were conducted in a language the accused did not understand, English. The scholarly tomes in the library had not mentioned this fact, perhaps because it was so taken for granted that none of the commentators thought it remarkable, or even requiring explanation, or justification.[11]

When I interviewed the members of the Armed Robbery Tribunal, one Judge, who was a police officer, assured me that the purpose of the public executions was to deter crime, to stop the post civil war violence by showing the criminals what happened to those who were caught. Certainly there was widespread civil mayhem. No one with a car drove at night or on unknown roads, and there were many guns in the hands of people with grievances and no jobs or money.

The Judge looked sternly at me and said, it was all very well to be against capital punishment in America – he had been to Atlanta for training at the United States Federal Bureau of Investigation (FBI) headquarters – where there was a well established tradition of respect for law and order (perhaps I demurred on the subject of the public executions, although I do not remember doing so), but the present chaos in Nigeria called for capital punishment, and public executions.

Neither the judges of the Armed Robbery Tribunal, nor the military officers who created the Tribunal, nor the general population of Nigerian millions, most of whom were law abiding, nor I, can say with authority whether the public executions deterred any armed robberies or murders (Ilo, 2004),[12] beyond the possible future robberies and murders not committed by those thrown to the sharks at Bar Beach on a particular day.[13] The Judge, however, firmly believed that these executions were a deterrent to further civil disorder and to future armed robberies and murders. It is certain that the violence did not stop.

My recollection is that the public executions usually took place on a weekend, so that more people would come. Probably they didn't take place on a Sunday. This was then a Christian part of the country. The carnival atmosphere of these occasions was striking. The crowds at the Bar Beach were market women and babies, pickpockets, boys with sticks and girls in colorful wrappers, according to the photographs and published reports – I never attended an execution – and what seemed to be a random, ordinary collection of men and women who had nothing better to do that day. People seemed to become exhilarated at the prospect of a killing, and some of the condemned commanded attention from their brief position on center stage.

Whether or not public executions deterred murder and armed robbery, at the end of the academic year, I was completely seduced by this research. The death penalty has remained an abiding preoccupation. Every time I plan on moving away from it, some new development will bring me back. In the 1970s I collected all of my data points on 114 homicides in Western Nigeria, observed every level of adjudication, including several murder trials, and interviewed every level of judge in the court system, as well as defense attorneys and prosecutors and legislators. I came to Nigeria prepared to leave law school when I returned to America. I returned as a homicide researcher. My first job after law school, on the recommendation of Marvin Wolfgang, was working as a research attorney for an NIMH study of sexual assault in Philadelphia. I spent 15 years as a Public Defender working on homicide and capital punishment in New Jersey and conduct similar research now in Illinois, all because I was mesmerized by the contradictions of capital punishment in Nigeria 35 years ago.

ILLUSTRATIVE CASE NO. 2 – NEW JERSEY, 1980–1992

A few years after graduating from law school I went to work for the New Jersey Office of the Public Advocate, which then included the statewide Office of the Public Defender. When I brought up my research background, working on capital punishment and homicide in Nigeria, to the lawyer who would basically be my supervisor for the next 15 years, he crisply informed me that New Jersey had no death penalty. The last execution occurred more than 20 years ago.[14] And, he continued, it was unlikely there would be a death penalty in New Jersey in the future. The then governor had promised to veto any capital punishment bill out of the legislature, and the votes are not there to override his veto. Besides, he added, we do not do social science type research at the Office of the Public Defender. This is a law office. By this time I had spent several years working on a scientific study of all reporting rape victims in Philadelphia and was familiar with the quantitative analysis of legal issues in the context of sexual assault. Statistics and the abstraction of legal analysis were a rudder and a distancer in the area of rape, as well as homicide, for me, for the courts, and for the legal system.

The year was 1976, when state legislatures had received the green light from the United States Supreme Court in *Gregg v. Georgia* (1976) to go ahead with capital prosecutions. New Jersey had reluctantly declared its system of capital punishment unconstitutional in *State v. Funicello* (1972).[15] After monitoring the passage of a new criminal code, which eventually included a death penalty, I ended up spending 10 of my next 15 years as a Public Defender constructing an empirical study of homicide in New Jersey. It was another attempt to impose objectivity, the science of quantitative analysis, on the chaos and confusion brought on with the reimplementation of capital punishment. It was the rationalist's hope that if only we could get enough information, and analyze it with sufficient scientific objectivity, we could control and understand what was happening. The application of the death penalty would be principled, under the law. That impulse, to make the application of capital punishment consistent and predictable, would come again in Illinois, and is seen in the lethal injection cases as well.

My colleague had been correct in predicting that the reenactment of capital punishment in New Jersey was not a foregone conclusion, even after *Gregg v. Georgia* (Bienen et al., 1988).[16] When constitutional provisions prevented Governor Brendan Byrne from running again in 1982, the newly elected Republican Thomas Kean did sign the bill reinstating the death penalty. The effective date of reenactment was August 6, 1982, the date that Governor Bryne's successor signed the bill. The first capital prosecution in New Jersey occurred soon after, and the New Jersey Supreme Court immediately began to hear a series of procedural and systemwide challenges to the reimposition (Bienen et al., 1988, pp. 70–100).

The state legislators were unequivocally in favor of the death penalty, although it was never entirely clear why the state legislators were so keen to reenact.[17] The 'father of the death penalty,' Senator John Russo, was formerly a prosecutor, but it was not the county prosecutors who were pushing for the reenactment. New Jersey is one of the few states not to elect county prosecutors, or to elect judges. A majority of the 21 appointed county prosecutors in New Jersey did not favor reenactment of capital punishment according to an informal poll taken at a county prosecutor's meeting just before the effective date of reenactment. Nonetheless, they all pledged to follow the law and prosecute death eligible homicides as capital cases after reenactment.

The New Jersey legislature, which was so keen to reenact, never turned down a request for funds for capital defense from the Office of the Public Defender during the first decade after reenactment. The Department regularly spent more than a million dollars on a single capital case, especially in the early years of the statute when no one, including the judges, the prosecutors, and the defense attorneys, knew how to interpret or apply the new death penalty law with the two tiered trial and its statutory aggravating and mitigating factors. When New Jersey reenacted, Illinois was well on the way of filling up its death row, although the first execution in Illinois was not until 1990. The first death sentence in Illinois was upheld in 1981 (Bienen, 1996). New Jersey in 1982 was already well behind Illinois in reestablishing a capital punishment system which regularly turned out death sentences and executed defendants.

This is where I became a homicide researcher again. With the expert assistance of colleagues from the Criminology Center at the University of Pennsylvania, the Supreme Court of New Jersey and skeptical defense attorneys and prosecutors were persuaded that the entire system of prosecuting and trying homicide cases in New Jersey should be examined in detail, using the methodology of social science. The basic tenet of proportionality review is to inquire whether a particular death penalty imposed upon a particular defendant is 'just' or 'proportionate' when compared to other cases in which the death penalty has and has not been imposed.

Whether or not all death eligible cases as capital cases were prosecuted was one of the most important factual determinations of the long investigation into homicide and capital case processing which came to be known as proportionality review (Bienen, 1996).[18] It was surprising to the Public Defenders and others in New Jersey that jurors in the first capital trials in the state overwhelmingly rejected the imposition of the death sentence, even after finding the defendant guilty of a clearly death eligible murder, in spite of the high level of public support for capital punishment reported in the polls. Out of more than 130 initial capital prosecutions, only 25 defendants were sentenced to death (Bienen et al., 1988, p. 170, Table 2). The Public Defenders could congratulate themselves that the legal defense was effective, but perhaps it was that jurors, when faced with an actual defendant, even one who had been proved to have committed a horrific murder, did not want to vote to kill another human being. And these were jurors who had been death-qualified and were thus more likely than the general public to be in favor of capital punishment.

When the death penalty was reenacted in New Jersey in 1982, it was not clear who wanted it, except few highly vocal state legislators. State Senator John Russo claimed he persisted for years in reintroducing legislation reenacting capital punishment when it had no chance of becoming law to avenge his father who was a victim of murder. Senator Russo was a powerful state legislator, a member of the Senate Judiciary Committee during the time when the Criminal Code was being passed.[19] He also repeatedly said he wanted the death penalty to be fair and for defendants to have all due process rights. Ironically, Senator Russo was acquainted with several of the personages in the Robert Marshall case, the case from his county, Ocean County, which became the vehicle for the principal statewide challenge to the reimposition of capital punishment in New Jersey.

The facts in the Robert Marshall case were the perfect foil for the challenge to the reimposition of capital punishment in New Jersey (Bienen, 1996, pp. 183–212),[20] as evidenced by the fact that it was the subject of a best selling book and then a made for television movie (Bienen, 1993).[21] The case exhibited a motley cast of clowns and bumblers, including the private defense attorney who took what money Robert Marshall had, did not call his children to testify at the penalty trial, and then dumped the defendant and his death sentence on the Public Defender for what turned out to be more than 20 years of appeals. Not only was Robert Marshall the perfect hero–villain for the ensuing death penalty drama, but the attributes of his case made this the perfect case for the New Jersey Supreme Court to address the legal and ethical conundrums raised by the new death penalty.

Led by Robert N. Wilentz, the son of the Attorney General who orchestrated the drama which led to the execution of Bruno Richard Hauptmann in 1936 for the kidnapping and murder of the Lindbergh baby, the Supreme Court of New Jersey was in the 1980s the most intellectual and thoughtful state supreme court in the country. It was particularly known for developing state constitutional law doctrine, relying upon state constitutional principles at a time when the United States Supreme Court was becoming unwilling to reexamine the procedures in state capital convictions, look at state capital punishment systems or halt executions.[22] The Robert Marshall case became the occasion for the New Jersey Supreme Court to examine systemwide aspects of the legal ramifications of reenactment in New Jersey, before upholding his death sentence as constitutional in 1992, ten years after reenactment.

Robert Marshall was white, a college graduate, a successful insurance executive who seemed to live an ordinary small town American life until this aberrational murder. He was clearly guilty of planning to kill his wife. The outcome of the case at trial exemplified the quixotic aspect of capital trials: Robert Marshall was sentenced to death; one of the assassins, probably not the trigger man, was sentenced to time served; the other assassin was acquitted at trial; while the 'go between,' a clerk in a country store whose role was to allow his phone to be used and relay messages to the assassins, was sentenced to 30 years without parole. Recently, an interim governor commuted the sentence of the co-conspirator (Vaughan, 2006).[23] After 20 years of federal and state appeals, Robert Marshall's death sentence was set aside on grounds of incompetence of his trial counsel by the Third Circuit Court of Appeals in 2005 (*Marshall v. Cathel*, 2005).[24] The Attorney General of New Jersey asked for a writ of *certiorari* to the United States Supreme Court on the last day of eligibility.[25] He will not be retried with the possibility of being resentenced to death.

The New Jersey Supreme Court, under the strong leadership of Hauptmann's prosecutor's serious son, addressed the legal and ethical conundrums of the 'new' death penalty. Objective, statistical, and legal analysis was applied to the irrationality of murder and the bizarre outcomes at trial. This juxtaposition presented many conundrums. The reenactment of capital punishment in a number of states had been tarnished by the continuing taint of racial and economic bias in prosecution and sentencing. The poor, and mostly minorities, were sentenced to death. While that was uncontested, the reasons for it were confounded and, for some, inextricable from inequities which plagued the criminal justice system as a whole. Robert Marshall himself was not poor, mentally retarded, or socially or culturally disadvantaged. Nor was he mentally ill, psychotic, sadistic, a mass murderer, or any other kind of madman whose fate at the hands of an executioner would raise different legal and ethical issues. Although there was widespread publicity at his trial, Robert Marshall's death sentence presented a relatively straightforward case for the court to use as an occasion to consider systemwide inequities and procedural problems with the reimposition of capital punishment. His appeal also arose at a fortuitous moment in the development of capital punishment jurisprudence in New Jersey.

The Supreme Court of New Jersey did not uphold the statute as constitutional until five years after reenactment, and only after reversing 27 consecutive death sentences. This along with the court's controversial stand on other issues caused the Chief Justice Wilentz serious problems at his seven-year confirmation hearing.[26] Several state legislators expressed their unhappiness with the fact that four years had passed since reenactment and no one had been executed under the new statute (Bienen, 1996, p. 209, n. 283).[27] Nonetheless he was confirmed, and the court continued to develop extraordinary constitutional doctrine regarding capital punishment. The Supreme Court of New Jersey was unpreturbed by the fact that the United States Supreme Court had in 1984 declared that proportionality review was not required by the federal constitution and had rejected a systemwide challenge to a state capital punishment system in 1987. The Supreme Court of New Jersey simply said that law did not apply in New Jersey; state constitutional principles controlled. The

Supreme Court of New Jersey also simply ignored a legislative provision restricting proportionality review in New Jersey to a limited comparison of death only cases (Bienen, 1996, p. 211, n. 295).[28]

Instead the Supreme Court of New Jersey took over the study of all homicides in New Jersey since the reimposition of capital punishment, which was started at the Office of the Public Defender, hiring as its own Special Master Professor David Baldus from the University of Iowa, the expert whose elaborate statistical study had not been persuasive to the United States Supreme Court. He had been the academic, principally in charge of the Georgia studies brought before the United States Supreme Court over decades of litigation, culminating in 1987. In New Jersey Professor Baldus and others devised a new methodology for comparing the characteristics of the offense and offender to determine whether the imposition of the death sentence in a particular case was proportionate, or just (Bienen, 1996, pp. 183–207, n. 193).[29] The defining of this procedure and its application to individual cases took years and resulted in an elaborate jurisprudence, culminating with the upholding of Robert Marshall's death sentence as proportionate (*State v. Robert O. Marshall, II*, 1992).

No other state Supreme Court before or since has been willing to hold an entire criminal justice system up to the light. Then, the times changed, and the court's personnel changed. Chief Justice Wilentz died, and Justice Handler, who had been one of the most thoughtful of the contributors to the inquiry, retired, and other justices of the Supreme Court of New Jersey retired or were replaced (Bienen, 1996, p. 209, n. 284).[30] After 10 years of research on homicide and the death penalty in New Jersey, after, as Justice Handler of the Supreme Court of New Jersey noted, thousands of hours and thousands of pages of New Jersey Supreme Court opinions, the grinding of many computers and miles of green bar printout – that was where the technology was then – what was accomplished by proportionality review in New Jersey? Robert Marshall himself will not be executed, but for other reasons.

In the Robert Marshall case, after all of the statistics, after all of the systemwide analysis, after all of the technicalities of proportionality review, the most difficult fact for the court to reconcile was that there was another case from another county in New Jersey which was almost a twin of the *Marshall* case on its facts (Bienen, 1996, p. 196, n. 234). In another case a relatively well-off, white man – I do not use the term 'middle class' because there were suggestions of an organized crime association – hired two assassins to kill his wife. In some respects the circumstances of this case were 'worse' than those of *Marshall*. The wife was tortured before being killed by the two thugs hired to kill her.

As in *Marshall* there was no question of the guilt of the defendant, and it was a killing for hire. And yet the County Prosecutor in that case chose not to prosecute the case as a capital case, in spite of the fact that there was a strong factual basis for more than one statutory aggravating factor: the cold blooded hiring of two assassins to kill, and the torture of the victim. How could the principle of proportionality be maintained in the face of such a contradiction? More than the statistics, more than the regression analysis, more than the philosophical principles, this simple intuitive comparison between two cases, one where death was imposed and a similar case where it was not because of a prosecutor's choice, proved to be intractable.

Yet, at the end of all of these extraordinary legal proceedings, after all the complicated methodology, the Supreme Court of New Jersey was still stuck with the death penalty. The Court had been successful in postponing executions, at least for some time. Now the New Jersey legislature has taken an unprecedented step in imposing a moratorium on executions and creating a Study Commission whose mission it is to come up with reasons for keeping the death penalty. Probably the legislature could not have taken this stance if the Supreme Court of New Jersey had not engaged in 15 years of extensive dialogue about the reimposition of capital punishment in New Jersey. The methodology developed for the *Marshall* case has been and will continue to be applied to others sentenced to death whose sentences automatically come to the New Jersey Supreme Court for review, as long as there is a death penalty in New Jersey.

There was a great deal of expense and little entertainment value in proportionality review, although, as with every aspect of the death penalty, there were many ironies. As a homicide researcher it was enormously satisfying to be able to collect the data on all homicides in New Jersey since the reimposition of capital punishment in 1982, to participate in the creation of a workable model for analyzing cases by category of offense and offender, and then to watch the results and the contradictions rise to the surface in this relatively straightforward and scientific process. Though proportionality review did not result in the Court declaring the system unconstitutional, it did result in a substantial body of jurisprudence.

As of January 2006 there is a legislatively imposed moratorium on executions in New Jersey, and that same bill passed in January 2006 created a Study Commission to submit its findings to the New Jersey legislature before November 15, 2006 ([6]An Act Creating a Study Commission on the Death Penalty and Imposing a Moratorium on Executions, 2005).[31] The Study Commission has published a cost study, detailing the entire cost of the reimposition of capital punishment in the state and the cost of individual cases. The bill asks the legislature to repeal the death penalty unless there can be shown a reason to continue it. It is the only legislatively imposed moratorium, and the legislative findings announced in the statute are extraordinary.[32]

To understand what happened in New Jersey, it is very important to remember that the 21 county prosecutors are not elected, and that the last execution was in 1963. The legal institutions are not dug in with regard to a commitment to the death penalty. This is probably the most significant difference between Illinois and New Jersey. In Illinois the Supreme Court could hardly wait to affirm the first death penalty. They never recognized that the old statute was unconstitutional. In Nigeria the constitutionality of capital punishment was not even discussed. New Jersey is a unique political and legal culture, one without much interest or commitment to the reimposition of capital punishment. That cultural context was critical, as was the long standing tradition of judicial independence and the respect in the legal community for the Supreme Court of New Jersey.

As always, there were unpredictable elements in New Jersey as well. The former Governor of New Jersey, who opposed the bill creating the Study Commission and the moratorium on executions, resigned for reasons unrelated to the death penalty. The interim Governor, having nothing to lose politically, was willing to sign the legislation establishing moratorium and the bill with the findings creating the Study Commission. The present Governor, John Corzine, supports the moratorium and the bill. The former Attorney General of the State, Zulima Farber, who has since resigned for reasons unrelated to capital punishment, also was not in favor of capital punishment, and it remains to be seen whether her successor will take the same position.[33]

In New Jersey the death penalty does seem to be dying, but the death penalty had not for decades been strongly entrenched in the political or legal culture. It is as if the entire state is still recovering from the Hauptmann execution. For a critical decade the state Supreme Court was willing to distinguish its death penalty rulings from the trend at the United States Supreme Court and rule on the basis of the state constitutional law. The leadership and tenacity shown by Chief Justice Wilentz in this area could not have been predicted and will not be replicated. It is also important that the executions never started after reenactment, and few death sentences have been imposed or upheld by the state supreme court (National Association for the Advancement of Colored People Legal Defense and Education Fund, 2006).[34]

THE CHANGE IN THE POLITICAL CLIMATE
IN THE 1990s

In the 1990s the legal arguments in capital cases were becoming increasingly technical and incomprehensible to the public, replacing the dramas of revenge in some of the first death penalty cases after *Furman*, cases such as those involving Ted Bundy or Gary Gilmore. Perhaps the most telling analysis of the changes in the 1990s will be made by a demographic study of criminal defendants and the changes in the prison population during this decade. Nuances of federal appellate procedure were cast as rule interpretations and refined to tell death row inmates that they had no more avenues of appeal, even if they brought a new claim of innocence. The composition of the United States Supreme Court had changed, and the court had become impatient with protracted appeals in death cases. Lawyers who made careless mistakes, such as filing papers a day late, were responsible for sending their clients to the execution chamber. The technicalities of the questioning of jurors, who were qualified to vote for or against death based upon what they said in *voir dire*, was weighed down by an increasingly arcane body of precedent. Each state had different rules, and cases in the federal system were being bounced back to the states. Somewhere along the way the moral high ground was lost by those who had championed capital punishment as the return to a more principled criminal justice system based on the harsh punishment of murderers.

At the same time stories of death row inmates who were drugged, mentally incompetent, who did not realize they were not coming back from the execution chamber to eat their dessert, and inmates who were abused and brutalized as children became common currency, offset by the increasingly vocal victims' rights advocates. The discourse was all about pain and suffering on both sides. The reports were of local prosecutors running for reelection based on the number of murderers they sent to the gallows, of drunken and incompetent defense attorneys who were assigned cases after contributing to a judge's reelection campaign, of courts and counties who would not pay more than a few hundred dollars to defense attorneys, as well as allegations of false confessions, torture at the police station, rigged or mistaken identifications by eye witnesses, lost evidence, forged evidence, suppressed exonerating evidence, and on and on (Medwed, 2006).

As the new death penalty was bringing forward tales of less than a clean cut or wholesome death penalty prosecutions, the innocence movement was gaining momentum. Dozens of inmates on death row were proved to be entirely innocent of the crime for which they had been sentenced to death.

In state after state defense attorneys, who were learning to coordinate and collaborate on what came to be recognized as common patterns, were able to show that some people on death row were there because their false confessions were coerced, or because evidence of their guilt had been manufactured and evidence of their innocence suppressed or ignored. Or, just too many sloppy mistakes had been ignored, and no one cared. In trial courts across the country there were reports of things going on which did not comport with what many observers thought was fair or just. And the issues of race, of race and economic status, of race and ethnicity never went away. Meanwhile, courts and administrators of the death penalty seemed to be increasingly impatient with rational argument and objective evidence and what they called legal technicalities. It was time to move on with the executions.

As those on death row came out from the shadows, and the stories of their wrongful convictions were told, they were seen to be human, often pathetic bumblers with a record, who were in the wrong place when the police arrived. When dozens of claims of innocence became credible, prosecutors were backed into a corner. To admit prior mistakes was disloyal to their colleagues and institutions. People on death row were found innocent and released, but the number of people sentenced to death continued to grow. With the exception of Texas, no state was executing enough people to bring the numbers down. In the meantime our commercial entertainments became increasingly violent: showing widespread carnage, murder, and the dead stacked up like jacks or poker chips. The demographic of young men most likely to kill or be killed was especially addicted to ritualized violence on small and large screens. While the impact of this may be difficult to measure, arguments about the inhumanity of capital punishment seemed dated, or irrelevant, as the public became increasingly inured to public representations of violence and killing, and as the number of people sentenced to death continued to increase.

ILLUSTRATIVE CASE NO. 3 – ILLINOIS, 1998–2003

When I left New Jersey in 1995 to come to Illinois I was convinced I would never again do research on homicide or the death penalty. After all, nothing was happening in Illinois in 1995. There was a very large death row population. The Public Defender did not have the advantage of a strong statewide administrative structure or a budget similar to that which allowed the New Jersey Office of the Public Defender to spend millions of dollars on the defense of a single capital case. The Illinois Supreme Court had declared that it did not and would not conduct proportionality review. The court regularly affirmed death sentences. The then Governor was in favor of capital punishment, and executions had begun. Public support for the death penalty was high, although not significantly higher than the national levels.

The Illinois Supreme Court had through the 1970's and 1980's repeatedly affirmed death sentences (Bienen, 1996, p. 166, Table 1). There was a brief moment first in 1979 and then again in 1984 when the constitutionality of capital punishment was a live issue before the state Supreme Court and federal courts in Illinois (*People ex rel. Carey v. Cousins*," 1979; *People v. Lewis*, 1984; *People v. Silagy*, 1984).[35] Since that time the Supreme Court of Illinois indicated in numerous opinions that it was uninterested in system wide challenges to the capital punishment system. There had never been the institutional will or the leadership within the Illinois criminal justice system for an enterprise such as the comprehensive analysis of criminal justice system undertaken by the Supreme Court of New Jersey with the participation and cooperation of numerous other courts and state agencies, including the Office of the Public Defender, the county prosecutors, and the Attorney General.

The Illinois prosecutors, the State's Attorneys, are individually elected and answer to no higher legal authority than the voters in their individual jurisdiction. And there are 102 of them. They are elected as county officials, and there is no limitation on the number of terms they may serve. These are 102 very autonomous local officials, each with the independent and unreviewable authority to select a case for capital prosecution, or not.[36] Given the breadth of the Illinois statutory aggravating factors, when I arrived in 1995 and began reading the daily newspapers, it seemed as if a capital case was always on deck, on trial, being investigated, or one of the more than 160 inmates on death row was coming up for execution. The culture of capital prosecutions was and is well entrenched in Illinois.

The State's Attorney of Cook County is the most visible State's Attorney in Illinois, and one of the most powerful and autonomous political figures in the state. Prosecutions by the Cook County State's Attorney, like those by equivalent offices in Los Angeles and New York, regularly make national news. The State's Attorney of Cook County and the other Illinois State's Attorneys have always been visible and vocal advocates for the death penalty in the state, both in theory and practice. Cook County regularly accounts for about three quarters of the State's murders and the largest number, and the most visible, if not the largest proportion of capital prosecutions (Illinois State Police, 2003).[37] The State's Attorneys in Illinois have often been legendary political figures. There has long been a well-marked path from the State's Attorney's office, especially the Cook County State's Attorney's office, to the state legislature, to the judiciary, to the Illinois Supreme Court, and to other state and occasionally national political offices.[38] The elected state judiciary, and the state supreme court, have always traditionally included many former State's Attorneys.

In 1995 the Republican Governor of Illinois, James Edgar, did not seem to be particularly eager to carry out executions. The first execution after reenactment in 1990, when James Thompson was Governor, was of Charles Walker, who decided not to pursue further appeals (Warden, 2005, p. 398). The next execution in May 1994 was of John Wayne Gacy, the notorious murderer of young boys and men. Governor James Edgar included in his campaign for governor in the fall of 1994 extensive publicity of his opponent's opposition to the death penalty (Warden, 2005, p. 399). After his election, Governor Edgar signed five death warrants. One of those cases was based upon a problematic confession, and this case attracted some attention from columnists after Northwestern University students investigated the case and launched a campaign on the defendant's behalf. In 1996 Governor Edgar did commute one death sentence, that of Guinevere Garcia, 14 hours before she was to be executed (Warden, 2005, p. 401, n. 85).

In 1995 I and many others could not have anticipated what happened in the next several years. The institutional system supporting capital punishment did not change; the State's Attorneys remained enthusiastic prosecutors of capital cases. The Illinois Supreme Court did not abandon its bizarre electoral system for state Supreme Court judges that divided representation, ensuring factionalism and precluding establishing, at least in recent decades, a court known for intellectual leadership and political independence. The public defender in Illinois did not become institutionally stronger, richer, or more capable of addressing issues on a statewide basis. Factors outside of the institutionalized criminal justice system were critical.

In 1998 the innocence movement was gaining momentum. An extraordinary conference at Northwestern University School of Law, organized by Professor Lawrence Marshall and others, brought together some 1,500 advocates, representatives of the national and international press, and, most importantly, 29 men and women who were the living embodiment of the fact that the innocent could be wrongfully convicted of capital murder (Sarat, 2005, chap. 1).[39] When these men and women told their individual stories of how they ended up on death row, the world began to watch and listen.

The sympathy of the public for the innocents did not happen overnight or because of one event, and it did not happen without an enormous amount of expert effort and coordination between old and new advocates for capital defendants. Many of those who ended up on death row for crimes they did not commit had committed other crimes, or had problems with addictions, and few were articulate enough or in a position to tell their stories effectively to a skeptical American public. A group of articulate and highly skilled advocates, writers, and journalists brought these cases and the national discussion of capital punishment to a new level. This is where individuals and the advocacy movement as a whole, as well and the journalists and the larger legal community, made an enormous difference. The mention of the conviction of the innocent formerly could elicit the response, that this was just one of the unintended costs of the criminal justice system, analogous to highway deaths. And one case could always be dismissed as an aberration, or the result of the particularity of its circumstances.

In 1998 after the Northwestern University School of Law National Conference on Wrongful Convictions and the Death Penalty, there was a step level change in public perceptions and public discussion. The political climate changed, and support for a statewide moratorium gained momentum (Roper Center for Public Opinion, 2003).[40] I use those vague and impalpable terms because the change was like a change in the seasons, if you had been working on the death penalty for decades you could sense it in the air. No one was more surprised in 1998 than the old hands who been seeing the same 50 people at death penalty conferences since *Gregg*. In 1998 it felt like the coming together of elements which had been waiting to happen for some time. This change in the political weather was not immediate, nor was it the work of one person or group, or one case or series of events, although there were people without whom it would not have happened. But, once the political atmosphere changed, there was no going back to the old assumptions.

For several years the national Innocence Project, under the direction of Professor Barry Scheck at Cardozo Law School and others, had been pursuing evidence of the actual innocence of some capital defendants by reexamining identification evidence with newly sensitive DNA tests. The DNA analysis offered a whole new avenue for the uncovering of wrongful convictions. The seminar on capital punishment taught in the Medill School of Journalism at Northwestern University by Professor David Protess had for more than a decade been working with undergraduates and law students in researching the factual basis for questionable capital convictions. The founding of the Center on Wrongful Convictions at the Northwestern University School of Law was another milestone. These activities came together in an extraordinary way after 1998 (Warden, 2005, pp. 399–410).[41]

Another critical factor in Illinois was the expertise and experience of the columnists and crime reporters for the *Chicago Tribune* and several other prominent Chicago papers and legal journals. Television commentators also played an important role. For years, staff reporters and editors at the *Chicago Tribune* had collected data on capital cases, and on homicides in Cook County, and had written extensively about individual capital trials and appeals, and, the questionable tactics and practices of all participants in the Illinois capital case processing system. No newspaper in New Jersey played a similar role. Then, the perfect storm occurred: the case of Anthony Porter. The legal community and the public were forced to acknowledge that something was drastically wrong with a criminal justice system which could sentence Anthony Porter to death for a crime he did not commit.

The highly dramatic unraveling of the Anthony Porter death sentence was told in real time by several people simultaneously: his attorneys, newspaper columnists and reporters, who quickly realized something extraordinary was happening, and by the newly galvanized coalition of lawyers and advocates against capital punishment.[42] These were the unpredictable and mutually reinforcing elements of the Anthony Porter case: his actual innocence, that he came within hours of being executed, the fact that his case and the circumstances of his conviction matched system-wide defects in the national criminal justice system (the evidence against him included uncorroborated eye witness testimony and what turned out to be a false confession shortly after his arrest); he was an African American man with a prior record, possibly mentally retarded, with no job or social support system at the time of his conviction; he was arrested because he was near the crime scene at the time of the murder; and there was no physical evidence connecting him to the murder. Yet he was sentenced to death, and the sentence upheld.

I was teaching a seminar on homicide and capital punishment at Northwestern University School of Law before the Anthony Porter case began to unravel, and the seminar read the Illinois Supreme Court opinion unanimously affirming Anthony Porter's conviction (*People v. Porter*, 1986, pp. 1329–1330).[43] It contained several quotes, allegedly his statements, presumably from the police reports. At the time I recall saying to the students that the quotations sounded 'canned', the kind of obviously incriminating, aggressive, hostile statements which I had seen attributed to defendants time and time again in police reports in New Jersey. It was not that defendants did not sometimes incriminate themselves, or confess, or make hostile and insensitive comments, but they did not all use the same language, the same phraseology, the same syntax and diction, especially those defendants who barely spoke English, or were incoherent, inarticulate, or struck dumb by their arrest. Indeed there is now a phalanx of experts trained to compare questionable statements attributed to defendants with the defendant's actual ordinary speech patterns.

When I mentioned my suspicions to one of Anthony Porter's attorneys at the time, he replied, correctly, that the Illinois Supreme Court had unanimously affirmed the conviction twice, and the conviction was the result of a jury verdict. There was no live challenge to the conviction. At that point no one had ever suggested Anthony Porter had not committed the murder. This same attorney uncovered evidence suggesting Anthony Porter might be retarded, an issue which had never been raised at trial, and it was the possibility of this – the question of his competency to be executed – being a valid legal issue which temporarily postponed Anthony Porter's execution. When his actual innocence was revealed, the facts and circumstances of Anthony Porter's conviction and appeals raised questions about the entire capital punishment system in Illinois at a time when people were prepared to listen.

In Illinois there were other totally unpredictable circumstances in the Anthony Porter case: that the Northwestern University team videotaped the recantation of the eyewitness who lied at trial, and then videotaped the incriminating statements of the actual killer (these statements were later retracted). Not only was this persuasive, but the drama of the revelations was bolstered by the luck that both the recanting witness and the 'actual' killer were alive and found by students and investigators. The unraveling of the foundation of Anthony Porter's death sentence took place in daily installments in the media, masterfully and expertly chronicled by the *Chicago Tribune*'s prizewinning reporters, columnists and editors, and others (Warden, 2005, pp. 403–404).[44]

Of course the real wild card, the card that trumped all others, was the character and circumstances of George Ryan himself. Most importantly, his political career was not associated with any of the Illinois State's Attorney's Offices, and thus he was not politically beholden to the entrenched pro-death penalty legal establishment (Sarat, 2005, pp. 1–33).[45] Like the majority of the public George Ryan was a *naif* when it came to the politics and realities of capital punishment, and the criminal justice system generally.

George Ryan repeatedly announced that he had voted for the reinstatement of capital punishment in 1977 when he was a legislator. He could sincerely express shock and outrage, thus taking the moral high ground, when it developed that in Illinois more people on death row had been exonerated than executed since reenactment. And at the time when the possibility of a blanket commutation arose, he was leaving office and leaving political life. He had nothing to lose by taking an unpopular position, and much to gain. There were other unreproducible circumstances of George Ryan's personal life and political position. George Ryan neither looked nor acted like a 'liberal'. George Ryan was not a Catholic, and thus the support of a the Catholic Church, the Pope, and anti-death penalty advocates, such as Sister Helen Prejean, counted doubly on the credit side, as did his lifelong membership and allegiance to the Republican Party. And, equally important, after the appointment of the Governor's Commission there was time for public support to build, with the help of a well-organized group of lawyers, judges, and other anti-death penalty advocates who had been working for a national and state moratorium on executions for years. When the moratorium was announced, it seemed inevitable.

The tale of the massive, unprecedented Ryan commutations, the emptying of Illinois' death row, has been told often and elsewhere. As a highly interested observer at the scene, my strongest impression was of the fortuitousness of the political circumstances: the luck and the hard work of the students and faculty at the Northwestern University School of Law and Medill School of Journalism and many others in uncovering the actual innocence of so many people on death row; the 1998 National Conference on Wrongful Convictions and the Death Penalty at Northwestern University; the appointment of a credible and expert, bipartisan Governor's Commission which published a scholarly, factual analysis of the Illinois capital punishment system (Turow, 2003);[46] the new public seriousness after 9/11; the guidance of Governor Ryan's professional staff, especially his close adviser, former Assistant United States Attorney Matthew Bettenhausen, in shaping the Governor's Commission and its thoughtful Report; the twists and turns of the Rolando Cruz case as a precursor and warm up for the Anthony Porter case; the consistent, steady involvement of Professor Lawrence Marshall, Rob Warden, the Center on Wrongful Convictions, the Innocence Project, and many other long time advocates; the careful cultivation and then the snowballing participation of the national, international, and local legal community; and the role of the media and especially the expert and experienced editors, feature writers, such as Eric Zorn, and reporters of the *Chicago Tribune*. So many pieces had to fall into place, to reflect off of one another, and reverberate and magnify one another, for that unique historic moment in the history of capital punishment in America to happen. And lest we forget, the commutations almost did not happen (Halt the Anguish, Gov. Ryan, 2002).[47] A ground swell of opposition to any commutations built in the fall of 2002 and came close to preventing them. George Ryan always said that he did not make up his mind until just before the commutations were announced.

While there has been some backlash, some retrenching since the commutations, support for the moratorium remains high in Illinois. Politicians running for office in 2004 discovered that the popular political position was the contradiction: to be in favor of the moratorium and to simultaneously express support for capital punishment itself. After the commutations, and after George Ryan left the Governor's office, the Illinois Legislature created the Capital Punishment Reform Study Committee in 2003, and that Committee, of which I am a member, is collecting information and preparing a Report, to be filed in 2009 (Capital Punishment Reform Study Committee Act, 2003).[48] In the meantime the statewide moratorium on executions imposed by Governor Ryan remains in effect. The number of death sentences imposed has been falling from before the commutations and the moratorium. But that is true elsewhere. And the exoneration of the innocent continues (Center on Wrongful Convictions, 2006). The Illinois Supreme Court has held that the State could not seek the death penalty again for a person whose sentence of death was pending on appeal at the time of Ryan commutations, removing from death row several people whose status was unclear (*People v. Morris*, 2006).

Is the death penalty dying in Illinois? That question is too broad. The death penalty in Illinois does not exist as an abstraction. The Ryan commutations were a spectacular event, without precedent in Illinois or in the history of capital punishment in America. In Illinois, however, the very strong forces which have always supported the death penalty are still in place: the elected State's Attorneys; the elected judges; continued public support for capital punishment; and, perhaps most important of all, the institutional pull, the sheer inertia of the capital punishment system still being in place, still proceeding with capital prosecutions, still imposing death sentences and still pushing for executions.

There is less of that pull with the present moratorium on executions continuing, but the momentum of capital prosecutions and convictions, the preparation, the going forward with the trials, the training of the lawyers and judges, the publicity accompanying a capital trial and conviction, all continue to make the legal system, and the public, invested in keeping capital punishment. In Illinois the commitment to the prosecution of capital cases is deeply ingrained in the legal system. Capital prosecutions have been going without interruption since before reenactment in 1974, continuing a long tradition established well before *Furman*. The impetus may have slowed, but the death penalty is a long way from dying in Illinois. The situation in Illinois is very different from that in New Jersey where there is a good chance for the repeal of the death penalty under pending legislation. In Illinois the political impetus is in the direction of keeping capital punishment, although the enactment of the reforms of 2003, the continuing of the moratorium, and the appointment of the Study Committee signals to the contrary.

IS THE DEATH PENALTY DYING? – THE UNEXPECTED MOMENTUM OF THE LETHAL INJECTION CASES

This brings us to the present moment when the liveliest challenge to capital punishment as a system is, ironically, in the cases challenging the constitutionality of lethal injection. The United States Supreme Court recently agreed to head a case challenging the procedures for lethal injection, causing several states to suspend executions.[49] While the legal events in New Jersey and Illinois were challenging the operation of the death penalty as a system and as applied to individual cases, an entirely different legal challenge to capital punishment was being developed: the argument that the method of execution used by most jurisdictions, lethal injection, was itself the infliction of cruel and unusual punishment, and hence unconstitutional. There is a long history of challenges to methods of execution; classic challenges based upon the Eighth Amendment jurisprudence going back centuries. What is new in the lethal injection cases, what makes them 'the ringer' in this long series of legal challenges, is the presentation to courts of scientific and medical evidence documenting exactly what happens during a lethal injection.

The character of the evidence brought forward in these cases is unprecedented. This is what makes the lethal injection cases new. In addition, these are legal challenges to the entire system of capital punishment which are not based upon race, or economic status, or the abuse of prosecutorial discretion, or any characteristic of the defendant, the victim, or the circumstances of the offense or the case. This challenge is not all about the lawyers and judges not doing what they are supposed to do. This challenge has been gaining momentum just as all the reenacting states have either chosen lethal injection initially, or switched to it as the preferred or only method of execution.

Evidence of the mutilation of the body in the cut down procedures, the bleeding, the continued consciousness, all are being brought to the attention of the courts and the public. Procedures which are supposed to have been 'medical' and humane, controlled, highly civilized, are shown to have been the opposite. The people in the white coats are not doctors. The drugs are not just sedatives, but also paralytics. The evidence brought forward is 'objective,' couched in medical terminology, difficult to dispute. Those offering the evidence are strangers to the criminal justice system. It is not a question of how one judge interprets a statute or constitutional phrase. It is something anyone who has been inside a hospital can understand. The success of this legal tactic, as seen in cases postponing or halting executions in a number of states, is one of the surprises of the past decade and may have systemwide effects (Weinstein, 2006a, June 28).[50]

Lethal injection that the states adopted quickly when evidence of malfunction and mishaps came to light with the electric chair, seemed to be benign until academics and advocates began to pull back the curtain hiding the process (Denno, 2002).[51] There was the bizarre development of the equipment itself, the Rube Goldberg contraption invented by a self-promoting crank (Dr. Death and His Wonderful Machine, 1990).[52] Then, the embarrassing fact that all state and national medical societies have come out against medical doctors, and others governed by medical ethics provisions, participating in executions, although a recent poll of doctors showed that close to half of the doctors asked had no personal objection to participating in executions.

The fact is that many doctors, nurses, and other medically trained personnel are involved in executions. They do participate and observe executions, in spite of the ethical prohibitions and problems (Denno, 2002, Table 17). There is no sanction imposed upon doctors and medical personnel who participate in executions. Only half of all doctors are members of these professional societies. It is the state-licensing agency which can take away a doctor's license, not the professional medical society. Knowledge of doctors' involvement in the execution process is new, however. Their continued participation may be more problematic. The irony is that all of the trappings of a medical procedure which are supposed to make the death penalty more humane and civilized actually do the opposite. Through the Freedom of Information Act challenges information is now coming out about what actually goes on in execution chambers.

The state legislatures flocked to lethal injection in 1977 because it was politically palatable. The legislatures specified lethal injection and left it to the various state Departments of Corrections to figure out how to do it.[53] The procedures for lethal injection have not changed for 30 years. How it would work included what drugs would be used – the lethal cocktail, as it came to be called – and how and in what combination and sequence the drugs would be administered. Someone else, usually someone without much education who was afraid of losing a job with the State, was left to figure out the details, such as dosages and the implements for the dirty work of killing someone. And the results were not pretty (Denno, 2002, pp. 146–260).[54]

At the time of reenactment state legislators feared that doctors would not or could not participate in executions. The writers of the regulations engaged in elaborate distancing rituals to ensure that doctors were not the ones who actually pulled the trigger, so to speak (Denno, 2002, pp. 207–260).[55] Many states specify that doctors, usually the state or county coroner would only certify death. A new breed of civil employee, the Execution Technician, was created.[56] I was not aware until coming to Illinois of research by psychologists at Stanford and elsewhere which undertook an inquiry into the effects of execution upon those doing or observing the executions (Osofsky, Bandura, & Zimbardo, 2005).[57] Once again, the truth is more bizarre than the imagined situation, as details began to come to light about the protocols, the cavalier attitudes expressed by some legislators and judges, the training of personnel or its absence, and the ghoulish specifics of the procedures themselves.

Lethal injection procedures were adopted by corrections officials who received little or no guidance from the state legislators, and they turned out to be slap dash and designed to mimic a medical act, the giving of a medically appropriate injection. The rest was window dressing: the use of the hospital gurney or stretcher, the white sheets on the gurney, the curtain behind which the witnesses sat, the white coats of the technicians, and the giving of a sedative to the person to be executed. With the exception of the giving of the sedative, the rest of the procedures were all an elaborate stage show to reassure those observing or participating that what was going on was controlled and humane, and medically appropriate.

Evidence of botched lethal injections started to accumulate immediately. And the medical, legal and academic community challenged the procedure itself.[58] Meanwhile, everyone associated with its establishment could blame another institution for the conundrum: what was supposed to be a kind of 'euthanasia' was turning out to be tortuous. The legislators could blame the public for demanding capital punishment. The prosecutors and the defense attorneys could blame the corrections officials and the legislature, and say they were just following the law. The corrections officials and prison administrators, who had to figure out how exactly to put the new method into effect, could blame the lawyers, the judges, and the legislatures. And everyone could blame the convicted murderers about to be executed. After all, if they had not committed those terrible crimes they would not be causing more trouble by making everyone else worry about whether a method of execution was humane.

The moral disengagement and ambivalence described in the scientific idiom by the academic psychologists became the subject of narratives in photographic essays, first person accounts from death row inmates and their advocates, newspaper stories and books (some of which became best sellers), television shows and highly successful commercial films.[59] Lethal injection had appealed to state legislators as putting murderers to sleep – painlessly, mercifully, cleanly, on a stainless steel table, surrounded by people in white coats who looked like doctors but were not doctors. Some commented that this peaceful a death was too good for people who had themselves tortured and made their victims suffer. The truth was often to the contrary.

The procedure, with minor variations among the 37 states specifying lethal injection, is a three-stage process: the first drug is a sedative, the second drug has no other function but to paralyze the inmate; and the third drug stops the heart. The only reason for including the paralytic drug is to sanitize the process and mask the infliction of pain, to paralyze the person being executed so that there is no twitching, screaming, vomiting, or perceptible expression of pain. The only reason for including the second paralytic drug is because doctors did not know how long it would take for the other drugs to act. The veterinarians now use quicker and better drugs to euthanize animals. The veterinarians will not use the paralytic agent used in lethal injections in the killing of animals. The pain experienced, if the sedative is inadequate or has not yet reached the brain, is the pain of having a heart attack.

In 2001 only nine states mentioned in their protocols the amount of drugs they were using. Only with the Freedom of Information Act requests did information come out on how the procedures were actually being implemented. This information, available for the first time now is what makes these cases powerful. In 1978 the Texas Court was not even required to say what drugs were being used. The constitutional theory of the challenge to the method of execution is not new; it is 'cruel and unusual punishment,' the same as the challenges to hanging and the electric chair, under the principles of the Eighth Amendment. It is the detailed information about what actually happens in the execution chamber, the level of incompetence and indifference, which has caught the attention of the courts, the advocates, and the public.

A factual inquiry in Missouri in 2006 has brought to light that the physician preparing the injections – in violation of the state and national ethics provisions – unilaterally halved the dose of the sedative because of difficulty in dissolving the powder in the liquid because the supplier used a different package. This same doctor testified that he had not seen any written protocols for executions, and the only way in which they might have been written down is if someone observed what he was doing during an execution and wrote that down. This same doctor admitted that he was 'still improvising' his technique for executing people, and that he himself was dyslexic and thus it was not unusual for him to make mistakes with numbers. These mistakes, he alleged, were not critical to the work he does as a surgeon. The head of the Missouri Department of Corrections, to whom the doctor reported, had no background in corrections and no background in medicine. He told the dyslexic doctor that he was completely reliant on the doctor to advise him whether changes in the procedures for lethal injection needed to be made (*Taylor v. Crawford*, 2006, pp. 7–10).[60]

Once again raids and inroads are being staked out as to who will take the moral high ground as the lawsuits began to multiply. Recently and surprisingly the United States Supreme Court halted a Florida lethal injection in the last hours in May 2006, on a procedural question, whether the inmate could use Section 1983 to challenge lethal injection. This gives a broader legal theory for inmates to make substantive challenges to lethal injection procedures in the future. The Florida inmate was executed after another procedural ruling at the state level, however, no attorney today can bring a death penalty case without challenging lethal injection itself on constitutional grounds. It would be ineffective assistance to neglect to bring that constitutional challenge now.

At some point the United States Supreme Court will have to take a case addressing lethal injection challenges substantively, not just procedurally. And that is why these cases are 'the ringer'. Just as the United States Supreme Court appeared to have put to rest the last of the systemwide challenges to capital punishment in the United States, the lethal injection cases have gained a surprising amount of traction. The issue will reach the United States Supreme Court and have implications for all capital punishment systems currently in place in the 37 states. A federal judge in California has ordered a hearing to take place in September 2006 to review the constitutionality of California's procedures. The prospect of new, protracted proceedings on behalf of the more than 650 men and women on death row in California is a startling new development.

One of the interesting aspects of these lawsuits is that they halt an execution on medical grounds, yet they are nonetheless challenges to the legal system imposing the death penalty as a whole. There are no allegations about due process violations to defendants during arrest, incarceration or trial, or of discrimination based upon race of the victim or defendant, or socio-economic status of the defendant or victim, or allegations about the inequities generally in the 'criminal justice system.'

These are civil suits, mostly heard in the federal civil courts at the district level, by judges who are not typically criminal judges. They can and are also brought in state courts. This may be an important factor in the character of the decisions. Perhaps these judges, like former Governor George Ryan, are not inured to the brutalities of the criminal justice system. Although the cases may be brought under habeas corpus, they are also being brought as declaratory judgment cases, or simply as civil rights complaints under state or federal law.

For example, United States District Court Judge Jeremy Fogel in the *Morales* case in San Jose, California sent a questionnaire to both counsel, asking counsel what would comprise a constitutionally acceptable procedure for lethal injection (Weinstein, 2006c, Oct. 6). The judge wants to know how the drugs will act and what the qualifications are of the 'execution team.' This is highly unusual, and not the dismissive treatment which capital defendants may typically receive in the lower federal courts when everyone in the system has seen too many cases. In the *Morales* case the lawyers have objected that it is not their responsibility to come up with constitutional methods for killing their clients. New litigants are bringing these cases, new arguments are being made and being heard afresh. The faces in court are not only the public defenders and members of the anti-death penalty establishment from prior capital punishment battles. As an example of the reach of these cases, the most recent execution in Virginia was an electrocution. In Tennessee an inmate also chose electrocution. These inmates chose electrocution over lethal injection because they thought it was more humane (Death Penalty Information Center, 2006).

The lethal injection cases are straightforward and very democratic: a challenge to the system for implementing the death penalty itself, assuming the death penalty has been correctly applied to a person whose guilt is not in question. It isn't necessary to frame the legal arguments in subtle terms to meet the refinements of the most recent interpretation of the habeas corpus jurisprudence. The arguments are politicized along different lines and different alliances are being drawn. Having new advocates making the case adds another dimension of unpredictability. And since the other methods of execution have been problematic – hanging because it is too crude, and arguably 'cruel' (*Rupe v. Wood*, 1994),[61] the electric chair as demonstrably cruel – the system must figure out another way to execute, or find a way to make this method not cruel.

Perhaps it is because the arguments are more factual than legal, that certain groups, such as the American Society of Anesthesiologists, who say they are neither for nor against the death penalty itself, has advised its

40,000 members to 'steer clear' of participating in executions, saying: the legal system has painted itself into a corner with lethal injection, and it is not the responsibility of the professional anesthesiologists to resolve the legal issues. On the contrary, the Society advises, professional anesthesiologists should not be involved in lethal injections in any manner. This is not a medically appropriate sedation.[62]

The federal judges, the lawyers, the journalists, and the advocates have put the information out about the circumstances of botched executions (Capital punishment: Cruel and unusual, 1993). The fiction that this is analogous to putting the family pet to sleep is no longer tenable. Veterinarians and advocates for animals have gone on record as saying that the procedures used in lethal injections of people would not be sufficiently humane to use in the killing of animals. It will be awkward for state legislators to argue that executions should continue in the face of this evidence.

A federal judge can hold a hearing under Section 1983 for further fact finding. This is one of the few unobstructed powers of the federal judiciary. United States District Court Judge Fernando J. Gaitan, Jr. in an evidentiary hearing on lethal injection wrote the following as a factual finding:

> ...There is no dispute that if an inmate is not sufficiently anesthetized when the potassium chloride [the drug which stops the electrical activity of the heart] is administered, it will cause excruciating pain, as it is administered through the inmate's veins. The inmate, however, would be unable to show he was experiencing discomfort due to the paralyzing effects of the pancuronium bromide [the paralytic agent]. (*Taylor v. Crawford*, 2006, p. 6)[63]

The inquiry in California is pending and may prove to be the mechanism for Governor Schwarzenegger to declare a statewide moratorium on executions, or to find that there is no constitutionally acceptable method for carrying out the death penalty.[64] As the legal challenges to lethal injection in other state and federal courts proceed, each ruling halting an execution, each factual finding of pain and suffering is reinforcing similar allegations in other cases. Now a case has reached the United States Supreme Court. That case when it is decided may result in an unpredictable or surprising alignment among the new judges of this United States Supreme Court.

CONCLUSION AND SUMMARY

Is the death penalty dying? The illustrative cases put forward here do not answer that question. With the exception of the clear national trend in the lethal injection cases, no predictions are offered in this essay. If these reflections upon three very different case studies have a common theme, it is the unexpected nature of the events which resulted in a very dramatic change in the jurisdiction's application of the death penalty. Decades from now these end results may appear to have been foreordained and inevitable, but to this observer close to the ground individual decision makers and the particularities of circumstances created a wobbling, momentary coherence, unpredicted, and not likely to be repeated.

In Nigeria the government established an extra legal system for imposing the death penalty, the Armed Robbery Tribunal, and used the very public application of the death penalty to intimidate the public and convince the polity of its legal authority. In New Jersey in the 1980s and early 1990s the Supreme Court of New Jersey, which had a long tradition of independence, fashioned a constitutionally required system for proportionality review and other court imposed procedural due process guarantees under the leadership of a powerful Chief Justice who is no longer there.

In Illinois the way was paved for Governor Ryan's blanket commutation by more than two years of serious work by the Governor's Commission on Capital Punishment (2002), by the concerted efforts of the national and local legal community supporting a moratorium on executions, and by a set of unpredictable cases, some long in preparation, others not, which unfolded in a relatively compressed time period and revealed that 13 men on death row in Illinois were either innocent, wrongly convicted, or both.

Of course, Nigeria in the 1970s is *sui generis*, in time, distance, and in the difference of its legal system. There has been a moratorium movement in Nigeria, but executions, including the executions of political prisoners and executions under traditional *Sharia* law, continue. The Armed Robbery Tribunal is still in effect. There are so many other illegal and unconstitutional state and private killings in that country that capital punishment as an issue of legal principle receives attention only from a few activists and from international human rights groups.

In New Jersey, capital punishment may literally be dying. The support for the death penalty within the legal community seems minimal. There is a legislatively imposed moratorium on executions, and the legislative initiative to abolish the death penalty is pending. Importantly, executions in New Jersey never started again after reenactment in 1982. A legal culture supporting and institutionalizing capital punishment has not been firmly entrenched for decades. The former Attorney General, the present Governor, some Justices of the Supreme Court of New Jersey, as well as many legal organizations, have gone on record as being against the death penalty, and also as saying that capital punishment is a waste of government resources.

Illinois is very different from New Jersey, yet both jurisdictions at present have a moratorium on executions. Illinois continues to have a strong institutional commitment to capital punishment within the offices of the State's Attorneys, the elected judiciary, and the private bar. That the dramatic commutation of more than 160 death sentences occurred in Illinois is testament to the coming together of an extraordinary set of people, institutions, and circumstances, unlikely to be replicated elsewhere. The Illinois commutations have had national reverberations, however, and the innocence movement continues to be strong in Illinois with the presence of the Center on Wrongful Convictions and the other advocacy institutions involved in national and Illinois exonerations.

Finally, some observations on the serendipity of the crop of cases challenging the application of lethal injection as a method for imposing the death penalty. This challenge crosses state and federal jurisdictional lines and threatens to halt all executions in the United States without raising any legal challenge to the death penalty itself, with regard to the manner and constitutionality of its imposition in the state or federal criminal justice system. Lethal injection may well be the next vehicle for overturning a large number of death sentences. I do not think there is the national will at the present time to devote large amounts of energy or invention to 'improving' the method of execution in the face of unrelenting stories of execution botches and administrative bungling.

There is one caveat, however. That is, if this country finds itself in an international war, with substantial loss of life at home, then that would transform the political climate regarding domestic capital punishment in unpredictable ways. It might mean that in states such as Texas, executions would continue or escalate with no one paying any attention. Alternatively, it might be that the amount of time, effort, and resources spent on capital cases would suddenly seem to be an extravagant waste. There could be a general lack of interest in continuing our present capital punishment system.

Throwing out the death penalty because of the cruelty of the method has the great rhetorical advantage of not being a 'victory' for either the defense or the prosecution. It allows those committed to capital trials and prosecutions not to be blamed, to say that only the last step is unconstitutional. It allows defense attorneys and the general public to argue against executions without appearing unsympathetic to victims or sentimental about defendants on death row. Perhaps this can be the excuse, the face saving, for the country to realize how tired we all are of capital punishment. The federal constitutional principle of an evolving standard of decency incorporates the idea of 'progress' in a civilized society, and might encompass outlawing lethal injection.

As Americans, we like to think there are certain things we do not do, or at least certain things we do not officially sanction. We like to think of ourselves as a country of laws and strong, independent legal institutions. When the State kills, or is poised to kill, the public, those within legal institutions, and those who watch and monitor those systems pay attention and, it is hoped, hold accountable the institutions and their administrators – courts, judges, lawyers, police officers, and prison officials – who are responsible for action taken in the name of the rule of law.

The rule of law requires judges to ask the hard questions, and it asks lawyers to put the information before judges so that they may ask and answer those questions on the basis of facts. Our entertainment driven culture is addicted to dramas about murder, and will always address issues of guilt, innocence, and punishment on multiple levels. At the end of the day, however, the legal institutions, the courts, must take the responsibility for finding the facts and deciding upon constitutionality of the official criminal justice system and its methods for imposing the law.

NOTES

1. The cited work and the following summarizes some of the early studies of race and the death penalty after Wolfgang's work, *The Impact of Race in Pre-Furman Studies: 1900–1959; The Impact of Race in Pre-Furman cases: 1960–1970*, pp. 103–118 in Bienen et al. (1988). Race had been linked with different rates of homicide and the imposition of the death penalty prior to Wolfgang's work, but the study at that time brought issues of race to the forefront (see also the 'Race of victim' studies cited in Bienen, 1996, pp. 149–150, n. 66).

2. This research resulted in two publications, and also got me my first job out of law school, as a research attorney for a large, quantitative study of sexual assault in Philadelphia. The African monographs on homicide are Bienen (1974) and Bienen (1976).

3. There was another military coup in July 1975, deposing Gowon, and the subsequent military government handed over power to a civilian government in October 1979.

4. The law was enacted in 1970 and still in effect: The Robbery and Firearms Decree of 1970. It was amended at various times, in 1971, 1972, and 1977 and then replaced with a very similar provision in 1984 (An Act to Make Comprehensive Provisions for Matters Relating to Armed Robbery, 1984).

5. The Western State of Nigeria in 1972 had a similar legal structure to New Jersey: a largely autonomous state legal system, with its own court structure, layered within a larger federal system. In 1972 issues concerning the conflicting authority of the civil and religious courts was not an issue, at least not in the homicide cases I was

studying, and not in the Western State of Nigeria. Nor was it an issue for The Armed Robbery Tribunal in Western Nigeria.

6. My recollection is that there was little radio, and no television except a small, tedious state run network. The dominant role of the newspapers in reporting all political and international news, and especially crimes, was similar to the role played by newspapers in Chicago in the early twentieth century (see Bienen & Rottinghaus, 2002, pp. 456–460).

7. The language of the Decree incorporated in the statutory law reads: "... If ... [any offender] ... (b) wounds or uses any personal violence to any person, the offender shall be liable upon conviction under this Act to be sentenced to death. The sentence of death imposed may be executed by hanging or causing such offender to face firing squad as directed by the Governor. ... The Governor of each State is empowered to set up a tribunal for the trial of offences under this Act. The Act provides for a conviction to be subject to be confirmed or disallowed by the Governor of a State. No civil proceedings shall be or be instituted in any court for or on account of or in respect of any act, matter or thing done or purporting to be done under this Act by the Governor of a State or by any member or officer of a tribunal constituted under this Act ..." (An Act to Make Comprehensive Provisions for Matters Relating to Armed Robbery, 1984).

8. The 1984 version of the statute does not require that the person 'in the company of' the armed robber who wounds be sentenced to death. The 1990 version of the same statute states that any offender 'in company with' any person ... shall upon conviction be sentenced to death (Criminal Code Act, 1990, January 31).

9. The 1990 statute does not mention public executions; the 1984 statute specifies hanging or firing squad (see note 8, infra).

10. This essay does not address the complex and very interesting questions involving traditional Muslim law, *Sharia*, and the death penalty. In 1999 the *Sharia* courts were empowered across northern Nigeria under the new penal legislation to impose the death penalty for sexually related offenses (*Zina*). The *Sharia* does provide for executions, including public executions, and death sentences have been handed down by *Sharia*, at least four recently (see Amnesty International, 2006, *Nigeria*; United Nations High Commissioner for Refugees, 2006).

11. If an answer was required of the accused – 'where were you on Saturday night when the victim was stabbed?' – then an interpreter would be brought in and that question was asked and answered in a language the accused understood. Then the trial would go back to being a conversation among the lawyers and judges.

12. The most comprehensive report on the death penalty in Nigeria concluded that it did not deter additional armed robberies: "The introduction of [the] death penalty for armed robbery in Nigeria, which was targeted at reducing the increasing cases of armed robbery in the country did not result in any remarkable reduction in armed robbery cases" (Ilo, 2004). This same Report lists 487 persons on death row, including 11 women, as of July 2003 (p. 71). A government report in July 2005 recommended that the death penalty be applied to juveniles and that state governors should execute people on death row to relieve congestion in the prisons (see Amnesty International, 2005, *Appeal for the abolition of the death penalty in Africa*).

13. Sentences by tribunals are generally severe, particularly for armed robbery and treason, which carry a mandatory death sentence with no right to appeal. Some

of the death sentences are carried out in public, even though public execution has been outlawed in Nigeria. In July 1991, Amnesty International reported that a total of 15 armed robbery convicts were publicly executed in three states and were witnessed by hundreds of spectators" (Africa Watch, 1991).

14. Ralph Hudson, a 43-year-old white male whose crime was committed in Atlantic County, was executed on January 22, 1963, NJ Department. of Corrections. There have been no executions in New Jersey since 1963.

15. The then Chief Justice Weintraub's concurring opinion was particularly noteworthy: "… My point is the doctrines of the Federal Supreme Court have led to an impossible situation … I believe the case method should be replaced by a rule-making process in which the Federal Supreme Court can meet regularly with representatives of State Supreme courts, to become aware of their problems, to benefit from their experience, and to adopt rules of prospective application …" (*State v. Funicello*, 1972, Weintraub, C.J., concurring).

16. The then Governor of New Jersey, Brendan Byrne had kept his promise to veto any legislation reenacting the death penalty in 1978, and he was re-elected in 1978. As a judge he had declared the pre-*Furman* New Jersey capital punishment statute unconstitutional. He was prevented from being reelected by a limited term limits provision in the New Jersey Constitution (New Jersey Constitution). See also Waldron (1978, March 4). For a history of capital punishment in New Jersey and the reenactment in 1982, see Bienen et al. (1988, pp. 66–70).

17. By 1982 the majority of states had reenacted the death penalty, and the executions had begun again with the death by the firing squad of Gary Gilmore in 1977, under the authority of a Utah statute, which provided for death by firing squad at the election of the defendant.

18. Particularly note, Table 1 'Date of Reenactment, Date of First Capital Affirmance, Date of First Execution, and Time Period Between, by State,' p. 166.

19. When the New Jersey state legislature was enacting the Criminal Code which included the possibility of reenacting capital punishment, with the specter of the first execution in decades, the provision in the Code which attracted the most vocal opposition was the decriminalization of certain forms of consenting sexual conduct (see Sullivan, 1978, July 28).

20. For a detailed description of the litigation surrounding the Robert Marshall case, see; Statistics and Law; the Supreme Court of New Jersey's Implementation of Proportionality Review (Bienen 1998a, 1998b, pp. 183–212).

21. See also McGinniss (1991).

22. "It might be the best Supreme Court in the Country-state or federal," said Harvard law professor Laurence H. Tribe, as quoted in (Rosen, 1984, Nov 5). See also Hoffman (1996, June 30).

23. Robert Marshall was sentenced to death, and his co-conspirator, Robert Cumber, who let a man use his phone to set up the killing, got a 30-year life sentence. Cumber, now 68 and nearly blind, was released recently after former Governor. Richard J. Codey granted him clemency in the final days of his stay in office.

24. In the spring of 2005 Robert Marshall's death sentence was overturned by the Third Circuit Court of Appeals on grounds of the incompetence of his private trial counsel. The Ocean County prosecutor announced that they were not going to prosecute him again for capital murder in the spring of 2006. The Attorney General

of New Jersey did appeal the third circuit ruling by filing a writ of certiorari on the last day of eligibility. (Vaughan, 2006, February 2).

25. "At the end of an emotional 40-minute hearing in Toms River, Superior Court Judge Wendel Daniels gave Marshall the toughest sentence he could: life imprisonment with no parole for 30 years. The 66-year-old Marshall, who faced execution by lethal injection until the federal courts overturned that sentence, could be eligible for parole in December 2014–30 years from his arrest for arranging the murder of his wife, Maria, in 1984 ..." (Schwaneberg, 2006, August 19). The Ocean County Prosecutor recommended that sentence (*Ibid.*) The Ocean County Prosecutor tried the case in Atlantic County because of the publicity surrounding the crime.

26. "... In the summer of 1986 Robert N. Wilentz was very nearly fired. By then he had been Chief Justice for seven years, the point at which the [New Jersey] Senate considers whether to give a judge a lifetime appointment ..." (Hoffman, 1996, June 30, pp. 6–7). The New Jersey Supreme Court held the death penalty statute constitutional in *State v. Ramseur* (1987), soon after Chief Justice Wilentz's confirmation. The first capital conviction was not affirmed, however, until the first Robert Marshall case (*State v. Marshall*, 1991). Marshall II affirmed the death sentence of Robert Marshall after proportionality review. (*State v. Marshall II*, 1992).

27. This was typical. Legislators often expected executions to start soon after reenactment.

28. See also discussion of *Pulley v. Harris* (1984, p. 189).

29. This chapter provides a history of the proportionality review project in New Jersey prior to the appointment of Professor Baldus and the Order appointing Professor David Baldus as Special Master (see also Appendix E Order of July 29, 1988, pp. 371–372). For the history of proportionality review after the appointment of the Special Master, see Bienen (1996, pp. 159–212).

30. The Wilentz era ended in 1996, when the Chief Justice resigned for reasons of illness, dying a few months later in July 1996. Deborah T. Poritz, the former Attorney General and Governor's Counsel, was immediately appointed and confirmed as the new Chief Justice.

31. In January 2006, the interim Governor of New Jersey signed into law a bill requiring an immediate moratorium on executions and creating a Study Commission to study the economics, ethics, effects, and possible alternatives to the death penalty and report back to the legislature by November 15, 2006. A new study of the cost of capital prosecutions by the New Jersey Policy Perspective, said capital trials cost an average of $162,960, compared with 46,560 for non-capital trials (see Forsberg, 2005, November).

32. See, e.g. "... *The Legislature finds and declares that* ... [b] The experience of this State with the death penalty has been characterized by significant expenditures of money and time; [c] the financial costs of attempting to implement the death penalty statutes may not be justifiable in light of the other needs of this State; [d] There is a lack of any meaningful procedure to ensure uniform application of the death penalty in each county throughout the State; [e] There is public concern that racial and socio-economic factors influence the decisions to seek or impose the death penalty; [f] There has been increasing public awareness of cases of individuals wrongfully convicted of murder, in New Jersey and elsewhere in the nation; [g] The Legislature is

troubled that the possibility of mistake in the death penalty process may undermine public confidence in our criminal justice system; [h] the execution of an innocent person by the State of New Jersey would be a grave and irreversible injustice; ..." (An Act Creating a Study Commission on the Death Penalty and Imposing a Moratorium on Executions and Amending P.L., 1983, 1984). [emphasis supplied].

33. The Attorney General of New Jersey has supervisory authority over the 21 county prosecutors in New Jersey. See Consultation With and Supervision Over County Prosecutors; Uniform Enforcement of Criminal Laws, (2006): "The Attorney General shall consult with and advice the several county prosecutors in matters relating to the duties of their office and shall maintain a general supervision over said country prosecutors with a view to obtaining effective and uniform enforcement of the criminal laws throughout the State." Illinois does not provide that the Attorney General of Illinois shall have supervisory authority over the independently elected State's Attorneys.

34. As of the spring of 2006 only 13 people are on death row in New Jersey, more than 20 years after reenactment, and there have been no executions in New Jersey since 1963. There have been 1,016 executions in the country as a whole since *Gregg* (Death Row USA, Spring, 2006).

35. See also discussion in Bienen (1996, p. 235, notes 401–403) and Bienen (1998a, 1998b, pp. 197–209). And see Warden (2005, pp. 389–391).

36. Only recently has the Illinois State's Attorney's Association issued a set of guidelines for the prosecution of capital cases, and those have only recently been published and made public. The New Jersey county prosecutors published their guidelines in 1989 (see Bienen, Weiner, Allison and Mills (1990, pp. 791–793, Appendix B: Prosecutor's Guidelines for Designation of Homicide Cases for Capital Prosecution)).

37. In 2003 there were a total of 896 murders reported by the Illinois State Police and 696 were from Cook County. The collar counties around Cook, account for a sizable fraction, e.g. Kane County and Lake County, in 2003, 21 and 15, respectively. Other counties, such as Dupage (6 murders in 2003) have a strong, pro death penalty culture.

38. The present mayor of Chicago, Richard M. Daley, was the State's Attorney in Cook County from 1980–1989 and was elected Mayor in 1989. He was a member of the Illinois State Senate from 1972–1980 and a supporter of capital punishment.

39. See also Warden (2005, pp. 391–410); and in numerous articles and newspaper accounts.

40. See e.g. a 2003 Roper poll showing that 60% of those asked supported a moratorium on executions to allow government to reduce the chances that an innocent person would be put to death. Survey 1/15/2003 to 1/16/2003, telephone interview with 1,010 national adults. The same survey showed 64% in favor of the death penalty for individuals convicted of serious crimes such as murder. Q. 029 and Q 021.

41. See also Sarat (2005, pp. 1–33).

42. The nearly perfect storm was the Rolando Cruz case that brought Professor Lawrence Marshall into the vortex, but the Rolando Cruz case had too many ambiguities, too much baggage, and too many recent memories about the brutal

murder of a child for that case to capture the public imagination the way the Anthony Porter case did. The defendant himself, Rolando Cruz, was not sufficiently credible to prevent another jury from finding him guilty. At his third trial the judge directed a verdict of acquittal (see Warden, 2005. pp. 400–401 and n. 80–84).

43. See also *People v. Porter* (1995).

44. See Tribune features in this chapter.

45. See also Warden (2005, pp. 405–409). As a state legislator George Ryan had voted for the death penalty to be reinstated and then voted for it to be expanded (*Ibid.*, p. 388).

46. And see *The Report of the Governor's Commission on Capital Punishment* (2002).

47. The highly publicized hearings before the Prisoner Review Board in October 2002, consisting of testimony about the underlying crimes by victim's families, alienated many, including the Chicago Tribune which in an editorial called for Governor Ryan not to commute all death sentences.

48. The act was filed without signature of the Governor and after an amendatory veto was overridden. The Illinois Study Committee Act does not contain the sweeping declarations of the New Jersey law.

49. *Baze v. Rees*, No. 07-5439 (U.S. Sup. ct., cert. granted Sept. 25, 2007).

50. Discussing *Taylor v. Crawford* (June 26, 2006), Fernando J. Gaitan, Jr., J.

51. See also Denno (1997) and Denno (1994).

52. See also discussion in Denno (2002, n. 345 and surrounding text).

53. New Jersey, for example, specified lethal injection as the method of execution shortly after reenactment in 1982, years before the first death sentence was upheld.

54. Provides a state-by-state survey of the methods and drugs used, includes tables describing when individual states adopted lethal injection, and if there are protocols specifying procedures and participants.

55. See statutory language in the compilation of each state provision, e.g. Arkansas, Ohio, Oregon, or Arizona. The Arizona regulations declare that the procedure is 'not painful' (*Ibid.*, p. 207).

56. While observing this process in New Jersey I wrote a fictional account of the hiring and training of such a person, and his socialization into the task of killing for the State (see Bienen, 1998a).

57. See also Bandura (1999).

58. "… The high percentage of botches in Texas appeared to be partly attributable to the dearth of written procedures provided to the executioners concerning how to perform an execution. Originally, these 'procedures' listed little more than the chemicals to be used (in incorrect order or application) and a vague account of the content of the syringes. Moreover, there was no information specifying the nature and extent of the qualifications that executioners should have in order to perform an execution. … [Internal footnote omitted.]" (Denno, 2002, p. 111).

59. Tim Robbins' film "Dead Man Walking" based upon the 1993 book by Helen Prejean grossed more than $39 million in the U.S. alone, and was nominated for and won numerous awards (see Internet Movie Database, 1995).

60. U.S. District Judge Jeremy Fogel in San Jose California has scheduled a two-day hearing in September 2006 to review California's lethal injection protocol, which

prompted the State in February to call off the scheduled execution of Michael Morales in California (Weinstein, 2006a, June 28).

61. The challenge via habeas corpus was based upon the fact that the defendant would be decapitated by the hanging because he weighed 409 pounds. The case became moot when Washington changed its method of execution to lethal injection.

62. Dr. Orin F. Guidry, President of the American Society of Anesthesiologists has strongly urged members of his 40,000 member organization to 'steer clear' of any participation in executions. "Lethal injection was not anesthesiology's idea, ... American society decided to have capital punishment as part of our legal system and to carry it out with lethal injection. ... The legal system has painted itself into this corner, and it is not our obligation to get it out" (American Society of Anesthesiologists, 2006). The President of the Association said he was prompted to issue that message when the federal judge in Missouri ordering the halt to lethal injections said that a board certified anesthesiologist needs to be responsible for the mixing of drugs in the lethal injection process (Weinstein, 2006a, July 2).

63. And see Weinstein (2006b, June 28).

64. "A federal judge in San Jose has effectively halted the practice [of lethal injection] in California, after state officials said they could not satisfy his orders to have medical personnel take part in executing rapist-killer Michael Morales last week. Despite a widespread assumption that it is painless, courts around the country are weighing similar challenges from prisoners who contend that the most common method of lethal injection can still lead to physical suffering ..." (Bailey, 2006, February 26) and subsequent articles in this same paper on the Morales case.

ACKNOWLEDGEMENTS

The author gratefully acknowledges the continuing support of the Northwestern University School of Law and its Research Funds, and the unflagging assistance of the law school staff. Special thanks to Sarah Hager, Marcia Lehr, and Juana Haskin.

REFERENCES

The Report of the Governor's Commission on Capital Punishment. (2002).

Africa Watch. (1991). *Nigeria – On the eve of 'change' – Transition to what?* New York: Human Rights Watch, October.

American Society of Anesthesiologists. (2006). *Message from the President.* Retrieved on November 2006 from http://www.asahq.org

Amnesty International. (2005). *Appeal for the abolition of the death penalty in Africa.* Retrieved on November 2006 from http://www.amnesty.org/

Amnesty International. (2006). *Nigeria.* Retrieved on November 2006 from http://www.amnesty.org/

An Act Creating a Study Commission on the Death Penalty and Imposing a Moratorium on Executions and Amending P.L. 1983, ch. 245. NJ P.L Ch. 321 (2005).

An Act to Make Comprehensive Provisions for Matters Relating to Armed Robbery. Robbery and Firearms (Special Provisions) Act, Cap. (1984). 398 p. 14140.

Bailey, B. (2006, February 26). Lethal injection facing scrutiny, attention likely to amend but not end death penalty. *San Jose Mercury News, 1A*(February 26).

Bandura, A. (1999). Moral disengagement in the perpetration of inhumanities. *Personality and Social Psychology Review, 3*, 193–209.

Bienen, L. (1974). Criminal homicide in Western Nigeria, 1966–1972. *The Journal of African Law, 18*, 57–78.

Bienen, L. (1976). The determination of criminal insanity in Western Nigeria. *The Journal of Modern African Studies, 14*, 219–245.

Bienen, L. B. (1993). A good murder. *Fordham Urban Law Journal, 20*, 585–607.

Bienen, L. B. (1996). The proportionality review of capital cases by state high courts after Gregg: Only 'the appearance of justice?'. *Journal of Criminal Law & Criminology, 87*, 130–314.

Bienen, L. B. (1998a). Technician. *TriQuarterly, 104*, 192–271.

Bienen, L. B. (1998b). The quality of justice in capital cases: Illinois as a case study. *Law & Contemporary Problems, 61*, 193–217.

Bienen, L. B., & Rottinghaus, B. (2002). Learning from the past, living in the present: Understanding homicide in Chicago, 1870–1930; Newspapers and the political and intellectual climate of the times. *Journal of Criminal Law & Criminology, 92*, 437–554.

Bienen, L. B., Weiner, N. A., Allison, P. D., & Mills, D. L. (1990). The reimposition of capital punishment in New Jersey: Felony murder cases. *Albany Law Review, 54*, 709–817.

Bienen, L. B., Weiner, N. A., Denno, D. W., Allison, P. D., & Mills, D. L. (1988). The reimposition of capital punishment in New Jersey: The role of prosecutorial discretion. *Rutgers Law Review, 41*, 27–372.

Bohannan, P. (1960). *African homicide and suicide.* Princeton: Princeton University Press.

Capital Punishment Reform Study Committee Act. (2003). Ill. P.A. 93–605.

Capital punishment: cruel and unusual. (1993, January 23). *The Economist, 86.*

Center on Wrongful Convictions. (2006). *Illinois exonerations.* Retrieved on November 2006, from http://www.law.northwestern.edu/wrongfulconvictions/

Consultation With and Supervision Over County Prosecutors; Uniform Enforcement of Criminal Laws. (2006). 52 N.J. Stat. Ann. 17B–103. (2001 & Supp. 2007).

Criminal Code Act. (1990). In: Law Revision Committee (Eds), *The laws of the federation of Nigeria.* Portsmouth: Grosvenor Press Ltd., January 31.

Death Penalty Information Center. (2006). Statistics. Retrieved on November 2006 from http://www.deathpenaltyinfo.org/

Denno, D. W. (1994). Is electrocution an unconstitutional method of execution? The engineering of death over the century. *William & Mary Law Review, 35*, 551–692.

Denno, D. W. (1997). Getting to death: Are executions constitutional? *Iowa Law Review, 82*, 319–464.

Denno, D. W. (2002). When legislatures delegate death: The troubling paradox behind state uses of electrocution and lethal injection and what it says about us. *Ohio State Law Journal, 63*, 63–260.

Development Policy Centre Nigeria. (2000). In: O. Dina, A. Ajibade, M. Atinmo, & I. Mabawaonku (Eds), *Laws of the federation of Nigeria: A subject of analysis.* (pp. 262–263). Ibadan, Nigeria.

Dr. Death and his wonderful machine. (1990). *New York Times*, October 18, p. A24.

Forsberg, M. E. (2005). Money for nothing? – The financial cost of New Jersey's death penalty. *New Jersey Policy Perspective*, November. Retrieved on November 2006 from http://www.njadp.org/forms/Cost/Money

Gregg v. Georgia, 428 U.S. 153 (1976).

Halt the anguish, Gov. Ryan. (2002). *The Chicago Tribune*, October 20, 8p.

Hoffman, J. (1996). *His court, his legacy. New York Times*. sec. 13NJ, June 30, 1p.

Illinois State Police. (2003). *Uniform crime reporting program, crime in Illinois*. Retrieved on November 2006 from www.isp.state.il.us/crime/cii2003.cfm

Ilo, U. (2004. The Rope: Country report on death penalty application in Nigeria. In: *Report presented at the first African conference on death penalty application in Commonwealth Africa*. Entebbe, Uganda, May 10.

Internet Movie Database. (1995). *Dead man walking*. Retrieved on September 9, 2006, from http://www.imdb.com/title/tt0112818/

Laws of the Federation of Nigeria. Section 402(2)(a)(b) Criminal Code Act, cap. 77. (1984).

Marshall v. Cathel, 428 F. 3d 452 (3rd Cir. 2005).

McGinniss, J. (1991). *Blind faith*. New York: Random House.

Medwed, D. S. (2006). Anatomy of a wrongful conviction: Theoretical implications and practical solutions. *Villanova Law Review, 51*, 337–377.

National Association for the Advancement of Colored People Legal Defense and Education Fund. (2006). *Death Row USA*, Spring.

NJ Constitution, Article V, section 1, paragraph 5.

Osofsky, M. J., Bandura, A., & Zimbardo, P. G. (2005). The role of moral disengagement in the execution process. *Law and Human Behavior, 29*, 371–393.

People ex rel. Carey v. Cousins, 397 N.E. 2d 809 (Ill. 1979).

People v. Lewis, 473 N.E. 2d 901 (Ill. 1984).

People v. Morris, 848 N.E. 2d 1000 (Ill. 2006).

People v. Porter, 489 N.E. 2d 1329 (Ill. 1986).

People v. Porter, 647 N.E. 2d 972 (Ill. 1995).

People v. Silagy, 461 N.E. 2d 415 (Ill. 1984).

Pulley v. Harris, 465 U.S. 37 (1984).

Roper Center for Public Opinion. (2003). Survey. Retrieved on November 2006 from web site.

Rosen, B. S. (1984, Nov. 5). A bold court forges ahead. *National Law Journal, 1*(November 5).

Rupe v. Wood, 863 F. Supp. 1307 (W.D. Wash, 1994), pp. 1, 38–40, 44.

Sarat, A. (2005). *Mercy on trial – What it means to stop an execution*. Princeton: Princeton University Press.

Schwaneberg, R. (2006). Marshall gets life in prison. *The Star-Ledger (Newark, NJ)*, August 19, 1.

State v. Funicello, 286 A. 2d 55 (NJ 1972).

State v. Marshall, 586 A. 2d 85 (NJ 1991).

State v. Marshall II, 613 A. 2d 1059 (NJ 1992).

State v. Ramseur, 524 A. 2d 188 (NJ 1987).

Sullivan, J.F. (1978. Penal code revision easing curbs on sex passed in New Jersey. *New York Times*, July 28, 1p.

Taylor v. Crawford. (2006). No. 05-4173-CV-C-FJG (W.D. Mo., June 26).

Turow, S. (2003). *Ultimate punishment*. New York: Farrar Straus & Giroux.

United Nations High Commissioner for Refugees. (2006). Retrieved on November 2006 from web site.

Vaughan, B. (2006). New Jersey seeks appeal of Marshall ruling. *The Press of Atlantic City*, February 2, A1p.

Waldron, M. (1978). Byrne pocket vetoes death penalty bill. *New York Times*, March 4, 45p.

Warden, R. (2005). Illinois death penalty reform: How it happened, what it promises. *Journal of Criminal Law & Criminology*, *95*, 381–426.

Weinstein, H. (2006a). Federal judge orders Missouri to stop all executions. *Los Angeles Times*, June 28, A16p.

Weinstein, H. (2006b). Anesthesiologists advised to avoid executions. *Los Angeles Times*, July 2, A32p.

Weinstein, H. (2006c). Judge considering constitutionality of lethal injection posing tough questions. *Los Angeles Times*, October 6, B3p.

Wolfgang, M. E. (1958). *Patterns in criminal homicide*. Philadelphia: University of Pennsylvania.

FACTS AND FURIES: THE ANTINOMIES OF FACTS, LAW, AND RETRIBUTION IN THE WORK OF CAPITAL PROSECUTORS

Paul J. Kaplan

ABSTRACT

Recent trends against capital punishment raise the question of whether or when the U.S. is going to abolish the death penalty. One way of investigating this possibility is to study the work of capital prosecutors. In this chapter I analyze California capital prosecutors through a close reading of trial transcripts and interviews. The results show that prosecutor discourses evince a paradox – while instantiating powerful ideological themes that may underlie state killing, prosecutors also assert the primacy of 'facts' and 'law.' While this tension does not represent a strict measure of capital punishment's lifespan, its presence suggests that these types of tensions are not enough to change the law, thereby hinting that while the death penalty may be weakened in the United States, it is not close to dying.

Recent limitations placed on the practice of capital punishment by the U.S. Supreme Court, the prominence of 'miscarriages of justice,' and court-based moratoria in several states[1] suggest that the death penalty's days may be

Special Issue: Is the Death Penalty Dying?
Studies in Law, Politics, and Society, Volume 42, 135–159
Copyright © 2008 by Elsevier Ltd.
All rights of reproduction in any form reserved
ISSN: 1059-4337/doi:10.1016/S1059-4337(07)00405-X

numbered in the United States. However, state lawmakers in some jurisdictions have advocated – or actually passed – new laws *expanding* the use of capital punishment to include death sentences for defendants convicted of sexually assaulting children (see Hart, 2006).[2] These conflicting trends raise, once again, the question of whether or when the U.S. is going to cease the practice of state killing.

One way of investigating capital punishment's life or death in the U.S. is to examine the practices and consciousnesses of persons who vociferously promote its purported benefits-capital prosecutors. In this chapter, I analyze the work of California capital prosecutors on the basis of a close reading of trial transcripts and interviews with prosecutors from three large and diverse counties. The results of this analysis show that prosecutor discourse and consciousness evince a paradox of sorts – while instantiating powerful ideological themes that may underlie state killing (such as retribution and individualism) in trial discourses and also interviews, prosecutors also assert the primacy of 'facts' and 'law.' Why is this paradoxical? It is firstly because there is a tension between the formally rational, bureaucratic *process* through which prosecutors narratively construct reality, and the profoundly affective *content* of that constructed reality. Secondly, prosecutors' commitment to and valorization of the formally rational 'law' is at odds with their belief that the law's *purpose* is to provide retribution on behalf of the families of murder victims and also society in general. While this tension does not represent a strict measure of capital punishment's lifespan, its enduring presence in the operation of the law suggests that these types of tensions are not enough to change the law, thereby hinting that while the death penalty may be weakened and may well continue to be whittled down in the United States, it is not close to dying.

DATA AND METHODS

The data for this chapter consist primarily of: (a) the transcripts of the entire record of death sentence resulting trials from 1996 to 2004 for three large and diverse California counties ($N=37$) and (b) interviews with eight prosecutors from those counties. I coded the transcripts using the software program Atlas ti, which facilitated the process of constructing analytical categories out of the data. This process entailed carefully reading the transcripts and identifying passages that reflected analytical themes that I had already identified prior to the analysis, and also identifying new and sometimes unexpected themes that emerged from the data.[3]

The process thus resembled the method of grounded theory, to the extent that I formulated new codes and analytical themes as I analyzed the data. For example, before reading a single passage of the transcripts, I knew from prior experience with capital trials that a number of themes, for example, 'retribution' or 'incapacitation' would very likely be present as aspects of the narratives.[4] I did not know, however, that both defenders and prosecutors would sometimes disregard logical coherence when constructing their arguments. Noticing this general pattern of 'illogic' drew my attention to the strange tension that is the central topic of this chapter – prosecutors' contradictory devotion to both 'facts and law' and simultaneously to enraged retribution.

The interviews for this study consisted of semi-structured interviews with eight California capital prosecutors. I came to each interview with a set of open-ended questions with the goal of initiating a conversation rather than administering a questionnaire. Each interview lasted between one and three hours; I recorded several of the interviews, but decided not to record the others due to my impression that recording tended to inhibit the interviewees. I analyzed the interview transcripts similarly to the trial transcripts, coding for some pre-determined themes and developing new ones as I went along. Confidentiality has been maintained throughout the process.

It is through this grounded method that I identified the analytical themes of illogical narratives and a general contradiction between 'facts' and 'furies.' As I read, coded, re-coded, and analyzed the data along a number of theoretical dimensions,[5] I began to notice an unsettling mix of formal and bureaucratic processes and vividly horrific stories, as if an accountant were to walk up to the podium at a professional conference and proceed to intone in a calm voice the grisly details of the most recent shock movie to come out of Hollywood, interpolating bureau-speak and pleasantries ('If it please the court,' 'I hope you all had a nice lunch,' etc.) between colorful descriptions of blunt force trauma, slash wounds, and the necessity of state killing. Noticing this tension led me to develop the central idea expressed in this chapter – that the evidently unproblematic and enduring existence of this contradiction suggests that there may be something indelible about the U.S.'s continued commitment to state killing.

CAPITAL PUNISHMENT'S INDELIBILITY

The *source* of this (possible) indelibility is a complex and difficult to measure question – one taken up by several prominent death penalty scholars. Some have argued that 'American Exceptionalism,' in various forms, explains U.S. retention of the death penalty. The arguments range from Zimring's (2003) proposal that a commitment to vigilantism is the operative variable, to Whitman's (2003) suggestion that American harsh punishment[6] can counter-intuitively be explained by a uniquely American commitment to egalitarianism, to Poveda's argument that an individualistic American Creed[7] creates an 'executable class' of persons in the U.S. I have added elsewhere to these theories of U.S. retention that a key force underlying the death penalty, beyond vigilantism, egalitarianism, or individualism, is racialized inequality (see Kaplan, 2006). Executees in the U.S. almost never look anything like executioners – the 'race effect' of murder victims and the disproportionate representation of poor persons of color among the condemned and executed is well established, and 97.5% of prosecutors in death penalty states are white (Dieter, 1998).

However, another branch of what might be termed the 'culturist' literature on capital punishment finds that the death penalty may be abolished relatively soon in the United States due to changing norms. Sarat (2001), for example, argues that a 'new abolitionism' has been emerging in the U.S. that invokes 'evolving standards of decency' and constitutional due-process protections in taking on capital punishment's *legal* (rather than moral) standing (see p. 252). The essence of this new abolitionism is a valorization *of* the law – rather than a challenge *to* the law:

> The new abolitionism that Blackmun championed presents itself as a reluctant abolitionism, one rooted in acknowledgment of the damage that capital punishment does to central legal values and to the legitimacy of the law itself. It finds its home in an embrace, not a critique, of those values. Those who love the law, in Blackmun's view, must hate the death penalty for the damage it does to the object of that love. (Sarat, 2001, p. 253)

In Sarat's analysis of the 'cultural life' of capital punishment, a different set of cultural commitments – based on legality and fairness – is required to achieve abolition rather than the familiar moral or religious ideals that have long been associated with abolitionism.[8]

David Garland (2005) has more explicitly challenged the 'American Exceptionalist' theories of retention by proposing that retention is related not to *longstanding* cultural forces but instead to the *recent* crime control policies of late modernity (see p. 22). From Garland's perspective, certain aspects of the American polity – such as "the separation of powers between legislatures and courts; the local nature of criminal law jurisdiction; the elected nature of criminal justice officials; the political character of criminal justice decision making" (Garland, 2005, p. 23) – coupled with recent cultural developments in the penal landscape – such as "the 'crime complex' of the 1970s, the backlash against the Court's liberal activism, the conservative reaction against civil rights gains and the 'moral decay' of the 1960s" (Garland, 2005, p. 23) – together explain U.S. retention of capital punishment. From Garland's point of view, this situation adds up to a likelihood that the U.S. is simply lagging behind its European peers in abolishing the death penalty. After all, according to Garland's logic, if the *Furman v. Georgia* (1972) decision had never been reversed, the U.S. version of abolition would have taken place during the same approximate time as France.

In this chapter, I aim to add to the current debate that focuses alternatively on deep and longstanding 'American' ideologies or more recent cultural-penal developments by showing how a commitment to affective retribution in the practice of capital punishment operates against the prospect of abolition (albeit in contradiction to the law's rational and formal impulses). This argument is consistent with classic treatments of law and punishment that have long recognized the inherent tension in law between vengeful impulses and a 'modern' need for formal rationality.

CONTRADICTIONS OF CAPITAL PUNISHMENT

The general theme of contradiction or paradox within the realm of capital punishment has been addressed at length by many analysts. In the first place, the use of capital punishment seems, to some observers, inherently antinomic to modern liberal legal order purported to be exemplified by the United States:

> The fulfillment of Enlightenment that ought to have resulted in Kant's Maturity of reason, reason also ought to have been accomplished in such a way that criminal acts would come to be considered as irrational, and criminals would become known as beings who are subject to correction if possible and containment if not. Indeed, in a well-ordered, fully enlightened society, punishment is supposed to fade away and penalties would continue to exist only as forms of reassurance. To actually kill in the name of containment would be to abandon the reason that knows perfectly the fallibility of its all too human execution by persons not fully endowed with the capacity to reason – the insane, infirm, or imbecilic. (Dumm, 2000, p. 471)

Put less elegantly, it seems irrational or contradictory to execute within a purportedly modern, rational, and enlightened society.[9] Such a conceptualization of the death penalty is in alignment with Foucault's (1977) vision of punishment as delineated in *Discipline and Punish*, which imagines "criminal justice today as fundamentally rational and bureaucratic, and as a largely cold and routinized expression of growing administrative control" (Smith, 2003, p. 28). According to Smith (2003), Foucault's rationalist vision imagines a situation in which "primordial symbols and mythologies no longer play a significant part in punishment discourse. Punishment is now explicable as a rational and instrumental application of social control, not an expression of meanings" (Smith, 2003, p. 29). Indeed, as Dumm (2000, p. 471) argues:

> Michel Foucault's thesis – most fully announced in *Discipline and punish* (1977) – supposedly is that the rise of practices of visibility, order, and micro-management of bodies culminated in the penal reforms that ended the spectacle of the scaffold and gave rise to disciplinary society, effectively foreclosing any meaningful purpose in killing criminals. The practice of state killing as a punishment for crimes ought to have withered away as a disciplinary society extends its reach and the ensemble of corrective measures becomes more extensive.

Nevertheless, one wonders whether the death penalty is really so contradictory with the modern liberal legal order. A tautological response would be to argue that its presence proves its logical place in American society. This perspective underlies the pro-retention argument that the death penalty 'fits' in American society because it is apparently vaguely popular. A more convincing argument for the death penalty's fit within a rational society comes from Smith (2003, p. 31), who, invoking Durkheim's functionalist notions of punishment as expression of collective moral outrage, as well as empirical evidence of 'affective' and 'mythological' use of the guillotine in 18th century France,[10] argues that "there is no necessary antinomy between technological reason within the disciplinary complex and affective mythology." Smith's point is that a strict application of the Foucauldian notion of rationalized punishment overstates the relationship of rationalism to punishment, while bracketing out the empirically verifiable role of emotion and symbolism. More radically, Dumm (2000, p. 471) suggests that the death penalty may actually represent the ultimate aim, or telos, of the Enlightenment because it operates to establish order upon disorder:

> We still seek to bring back to order the disorder the polity suffers, a disorder initiated at the moment when a criminal confronts or evades the sovereign by violating the sovereign's laws. In a bloody paradox, we seek to re-order what has been disordered, by killing those who have introduced disorder into the fabric of polity.

I do not hope to adjudicate these competing explanations for the presence of an affective death penalty in a purportedly rationally formal legal system. Instead, I argue throughout this chapter that the sometimes vexing concomitance of emotion and rationality in death penalty discourses may itself offer a hint about its persistence – to the extent that the law can continue to abide both 'facts' and 'furies,' it is not, after all, an especially 'logical' institution, and thus perhaps not susceptible to the disciplining forces of *rational* arguments against legal state killing (such as a 'new abolition').

Beyond the complex and perhaps unresolved sense of contradiction between enlightenment ideals and state killing, capital punishment illuminates a number of other conflicts in American criminal law, such as the competing values of retribution and due-process (see Zimring, 2003), the paradox of distinguishing state violence from illegal violence (see Sarat, 2001), as well as other major legal tensions such as the competing values of rationality (non-arbitrariness) and individualization, and the contradictory doctrines of individual culpability and 'diminished autonomy.'[11]

In most capital cases, for example, the law requires that the defendant be 'contextualized' (in the penalty phase) while it – the law – maintains a respectable rationality. Unlike most criminal cases, capital cases are rather individualized – the punishment is as much connected to the *person* as to the *crime*. Indeed, the most important legal factor in capital cases – after guilt for homicide is determined – is the defendant's individual characteristics. And while it is not legally required for a verdict and penalty, the background of the victim (as well as the impact of his or her death on family members) is often prominently discussed in all stages of capital cases. This is one way that 'death is different,' and is an unexpected point of focus in American legal proceedings because it contradicts the value of generalization central to American formalism. This generalizing characteristic is often thought of as an essential tenet in modern liberal legal systems. As Milovanovic (1994, p. 41) puts it (discussing Weber), "'rationality' means 'following some criteria of decision which is applicable to all like cases.' In other words, it stands for generality; it means dealing with all similarly situated cases in a similar way." Rationality is important to modern states because it makes for a highly predictable, stable legal framework, which is necessary for a smooth-running capitalist political economy. The introduction of extensive and detailed evidence about the characteristics of individuals is generally *not* something that fits with a rational legal system.[12]

Indeed, recent capital jurisprudence is one prominent instance in which the tension in the law between 'individualization' and 'reliability' has been played out. Recall that the essence of the Supreme Court's ruling in

Furman v. Georgia (1972) was that death penalty statutes were too arbitrary. The eventual response by legislatures in many American states was to rewrite their capital statutes to adhere to the principle of 'guided discretion,' which gave adjudicators detailed guidelines for deciding capital cases. The post-*Gregg v. Georgia* (1976) era was supposed to bring rationality or reliability back to the practice of capital punishment. However, with cases such as *Woodson v. North Carolina* (1976), *Lockett v. Ohio* (1978), and *Eddings v. Oklahoma* (1982), the court required that capital adjudicators consider defendants' individual characteristics when determining death sentences. The result has been a rather contradictory and confusing body of jurisprudence that Zimring (2003) has described as 'a Frankenstein's monster.'[13]

Aside from these contradictions embodied by the death penalty, I describe in this chapter other legal tensions presented by capital punishment, namely the presence of illogical storytelling in prosecution narratives, and a disjunction between the purportedly neutral and self-evident *facts* and *law* valorized by prosecutors, and the *fury* of the content of their arguments about facts and within the law.

CONTRADICTIONS IN PROSECUTOR NARRATIVES AND CONSCIOUSNESS

One of the most striking illogics I discovered in this analysis was the prosecutor reliance on the narrative tactic of comparing defendants to animals or monstrous, non-human creatures. The 'defendant as animal' theme, as illustrated in the following quotes, is paradoxical because it contradicts a presiding theme of 'willfulness' that is necessary for the demonstration of mens rea:

> When this feral pig of a defendant stripped her of her clothing and stripped her of her dignity, what do you think Terena was thinking? (Nady, p. 5906)

> Don't you just wonder, too, what words this hyena was mouthing to her? (Nady, p. 5906)

> Thanks, Giles. Thanks. You miserable viper. You have ruined, shattered three generations of one family because anal sex is your specialty. (Nady, p. 5932)

> Don't forget, this reptilian predator of the pastor's wife has been in jail since January of '96. (Nady, p. 5958)

> Did you ever hear one word of remorse from that tattooed hyena, one word to his mother or anyone else about remorse? (Nady, pp. 5961–5962)

This man has no conscience. This man is a monster, you know, all the more so because he's able to convince people otherwise. (Bennet, p. 6509)

Not to mention that this is the same man they call Dragon, that is what he is known out on the street, ladies and gentlemen, Dragon, a mythical monster that breathes fire. That is what Dragon is. (Brents, p. 2588)

And not to patronize you, but there's a story about the scorpion and the frog, and maybe some of you have heard it. But the scorpion and the frog – there's a scorpion on the other side of the river and he wants a ride across the river. And scorpions, I don't know if you know this, don't know how to swim. Or so it's told. And the frog is going by on his merry way, and the scorpion says to him, 'hey, give me a ride across the river,' and the frog says, 'hu-huh. You scorpions have a habit of stinging us frogs and killing us.' The scorpion says, 'of course I'm not going to sting you because I'll die, too.' And the frog says, 'I'm not sure I believe you,' but the frog, against his judgment, goes ahead and gives the scorpion a ride. And they're swimming across the river. The scorpion is on the frog's back, and they're halfway across the river. And what does the scorpion do? He stings the frog. And they're both sinking now because the scorpion can't swim and the frog is paralyzed. And the frog looks up at the scorpion and says, 'Why? You just killed us both.' And the scorpion said, 'That's the way I am.' That's the way Ivan Gonzalez is. (Gonzalez, p. 12766)

Dangerous creatures such as scorpions, hyenas, or miserable vipers are *inherently* violent, and lack the ability to choose – to compare a defendant to such a creature thus contradicts the legal concept of mens rea – scorpions, unlike human beings, cannot possess a guilty mind. Moreover, in a purportedly rational society, the government would not *execute* dangerous animals – although it might destroy them in the name of public safety.

In a similar vein, prosecutors occasionally made the argument that defendants were *inherently* 'evil' – unable to help themselves from committing violence. This narrative theme resembles the 'defendant as animal' theme because it downplays the role of the defendant's will, thus diminishing his mens rea. For example, in the following examples, the prosecutors characterize the defendant's actions as 'his nature':

The key here, and what these felonies really tell you is that the two murders are more the product of his own nature as a human being that just a slip up along the way or happenstance crimes that he got caught up in. (Blacksher, p. 3945)

We have a guy here who has had some episodes of depression who underneath it all is a violent, angry person. His essence, who he is, he's a violent angry person. (Crawford, p. 12712)

According to the logic embodied in these passages, the defendant is *naturally* a murderer, which raises the question of how he could possibly *choose* to kill. There is a subtle but logically important difference between 'being' a killer and 'choosing to kill' – a difference that presents a logical conflict for the theory of mens rea, but nonetheless appears to be relatively unimportant to prosecutors. In her ethnography of maximum security prisons, Rhodes (2004) shows how the attribution of 'psychopathy' (or *inherent* or *natural* 'evil') to particular prisoners invokes a desire for incapacitation of those 'psychopaths' among prison workers (see Rhodes, 2004, p. 180). It may be that the emotional impulse driving these prosecutor arguments is fear (similarly to prison workers) – an emotion that makes some sense within the context of a maximum security prison or a murder trial, but presents a *logical* problem for the rationality of mens rea.

FACTS

Aside from these contradictory themes in prosecutor arguments, a noteworthy tension in these data involves an unsettling disjunction in prosecutor discourse and consciousness between the seemingly objective 'facts' of the crime and also the purportedly neutral 'law,' and the florid, affective, and sometimes perhaps hyperbolic nature of the arguments *about* facts and law.

The prosecutors I interviewed for this project all privileged 'the facts' as foremost in shaping the contours of the narratives they constructed in trials. For prosecutors, the most important thing to know when putting on a capital case is 'the facts' of the crime, which they understand to mean the details of the violent events that caused the death of the victim. The word 'fact' in the legal context is something of an idiom, a legal term of art, defined in a popular law dictionary as follows:

> Fact: An event that has occurred or circumstances that exist, events whose actual occurrence or existence is to be determined by the evidence. In deciding a case, a court will find facts on the basis of evidence presented to it, and then apply the law to those facts. In a jury trial, the judge will instruct the jury how to apply the law to the facts, and the jury will then find the facts and render a verdict. (Gifis, 2003)

In my interviews with prosecutors, the relevant 'events and circumstances' that guided their process of trying a capital case were limited to the temporally short details about the crime and the key characters involved, and were organized around three inter-related factual dimensions:

(1) the 'facts' of the crime,
(2) the 'background' of the defendant, and
(3) the victim's profile.

Prosecutors told me that their respective departments' policy was to bring cases to an internal committee that would consider these factors and make a recommendation for or against seeking the death penalty to the District Attorney.[14] None of the prosecutors I interviewed believed that all three factual dimensions had to seem 'death worthy' in order to bring a capital charge, but most believed that something like a rough guide of 'two out of the three' dimensions had to have certain characteristics in order to ask for the death penalty. Specifically, some combination of 'heinous' facts, a 'sympathetic' victim, and a 'threatening' defendant would prompt prosecutors to go for death.[15] For example, a crime where the victim was tortured by a defendant with a history of violence was enough, even though the lone victim was not particularly sympathetic, by conventional standards (a drug-abusing prostitute). In this case, two of the three dimensions – 'heinousness' and a 'bad' defendant – were satisfactory for the prosecutor to pursue a death sentence.

One of the notable things about this charging rubric is that prosecutors explicitly consider the status of the victim when deciding how to charge persons accused of homicide. This runs contrary to the formally rational law's egalitarian foundations and also suggests that prosecutors may act as personal advocates for victims rather than representatives of the state. Indeed, in these data, prosecutors sometimes represented themselves explicitly as advocates for the dead victim, as in the following quote: "I have a client too. The chair next to me appears to be empty, but his name is [the victim]. And I would like to introduce you to him" (Seumanu, p. 1556).

In a similar way, a different prosecutor constructed part of her penalty phase argument as a 'letter' to the victim: "[The victim] will not be forgotten. We promise that you will not die in vain. We promise that you will always be in our hearts, in our souls. We choose, we collectively choose to adopt you and to care for you" (Gonzalez, p. 12037).

As critics of the adversarial system, such as Givelber (2001), have pointed out, prosecutor advocacy for the victims of crime contributes to a general problem of indeterminate or contested 'truths' about the facts of particular cases. In an adversarial system, 'The Truth' is negotiated between competing knowledge-producing actors, a process that can, at the least, increase the likelihood of wrongful conviction of the innocent (see Givelber, 2001), and perhaps also result in a misleading or simplistic record of the crime, victim, and defendant.

But despite the adversarial nature of their arguments, prosecutors in interviews consistently emphasized the importance of a *seemingly* neutral 'truth' deriving from impartial 'facts,' as the following quote from an interview indicates:

> A: Well in any case I think our primary goal is, as a prosecutor, is to expose the truth. Our system, although it's the best in the world, is slanted towards not telling juries the whole truth ...
>
> Q: So your goal is to uncover the truth or display the truth for the jury? How do you do that?
>
> A: Well it begins in the very beginning of the assignment. You gather discovery. You make discovery available to the defense. You make all discovery available to the defense under the guidelines of either statutory requirements or Brady material. If it hurts you it hurts you. If it helps you it helps you. That's not the purpose of discovery. The purpose of discovery is to say here are the facts. This is what we know about this case and related facts. Then I think you have to be quite candid when you place things for a jury. You don't sugar coat things. You don't try to give things an aura of truth rather that they don't deserve. You don't make arguments that are disingenuous. Not as a prosecutor, that's not our job. You can expect those things from the defense of the defendant but prosecutors have one duty. That is to do a factual expose of a scenario so the jury can make a decision. (Prosecutor #1)

For this prosecutor, the 'truth' is the prosecutor's (and not the defender's) 'not disingenuous' narrative of the 'relevant' events and circumstances. For prosecutors, the 'relevant' events and characteristics tend to have to do with the forensic details of the crime. Other events and characteristics – 'facts' brought up by defenders and deemed irrelevant by prosecutors – are red herrings, misleading, and 'disingenuous.'

The 'relevant events and circumstances' for prosecutors in the trials in this data set tended to be temporally very short, referring to the events causing the victim's death – except in cases where the defendant had a history of crime or violence, in which cases the relevant events and circumstances tended to equate to a temporally long narrative beginning with and including the forensic details of the defendant's earliest crimes or violent acts, but excluding other events and circumstances that might mitigate the defendant's 'bad' behavior. In this sense, the 'facts' of the defendant's background are only relevant for prosecutors to the extent that they fit into a narrative schema that corresponds to their conceptualization of the defendant as one of a set of stock stereotypical characters such as 'the gang banger,' or 'the lurking rapist,' or, in the following case, 'the child killer'[16]:

> Q: What I'm curious about are the stories that lawyers tell in these cases. So in asking for death in this penalty phase I'm wondering how you put together ... how you went about deciding what to say?

A: The facts of the crime were big because this particular defendant did not have a criminal record other than a DUI and so she was ... to walk into her house and see the pictures and achievements on the walls, framed, if you didn't know what she was like you'd say she was the mother of the year. So I was able to bring in some acts of violence against previous boyfriends. The main thing in this case was the crime itself. (Prosecutor #2)

For this prosecutor, the 'crime itself' equates to 'the facts.' As this same prosecutor points out later in the interview, the important facts are those involved in the violence that caused the victim's death:

A: Well I have to look at everything. I have to look for mitigating factors. I anticipated the poor little girl had a miserable upbringing and have to cut her some slack thing. But sometimes the facts are just so overwhelmingly premeditated and moving from one room to the other and reloading. (Prosecutor #2)

This defendant was classified by the prosecutor as a self-involved psychopathic mother who murdered her children to spite the children's father – these were 'the facts,' the only relevant events and circumstances.

And while the following prosecutor recognized the defense's discretion to tell a longer story, he explains how he emphasizes the defendant's background when it includes prior crimes or violence:

A: We're gonna play the hand that we're dealt. And you may have a horrible crime that was done in a short period of time. Then we're going to emphasize that. You may have someone who has a series of crimes in which case we would emphasize that. You would have a longer story. But then the defense would tend to make it even longer. Outside these crimes, no matter what the period is, what happened to make this guy act this way. You see how it's phrased. What happened to make this guy act this way? (Prosecutor #6)

Another prosecutor, who did not wish to be recorded, told me that the notion that public pressure on capital prosecutors might lead to over-zealousness is 'Hollywood stuff,' and that prosecutors in his office always 'go by the facts,' meaning that they take whatever events constitute the crime and straightforwardly and impartially deliver these to the jury (Prosecutor #3).

One lesson we can take away from these glimpses into the consciousnesses of prosecutors is that despite their invocation of the neutrality of 'facts,' they see themselves as vigorously engaged in a tough adversarial battle. That is to say, while their version of 'the facts' seem to speak for themselves for prosecutors, prosecutors are excising or ignoring other events and circumstances that, according to others (such as defenders) might seem also to speak for themselves, such as traumatic childhood abuse and neglect of the defendant. In my interviews, there was a sense of exasperation running through prosecutors' commentary, as if the 'facts' of the victim's death made it self-evident that the defendant deserved a death sentence. This sense of exasperation might help explain the affective and vociferous tone of their arguments in trials.

Another prosecutor explained the primacy of facts this way:

> Q: How do you go about developing your opening statement and your arguments? In guilt and in penalty?

> A: Fact driven. Fact driven on the case. Guilt argument is no different than any other argument in any other case. Is there a murder? Is he the guy that did it? And you try to explain to them what murder is and the various elements are. Then you pull in the various facts and say you've proven this you've proven that. I tell them, on occasion, the guilt decision is brain driven. (Prosecutor #5)

For this prosecutor, guilt phase arguments are *rational* and based on his interpretation of 'the facts.' Interestingly, however, this same prosecutor conceptualizes the penalty phase differently – as 'gut driven':

> The penalty decision is gut driven. It's a morality decision. You look at what is right and what is wrong. Is he deserving of the ultimate punishment or a lesser punishment? What is he all about? How bad is this crime? How vulnerable was the victim? What has he made of his life? Where did he come from? What did he have? What didn't he have? (Prosecutor #5)

This commentary on the penalty phase is notable partly because it acknowledges the significance of the victim's status. But it is also interesting because this particular prosecutor seems to understand the significance of the defendant's social history when developing a perspective on the suitability of the death penalty. Of course, his own answers to the questions he poses in his comments – What has he made of his life? Where did he come from? What did he have? What didn't he have? – may reflect an individualistic conceptualization of human beings, which might be different for defenders, or perhaps jurors.

LAW

Sometimes, prosecutors invoked the primacy of law rather than facts:

> Q: One of the things I'm interested in learning is what are the factors that shape the argument in the penalty phase? So I mean one could imagine that there's the facts, the evidence. But one could also imagine that there are legal constraints on what you can or can't say in sort of developing this story or argument, but also you've already mentioned sort a strategic decision where you choose to ask them. How do you go about shaping that argument? What are the factors that influence it?

A: Legally, obviously is the first place you start. And the law has changed a lot since I came to the DA's office. What you could argue. Victim impact was never appropriate. In the legal world it is relatively new. Obviously the only thing that was important in the penalty phase is that it always focused on the defendant. The arguments you could use for killing a defendant were always things like his prior record, the likelihood, this is new too, that he would be violent in the future even if locked up without the possibility of parole. (Prosecutor #1)

This prosecutor thinks of penalty phases as disciplined by the law's rules. Similarly, in the following quote, we can see how the formally rational discipline of the law is an important feature for this different prosecutor in developing his arguments:

A: And I think from a prosecutor's standpoint they do what we started this conversation with, they expose the truth and they make the logical arguments about why they believe the death penalty is appropriate for this case. And as you know we are not hanging out in this abyss, there are rules and regulations for the jury to consider. They have very specific directions. You may assign whatever weight you want to them, but these are the rules, the K factors that you can consider. So it varies. I would say that in this case that I just finished I would say that my final argument is ten minutes. Because I believe that it was my goal to say to this jury that these are the facts, here is what you heard in the way of evidence and this is why the death penalty applies. Here is what your social responsibility is in considering the death penalty. Then sit down and shut up. (Prosecutor #4)

In these quotes prosecutors are reflecting a commitment to the Enlightenment ideal of formal rationality that is supposed to control the law in a modern liberal legal state, as alluded to earlier in this chapter. But despite these prosecutors' emphasis on the predominance of the rigors of a disciplining law (as well as apparently neutral or self-evident facts), much of the tenor of prosecutor argumentation in the trials analyzed in this study was anything but neutral and rational.

FURIES

Prosecutor arguments in these trials were often floridly emotional when describing defendants and their violent acts:

Now after and during this nightmare then at the rape scene, she is taken by these two hyenas on the Bataan Death March, as I like to state it, 55 yards up from the rape scene where she was hogtied like a rodeo animal – you can see that very plainly in the series 5 pieces of evidence – and then she is executed. (Thomas, p. 6092)

Don't you just wonder, too, what words this hyena was mouthing to her? What terms of endearment do you think he was telling her once he spilled his seed of lust into her now damaged anal cavity? What do you think he was saying to her? Can't you just imagine? (Nady, p. 5906)

Thanks, Giles. Thanks. You miserable viper. You have ruined, shattered three generations of one family because anal sex is your specialty. (Nady, p. 5932)

But when you put in the context of Tara's account of what happened, he stuck it in her anus. Then he made her suck his penis, and then he ejaculates on her. She said that she could taste the ejaculate in her mouth, and it's all over the front of her sweatshirt, and down here there's something that looks like fecal material and could be a combination of fecal material and saliva, her saliva, her fecal material, his semen. (Martinez, p. 4738)

There was trauma to her breasts. At the site of the autopsy X-rays were taken. And it was discovered by X-ray that this mousse can – this is loreal freehold styling mousse – this item was found inside of [the victim's] stomach, her abdomen. It had got there by being rammed up through her rectum and through the wall that separates the rectal area from the stomach and left within her rectal area – excuse me, in her abdominal area. (Edwards, 1963)

In each of these graphic descriptions, the prosecutor depicted filmic vignettes of terrifying, gruesome violence, all delivered in the sanctimonious grammar of indignation. These 'facts' speak for themselves – but are spoken furiously – and declare that the defendant is utterly Other, an inhuman threat to the sanctity of the victim, and by implication to society.

Sometimes these frightening vignettes invited the jury to imagine being the victim:

Imagine, imagine what that child was thinking about the last 30 minutes, those torturous minutes of her life. Imagine the indescribable terror of having a gun in your face and seeing the finger on the trigger and seeing everyone around you trying to save you, unable to bargain for your life no matter how much they pleaded and no matter how hard you hoped; the absolute fear of knowing that you would never run to your mommy again, you would never feel her arms around you, knowing that your mommy isn't with you to make you safe and that your big brothers aren't there to protect you, that you're aunties and your uncles and your cousins are all gone, you're all alone, all alone, a helpless little vulnerable girl with this very mean man who keeps pushing this gun in your cheek and he won't let you go, no matter how hard anyone asks him. And even though everyone is telling him to let you go, even people who are begging him for your life, every time they did that, he just pushed that gun harder into your cheek. That soft little cheek and that cold hard metal. And he was so mean and you were so afraid. Your precious little eyes showed us the terror that you felt. And it was those same eyes that begged you, begged all of us, to save you. But he wouldn't let us save you. Imagine knowing that no one can save you, that he's not going to let them. (Lewis, p. 6873)

As she realized she was being caught by this guy capable of karate and manhandling someone, imagine the terror when she realized she was caught. Imagine the helplessness she felt as the handcuffs went on her. Imagine the fear and the terror that she had when she was taped. Imagine the feeling of impending doom as that gag went in her mouth. 'I can't scream anymore even.' It is out of this world. It is unimaginable. Where did her thoughts turn at the end? Maybe her dead [*sic*]. Maybe she can't help. I don't know. Imagine the impact on her not only physically but spiritually when she was beat those 31 times. (Famalaro, p. 6640)

What does it feel like to be a victim like that? How does it feel to have your skin come off? How does it feel to see your red body with your skin ripped off your body and know that you don't stand a chance to live; to be hung, to be stuffed in a box, to be shoved behind a door? How does that last second of agony feel before death mercifully takes over? (Gonzalez, p. 12047)

Regardless of whether or not these passages may violate legal norms about appropriate argument they seem to push the boundaries of the (purportedly) rational law's limits on 'inflaming the passions' and possibly prejudicing the jury.

Beyond colorful descriptions of the crimes and florid invitations for jurors to imagine being the victim, prosecutors occasionally invoked explicitly retributive rationales to support giving a death sentence. These sections of arguments are notable because they illuminate prosecutors' attitudes about the concept of retribution as a theory of capital punishment:

A pronouncement of death to Erven Blacksher says: the intolerable nature of the evil acts you have perpetrated, based on the quality of man that you are, must be punished to the maximum. It is a cleansing and it is a catharsis that restores in some vital sense, order and continuity to what we have. (Blacksher, p. 3916)

And when I say 'necessary,' I mean morally necessary. I mean that justice requires a verdict of death in this case. (Daveggio & Michaud, p. 8442)

A late social philosopher, Robert Nesbitt, says: until catharsis has been effected [*sic*] through a trial, through a finding of guilt and a punishment, the community is anxious, fearful, apprehensive and above all, contaminated. (Daveggio & Michaud, p. 8524)

The whole notion of the death penalty as punishment is a way that is our certainty and our community, that we express this denunciation of a wrong-doing. It's a way that we maintain order for the law. And it's essential that this punishment be reserved for the gravest of crimes and that it should adequately reflect not only your outrage but your revulsion at this crime, a revulsion that is felt by the great majority of citizens when they witness the murder of an innocent child. (Lewis, p. 8677)

Now, nothing you do obviously is going to bring or give life back to [the victim]. But you can give her something. You can give her something underneath that tombstone with the big pink heart down in Texas. You can give her a just verdict. You can give her a verdict called for by the evidence. Not because you're mad at anybody. Not because you want revenge. Not for any base thing. You can just say that we've looked at the evidence, what's been presented to us, and what's warranted. What there is [*sic*] reasonable grounds for is the punishment of death. (Thomas, p. 7013)

But one of the concepts that we kept was this concept of punishment. And punishment is necessary. Those of you who have raised children and those of you who are raising children and those of you who will raise children in the future, punishment is an important part of a family, and it is an important part of society. And the death penalty is an acceptable punishment. There comes a point in time where a person has crossed the line, and the only appropriate punishment is death. (Clark, p. 16470)

And what you are doing by choosing this punishment is you are stating the level of moral outrage that you feel at these crimes and at this defendant. When you choose the death penalty, you are stating the level of outrage that you have for kidnapping and terrorizing and then murdering a perfectly innocent little child. (Lewis, p. 8577)

These rationales for state killing are explicitly retributive, and contrast other, more rational and utilitarian theories of punishment, such as deterrence, and incapacitation. Retribution is fundamentally *irrational*, predicated on emotion and an unpredictable logic of vengeance – indeed, explanations of retribution border on the tautological. To argue that 'we must give him death because he deserves it,' is circular in its logic. But as I have pointed out, logical coherence is not a necessary ingredient for the production of trial arguments.

And while it is perhaps unsurprising that capital prosecutors used vividly affective and retributive rhetoric in their trial arguments, they also display similar illogics in interviews:

Q: Opening up the frame here, as somebody who has conducted a capital case, what do you think the role of the death penalty is?

A: Well I would hope it was deterrence, mostly. But I think that it is the appropriate punishment for certain people. I think that the death penalty should be extended to more crimes. But I think there are certain cases where there is no better punishment than death. Granted they sit around forever, the appellate process is very lengthy. Who knows if I'll even see [the defendant] executed. Deterrence it doesn't really deter people. I have a lot of job security because I keep seeing people come through the system over and over again.

Q: From my academic research on that issue and from talking to some judges, prosecutors, defense attorneys most people agree with you that it doesn't have a strong deterrent effect but its main function to be this sense of justice. What do you mean by that? What is it about doing that that equates to justice?

A: If someone is given LWOP they are still given the opportunity to read magazine and watch tv and to basically go on with their life in this confined environment. I don't think that's appropriate for some people. I don't think it should apply to all murders but I think it's something that should be reserved for the worst of the worst. And that one I prosecuted falls within that category. I've had other cases where it wasn't even a question, we didn't have special circumstance, but I'm just saying, it wouldn't apply to all people. Someone who kills a child by shaking will get 25 to life, yes they deserve to go to prison and hopefully not get out. But it's not necessarily a death penalty case. But if you have torture, a special circumstance, have you talked to Judge Smith [a pseudonym]? He prosecuted an aunt and uncle who tortured [a victim]. Horrible. They are the poster children for the death penalty. To me that's justice. (Prosecutor #2)

For this prosecutor, the death penalty is 'appropriate' for certain 'worst of the worst' defendants. The 'worst of the worst,' of course, is a subjective construct, akin to pornography – it is hard to define but you know it when you see it, depending on your perspective on 'it.'

The following prosecutor struggles somewhat with the *purpose* of the death penalty as he delineates a rationale that resembles retribution:

A: It's obviously tough to decide what the death penalty does. The death penalty does for sure is insure that that defendant does not ever commit another crime or kill someone else. Whether or not someone says 'I think I won't kill this person because I don't want to get death' there is no way of knowing because you can't prove the negative. I also believe that that's probably not likely anyway, that people who are willing to commit capital crimes aren't probably thinking of the consequences of death.

Q: Not weighing carefully should I shoot the guy in the liquor store or not?

A: Right. I don't think that's part of it. I think in California and in the United States the idea of the death penalty is that there are some crimes that are so horrific to the public in general that they don't believe that any other penalty is appropriate. Of course, in California that's kind of an odd comment anyway since they never die.

Q: So I'm going to use the sort of sociological terminology now. It sounds to me like you're saying that there's an incapacitory effect, meaning that this guy isn't going to be able to hurt anybody because he is not going to be alive anymore. And there's something some kind of symbolic message effect that we society has decided that some crimes are bad or heinous enough that they deserve the most harsh punishment that we as a society can give.

A: I think it's cathartic for the public at some point, even though the death may never be carried out or something happens that it is postponed for 15 to 20 years, even though it is expensive and it is more expensive to put somebody to death in California only because of the appellate process, but it feels cathartic somehow to say that 'you will die for killing [a young female victim]'. That cute little girl kind of thing. I think it serves a purpose even if it's not carried out. (Prosecutor #1)

This prosecutor envisions lethal retribution as cathartic and symbolic, a necessary act that provides a cleansing for a society soiled by the murder of a sympathetic victim such as a female child. This commentary is notable because it invokes a particular theory of the state's role in managing violence – namely that the state's job is to intervene *after* the violence and enact retribution upon the perpetrator for symbolic reasons. This rather Durkheimian way of conceptualizing state punishment fits with the general trend in death penalty discourse of bracketing out social causes of violence and focusing instead on a sort of ex post facto 'easy solution' to the complex problem of racialized inequality that is involved in producing violent and impoverished communities and persons.[17]

For another prosecutor, retribution is 'simply' appropriate:

Q: So this is just a big open ended question, but as a person who has participated in capital trials, what do you think is the role of the death penalty in the US? What is its function or purpose?

A: The role of the death penalty is to serve as the appropriate punishment for certain crimes.

Q: That's it?

A: That's it.

Q: Okay. When you have done these capital trials ... let me ask you to elaborate on that response a little bit. Because what I assume you mean by that is that you don't see it as having a great deterrent effect? But you think of it as a just punishment and that's essentially its role.

A: It has a tremendous deterrent effect on the perpetrator.

Q: On the guy. The one guy?

A: Right. The recidivism rate amongst people who are on death row is zero. Deterrence regarding whether or not other people are deterred by the fact that someone else received the death penalty for their conduct, in my view, is not a factor. It's not relevant. Frankly, I think it's a diversionary tactic. As if the existence or the non existence of deterrence is somehow for or against support for the death penalty.

Q: Why do you think it's a distraction?

A: Because I think it's very difficult for people to argue the nuts and bolts aspect of the punishment. Some people just don't like the thought that the government is going to take someone's life. And they don't want to or can't argue whether that's appropriate. So instead it becomes a diversionary tactic of let's talk about something else. Because in no other type of crime do we talk about punishment being a diversion to others. I can't think of any other type of crime where we talk about deterrence. The nature of the punishment, certainly the fact that you might be caught and punished might have some deterrent effect on someone who is thinking about committing a crime, but the specific nature of the punishment, whether it's two years in state prison or three years in state prison. (Prosecutor #4)

For this prosecutor, deterrence is a red herring because, for him, it is irrelevant to the real question of capital punishment's appropriateness. For him, the death penalty is simply 'the appropriate punishment for certain crimes,' although he also believes it manifests specific deterrence on the defendant. This is an exclusively retributive and rather tautological rationale for defending the use of capital punishment.

These affective 'furies' – vivid descriptions of violent deaths, invitations to imagine being murdered, and invocations of affective retribution – are constructed within the formally rational context of 'facts' and 'law.' This situation presents yet another paradox in U.S. capital punishment, a paradox that can be partially explained by the social rules of the legal institution, yet may also shed light on the question of U.S. retention of the death penalty.

INSTITUTIONAL NORMS

It is important to note that the contradictory predicaments I have described in this study can be partially understood as the product of legal-institutional norms that operate to filter or discipline emotionally driven actions such as prosecuting a capital trial. Prosecutors are taught to 'play by the book' and 'uphold justice' no matter how angry they become over the particulars of any given case. These values are embedded in jurisprudential rules prohibiting 'emotional' or 'inappropriate' rhetoric in closing arguments (such as *Darden v. Wainwright*, 1986), as well as quasi-regulatory documents such as the American Bar Association's Standards for Criminal Justice (see American Bar Association, 2007, Standard 3–5.8).[18]

These institutional conditions help explain, to a certain extent, the legal antinomies elucidated in this chapter. There is an inherent tension in contemporary criminal legal processes between the affective urge toward retribution that arises in human beings when confronted with a terrifying and offensive killing, and the law's (purported) necessity for formal rationality. Durkheim alluded to this tension long ago when he argued that "[modern] punishment constitutes a reaction of passionate feeling, graduated in intensity, which society exerts through the mediation of an organized body over those of its members who have violated certain rules of conduct" (Durkheim, 1984, p. 52).[19] When prosecutors tell their vivid horror stories in the grammar of bureau-speak, they *embody* this tension.

CONCLUSION: THE VEIL OF FACTS AND LAW

Prosecutor reliance on the purportedly neutral and self-evident 'facts' and the purportedly formally rational law operates like a veil covering the affective spirit of their retributive arguments. This situation represents yet another contradictory aspect of state killing. While prosecutors shrug and point to the seemingly obvious, straightforward, and neutral 'facts' and 'law' when making their arguments and describing their processes of constructing their arguments, they do so in the emotional grammar of sanctimonious outrage – all toward a goal of irrational retribution. This situation suggests that, while there appear to be societal trends that cast a suspicious light on the retention of capital punishment in the United States (at least some), practitioners of state killing are deeply and emotionally committed to its symbolic necessity.

Can this commitment be a measure of the death penalty's life or death? The contradiction in prosecution discourses between 'facts' and 'furies' suggests that not only is logical coherence not especially important in legal discourse, but also that the (purportedly) formally rational law in the United States has *not* disciplined the urge toward vengeance described by Durkheim (and others). If this is so, it may indicate that, in spite of some trends against state killing, the law itself seems to be enduringly comfortable with the tension-riddled 'Frankenstein's monster' of what the death penalty has become in the United States, and is not likely to abandon it any time soon.

NOTES

1. A California judge recently placed a ban on executions until officials are able to demonstrate that lethal injection is not a cruel and unusual punishment. Other states, including Maryland, Florida, and Missouri have halted executions over similar concerns (see Times Wire Report, 2006).

2. It remains to be seen if these statutes will withstand constitutional challenges.

3. I focused almost exclusively on the opening statements and closing arguments in both the guilt and penalty phases, although I also sometimes read parts of the pre-trial materials and evidence.

4. From 1996 to 2003, I worked as a capital mitigation investigator.

5. My initial analytical goal in this project was to investigate the ways in which prosecution and defense narratives in capital trials sustain or challenge a nexus of ideologies (individualism, egalitarianism, liberty, populism, and laissez-faire) known as 'The American Creed' (see Kaplan, 2007b). The current paper is thus a somewhat unexpected offshoot of my original investigative goal, and thus an example of how the grounded approach I employed produced new analytical categories to investigate.

6. Whitman's theory includes, but is not limited to, capital punishment.

7. See FootnoteN 5 for an explanation of the American Creed.

8. More recently, Sarat (2005) has analyzed an empirical instance of 'new abolitionism' in Illinois gGovernor George Ryan's (in)famous mass commutation of Illinois' condemned that was principled not on 'mercy' but on ideals of legality and fairness.

9. I qualify 'modern,' 'rational,' and 'enlightened' with the word 'purportedly' because these terms are perpetually under debate; regarding the law in particular, formal rationality is always under the threat of indeterminacy.

10. Which is precisely the technological example Foucault drew upon in *Discipline and Punish*.

11. See Stetler (1999) for a discussion of 'diminished autonomy.'

12. Although it is relatively rare in the criminal law, this situation is not totally unique to capital cases. As Coutin (2000) shows, political asylum and immigration cases often focus on the individual. Like capital defendants, asylum applicants are required to fit a general category but simultaneously individualize their cases.

13. See Ewick and Silbey (1995) for a discussion of the basic and abiding conflict between individualization and generalization in the law.

14. I was told that prosecutors usually invite the defendant's lawyers to these meetings to make an argument about why the case at hand should not be a death penalty case. Ultimately, the decision is up to the District Attorney.

15. I put these terms in scare quotes because their meaning is indeterminate – different for prosecutors and defenders, and probably also different for judges, jurors, and the public.

16. I have elsewhere developed a typology of prosecutor (and defender) stock 'characters' in capital cases (see Kaplan, 2007a).

17. See Sarat (2001) on the notion of capital punishment as an 'easy solution to a complex problem,' and Kaplan (2006) on racialized inequality.

18. Although *Darden v. Wainwright* delineates the conditions of inappropriate prosecutor argument, the court found that the prosecutor involved in this case did *not* cross the boundaries into inappropriate argument. Indeed, courts often find that inflammatory prosecutor argument is 'harmless error.'

19. Durkheim's arguments about law and punishment in 'primitive' societies with 'mechanical solidarity' and 'modern' societies with 'organic solidarity' are open to criticism, particularly to the extent that 'modern' societies have turned out to be as harsh or harsher than 'primitive' societies. Nevertheless, Durkheim's insight about the tension between 'passionate feeling' and 'the mediation of an organized body' resonates well with the argument in this chapterpaper about 'facts' and 'furies.'

ACKNOWLEDGMENT

The author wishes to thank Austin Sarat, the anonymous reviewers of *Studies in Law, Politics, and Society*, Valerie Jenness, and Kate Coyne for their helpful comments on drafts of this chapter.

REFERENCES

American Bar Association. (2007). *Criminal Justice Section Standards.* http://www.abanet.org/crimjust/standards/pfunc_blk.html#5.8

Coutin, S. B. (2000). *Legalizing moves: Salvadoran immigrants' struggle for U.S. residency.* Ann Arbor: University of Michigan Press.

Dieter, R. C. (1998). *The death penalty in black and white: Who lives, who dies, who decides.* http://www.deathpenaltyinfo.org/article.php?scid = 45&did = 539

Dumm, T. L. (2000). Death, modernity, and enlightenment. *Punishment and Society, 2*(4), 471–476.

Durkheim, E. (1984). *The division of labor in society (Translated by W. D. Halls).* Macmillan.

Ewick, P., & Silbey, S. S. (1995). Subversive stories and hegemonic tales: Toward a sociology of narrative. *Law and Society Review, 29*(2), 197–226.

Foucault, M. (1977). *Discipline and punish: The birth of the prison.* New York: Vintage.

Garland, D. (2005). *Capital punishment and American culture: Some critical reflections.* http://research.yale.edu/ccs/papers/garland_cappunishment.pdf

Gifis, S. H. (2003). *Barron's law dictionary.* Hauppauge, New York: Barron's.

Givelber, D. (2001). The adversary system and historical accuracy: Can we do better? In: S. D. Westervelt & J. A. Humphrey (Eds), *Wrongly convicted: Perspectives on failed justice.* New Brunswick, NJ: Rutgers University Press.

Hart, L. (2006). More calls for death penalty in child rapes. *Los Angeles Times,* Tuesday October 10, 2006, p. A15.

Kaplan, P. (2006). American exceptionalism and racialized inequality in American capital punishment. *Law and Social Inquiry, 31*(1), 149–175.

Kaplan, P. (2007a). *Anatomy of a capital trial.* Unpublished manuscript, available from the author.

Kaplan, P. (2007b). *The subject of execution: The American creed in prosecutor and defender narratives.* Unpublished manuscript, available from the author.

Milovanovic, D. (1994). *A primer in the sociology of law* (2nd ed.). New York: Harrow and Heston.

Rhodes, L. A. (2004). *Total confinement: Madness and reason in the maximum security prison.* Berkeley, CA: University of California Press.

Sarat, A. (2001). *When the state kills: Capital punishment and the American condition.* Princeton, NJ: Princeton University Press.

Sarat, A. (2005). *Mercy on trial: What it means to stop an execution.* Princeton, NJ: Princeton University Press.

Smith, P. (2003). Narrating the guillotine: Punishment technology as myth and symbol. *Theory, Culture and Society, 20*(5), 27–51.

Stetler, R. (1999). *Capital cases.* http://www.criminaljustice.org/public.nsf/0/bee3ff4450880bb485256704006793eb?OpenDocument

Times Wire Report. (2006). Executions put on hold until review. *Los Angeles Times,* December 20, 2006. p. A26.

Whitman, J. Q. (2003). *Harsh Justice: Criminal punishment and the widening divide between America and Europe.* Oxford: Oxford University Press.

Zimring, F. E. (2003). *The contradictions of American capital punishment.* Oxford: Oxford University Press.

CASES CITED

Darden v. Wainwright, 477 U.S. 168 (1986)
Eddings v. Oklahoma, 455 U.S. 104 (1982).
Furman v. Georgia, 408 U.S. 238 (1972).
Gregg v. Georgia, 428 U.S. 153 (1976).
Lockett v. Ohio, 438 U.S. 586 (1978).
Woodson v. North Carolina, 428 U.S. 280 (1976).

CALIFORNIA TRIAL TRANSCRIPTS CITED

Bennett, E. W. No. 95ZF0007.
Blacksher, E. R. No. 125666.
Brents, G. G. No. 96NF2113.
Clark, W. C. No. 94CF0821.
Crawford, C. No. H-23269.
Daveggio, J., & Michaud, M. Nos. 134147A and 134147B.
Edwards, R. M. No. 93WF1180.
Famalaro, J. J. No. 94ZF0196.
Gonzales, I. No. SCD 114421.
Gonzales, V. No. SCD 119402.
Lewis, K. A. No. 128675.
Martinez, M. M. No. H-15696.
Nady, G. A. No. 129807.
Seumanu, R. No. H24057A.
Thomas, K. T. No. 118686B.

INTERVIEWEES

Eight anonymous California prosecutors.

THE JUDICIAL USE OF INTERNATIONAL AND FOREIGN LAW IN DEATH PENALTY CASES: A POISONED CHALICE?

Bharat Malkani

ABSTRACT

This chapter addresses the possible consequences of the United States Supreme Court's increasing attention to international and foreign human rights law in its death penalty jurisprudence, particularly with respect to the Eighth Amendment. I question the belief of those commentators who argue that such attention might assist with efforts to abolish the death penalty in the United States, and argue instead that the perceived threat to state sovereignty that the invocation of international and foreign human rights law poses might result in attempts to retain the death penalty as a means of reasserting state autonomy.

INTRODUCTION

The United States Supreme Court's invocation of (a) international human rights law and (b) the laws and practices of foreign countries in its death

Special Issue: Is the Death Penalty Dying?
Studies in Law, Politics, and Society, Volume 42, 161–194
Copyright © 2008 by Elsevier Ltd.
ISSN: 1059-4337/doi:10.1016/S1059-4337(07)00406-1

penalty jurisprudence has been both celebrated (Koh, 2002; Steiker, 2006) and criticised (Alford, 2004; Rothenberg, 2004). Rather than add to this normative debate, this chapter examines the possible consequences of this judicial enterprise, which I term: the *judicial domestication of external death penalty norms*. Ultimately, I argue that the Court's current method of judicial domestication may actually result in a strengthening of the retention of the death penalty in America, contrary to the arguments put forward by those who hope that international and foreign norms will assist with efforts to abolish the death penalty (Koh, 2002, p. 1130).

My argument rests on the following line of reasoning. First, I show that the hopes of such abolitionists are misplaced, because there is not yet a sufficient international consensus that can lead to the identification of an *abolition norm* in international and foreign law. Rather, I argue, the *regulation norm* in international and foreign law is stronger. By regulation norm, I mean the norm that accepts the legality of the death penalty, but demands that its imposition is regulated and is subject to certain limitations. Second, I apply this understanding of the worldwide status of the death penalty to an analysis of how the Supreme Court actually uses external norms in its Eighth Amendment jurisprudence.[1] I show that the Court only uses external norms that are considerably strong, and only cites them after considering (a) American standards of decency, as evidenced by the laws and practices of individual states and (b) the Court's independent proportionality analysis. External norms are only used in a *weak* manner, in order to *confirm* the reasonableness of an American consensus and the Court's own determination. With this in mind, the third part of this chapter illustrates the potential consequences of this state of affairs. Those who criticise the Court for embarking on the enterprise of judicial domestication have argued that the invocation of external norms into the domestic legal order, by an unelected and unaccountable judiciary, poses a threat to sovereignty and democracy, and represents an affront to states' rights under federalism. While abolitionists struggle to convince a reluctant Court to consider a weak abolition norm, those who fear and criticise judicial domestication are in a stronger position to consolidate the death penalty as a means of reasserting state autonomy. And, given the primacy attached to the laws and practices of individual states in its Eighth Amendment analysis, it is submitted that the Court will therefore not find the death penalty to violate "evolving standards of decency" (*Trop v. Dulles*, 1958, at 101), as determined by reference to the laws and practices of the individual states in America.

THE STATUS OF THE DEATH
PENALTY WORLDWIDE

The issue of the death penalty is addressed in the international legal system and in the various domestic legal orders across the world. Some instruments of international law, and some domestic laws, invoke the abolition of the death penalty, while other instruments of international law and domestic laws allow for its retention, but seek to regulate its imposition. In other words, it can be said that a particular legal order gives predominant strength either to a norm that espouses *abolition* or to a norm that espouses *regulation*. The following examines the relative strength of each norm in non-U.S. legal orders. As such, I will consider the status of the death penalty in (a) the international legal system and (b) domestic legal orders.

The Death Penalty in Public International Law

It is well established that, under Article 38 of the Statute of the International Court of Justice, there are two primary sources of public international law – treaty law and custom (Dixon, 2000). Therefore, it needs to be determined what treaty law and custom say about abolition and retention of the death penalty.

It is true that some multilateral treaties of international law – specifically international human rights law – prohibit the death penalty outright. Indeed, prohibition of the death penalty is the sole concern of treaties such as the Second Optional Protocol to the International Covenant on Civil and Political Rights (1989), Protocol 13 to the European Convention on Human Rights (2003), and the Protocol to the American Convention on Human Rights (1990). Such treaties point towards an *abolition norm* in international law.

However, there are instruments of international human rights law that explicitly permit such a punishment. The Universal Declaration of Human Rights [UDHR] (1948), though not a binding treaty, is arguably the bedrock instrument of contemporary international human rights law and, although Article 3 protects the "Right to Life," Mary Ann Glendon (2001) has argued that the drafting history shows an express intention to not include a prohibition of capital punishment in the Declaration. Indeed, Glendon defines the exclusion of such a prohibition as a "defeat for the representatives of ... the Soviet-bloc delegates, who had argued for a ban on capital punishment" (Glendon, 2001, p. 92). Clearly, a vocal majority of the Drafting Commission sought to allow the retention of the death penalty.

The International Covenant on Civil and Political Rights [ICCPR] (1976), the European Convention on Human Rights [ECHR] (1953), and the American Convention on Human Rights [ACHR] (1969) all permit the application of the death penalty, but seek to regulate its imposition. Although each one speaks in favour of eventual abolition, the regulation norm is clearly stronger than the abolition norm – abolition is an aspiration, regulation is an imperative. Furthermore, if we assume that the normative strength of an instrument of international law depends on its number of ratifications, it is arguable that the ICCPR, ECHR, and ACHR enjoy greater normative strength than their respective Optional Protocols that seek to abolish the death penalty.[2] Put another way, the more widely accepted instruments of international human rights law, namely the UDHR, ICCPR, ECHR, and ACHR, all expressly permit the retention of the death penalty. More recent instruments seek its prohibition, but these instruments do not enjoy the same normative force. Therefore, if the U.S. Supreme Court were to engage in an analysis of international treaty law in order to determine whether the retention of the death penalty is contrary to "evolving standards of decency," the Court would most likely be compelled to conclude that retention of the death penalty does not contravene worldwide "standards of decency."

Rules of custom are traditionally determined by reference to norms that are practiced by a significant number of states out of a sense of legal obligation (opinio juris), over a lengthy period of time. With this definition in mind, it becomes difficult to argue that abolition of the death penalty represents a norm of custom (Rothenberg, 2004, pp. 555–557). Since state practice is a significant criterion for the definition of custom, the justification for this assertion is explained below, in the section on the death penalty in nation states. At this point, it suffices to repeat the observation of the Constitutional Court of South Africa: "Capital punishment is not prohibited by public international law" (*State v. Makwanyane and Another*, 1995, at para 36).

The Death Penalty in Nation States

As an organisation committed to the abolition of the death penalty, Amnesty International is keen to state that "over half the world's countries have abolished the death penalty in law or practice" (Amnesty International, 2006). However, the statistics that Amnesty provides are not compelling: 87 countries have abolished the death penalty for all crimes; a further 11 have abolished it for ordinary crimes; and 27 are said to be abolitionist in practice, as they have not carried out any executions for 10 years or more. Adding these numbers, according to the Amnesty, means that 125 countries can be considered abolitionist in law or practice, while just 71 retain the death penalty. However, the numbers could be interpreted differently. The 27 who are abolitionists in practice are still retentionists in law, and it is plausible to argue that 98 countries are abolitionists for ordinary crimes while 98 are retentionists in law. In fact, it could be argued that just 87 countries are abolitionists, whereas 109 countries retain the death penalty in some shape or form.[3] It cannot be convincingly argued that a comparative analysis of death penalty abolition and retention leads to the conclusion that a majority of the world's countries reject the death penalty outright.

It is true that countries in the world appear to be moving towards abolition – since 1977, the number of abolitionist countries has risen from 16 to 87, and, although 4 countries have reinstated the death penalty during that period, 2 of those 4 have since reversed their position (Amnesty International, 2006). However, this analysis could also be used to strengthen the argument that the abolition of the death penalty is far from representing a rule of custom – the trend towards abolition has only picked up speed during the last 30 years. Ultimately, the abolition norm may take root in some years to come but, at present, comparative death penalty analysis cannot lead to such a conclusion.

Conclusions

In sum, it is clear that in international law and in the domestic legal orders worldwide, there is a greater emphasis on regulation than on abolition of the death penalty. I do not mean to suggest that the two norms are mutually exclusive – a legal system can promote abolition while ensuring that the imposition of the death penalty meets certain standards. In fact, Article 6 of the ICCPR seeks to do just this: Article 6(6) reads: "Nothing in this article [i.e., the safeguards set out in the preceding sections] shall be invoked to delay or to prevent the abolition of capital punishment by any State Party to the Covenant." However, as stated above, abolition is an aspiration, whereas regulation is a requirement. The second part of this article therefore illustrates how the death penalty is regulated, both worldwide and in the United States of America. Specifically, I examine how the U.S. Supreme Court uses external regulation norms when internally regulating the administration of the death penalty.

HOW THE UNITED STATES SUPREME COURT USES EXTERNAL DEATH PENALTY NORMS

External Regulation Norms

Before examining how the U.S. Supreme Court has used external death penalty regulation norms, we need to define what is meant by *regulation*, and we need to determine what the external regulation norms are. Of the 156 states that have ratified the ICCPR, only Thailand and the United States have entered declarations or reservations to Article 6.[4] Therefore, it can be said that the other signatory states that retain the death penalty at least purport to regulate the death penalty in a manner consistent with Article 6, and thus it is logical to consider these standards as a starting point in order to determine the content of external regulation norms.

Article 6(2) states that the sentence of death may only be imposed for "the most serious crimes" after due process of law. The right to seek "pardon or commutation" is granted in Article 6(4), and Article 6(5) establishes that juvenile offenders and pregnant women are to be exempt from capital punishment. For definitional purposes, these standards can be divided into three areas. First, there is the question: for what crimes, or *when*, can the death penalty be imposed? Second, there is the question of which class of offenders, or *who*, the death penalty can be imposed upon? Third, there is the question of the manner in which, or *how*, the death penalty is administered. These three questions of *when*, *who*, and *how* can be termed the *"triumvirate of death penalty regulation."* The international legal system, and the domestic legal systems of countries that retain the death penalty, seek to regulate the imposition of the death penalty in accordance with this triumvirate.

U.S. Regulation Norms

As will be shown, the U.S. Supreme Court's Eighth Amendment jurisprudence is analytically similar to the Article 6 framework. The Court has, on occasion, dealt with the question of whether it is cruel and unusual to impose the death penalty for certain crimes, or on certain classes of offenders, or in a certain manner. The question, therefore, is: to what extent has the Supreme Court substantively followed external death penalty regulation norms? In other words, how has the Court used external regulation norms such as the prohibition of the death penalty on juvenile offenders, or for crimes other than "the most serious," in its Constitutional determinations?

Before examining how the Court has, or has not, used external norms, we need to clarify what is meant by the phrase: "use external norms." The process of a national court "using external norms" can be entitled *judicial domestication*, reflecting the domestication of external norms by the judiciary. The following considers the theoretical aspects of judicial domestication as a process.

Judicial Domestication in Theory

Judicial domestication is a multi-faceted process, and the following provides an overview of the ways in which the Supreme Court can in theory, and does in practice, use external norms in its death penalty jurisprudence. As will be seen, the Court has taken a starkly conservative approach to considerations of external norms in its Eighth Amendment determinations, in spite of the possibilities available.

It has been argued that the U.S. Supreme Court has failed to offer a sound theoretical foundation for its citation of international and foreign norms. Jeremy Waldron (2005, p. 129), writing about a recent case in which the U.S. Supreme Court consulted external death penalty norms when ruling the juvenile death penalty to be unconstitutional, has opined:

> One of the frustrating things about *Roper* ... is that no one on the Court bothered to articulate a general theory of the citation and authority of foreign law.

Roger Alford (2005, p. 639) too has argued:

> [P]roponents of [the judicial domestication of external norms] rarely offer a firm theoretical justification for this practice.

In spite of the Court's failure to expound a "general theory," there is an abundance of scholarly attempts to explain and justify the enterprise of judicial domestication.

To begin with, it must be appreciated that, although sometimes considered in tandem, *international* law and *foreign* law pose different conceptual and practical questions when considering their relationships with U.S. domestic law. The relationship between international law and domestic law in general often raises discussions on the doctrines of dualism and monism. With respect to the latter, Hans Kelsen (1920, as discussed in Capps, 2006, pp. 30–32) is perhaps the most famous proponent of the idea that, because international law and domestic law share the same properties, they can be considered to be a unified legal order, and therefore norms deriving from international law are immediately part of the domestic legal order. Significantly, Kelsen has argued that the international legal norm should take priority over a conflicting domestic legal norm, even if the dispute is being heard in a domestic court. Under Kelsen's doctrine, then, it is conceivable for an international norm to override a conflicting domestic norm.[5]

Kelsen's espousal of monism, as will be demonstrated, has been largely overlooked by the U.S. Supreme Court in favour of dualism. Broadly speaking, dualism is the theory that holds the domestic legal order to be "hermetically sealed" (Capps, 2006, p. 40) from the international legal system, and thus domestic law takes priority over conflicting interna tional law in cases before national courts. Under dualism, norms of international law are not directly applicable in domestic courts unless such norms have been transformed or incorporated into domestic law by the appropriately empowered authorities. In the United States, the Constitution stipulates that only the President, with the advice and consent of the Senate, can ratify treaties of international law (U.S. Constitution, Article II, Section 2[2], 1787). It has been well established that the executive and legislature have historically been reluctant to ratify and give domestic legal effect to multilateral treaties of human rights. Treaties are either not ratified, as in the case of the United Nations Convention on the Rights of the Child (CRC), or are ratified but subject to a declaration of "non-self-execution" which serves to essentially negate the legal effect of such treaties in U.S. courts (Henkin, 1995; Redgwell, 2003). With respect to customary international law, Bradley and Goldsmith (1997) have argued that the Supreme Court does not recognise the direct applicability of such law in domestic law.[6]

The doctrines of dualism and monism do not really apply to considerations of the relationship between the U.S. Constitution and other domestic constitutions, a study of which is usually termed "comparative constitutionalism" (Tushnet, 1999; Childress, 2004). This is because there is no potentially formal relationship between the constitutions of sovereign states, in contrast to the potentially formal relationship between international law and domestic law. As such, there is no question of whether, say, a Canadian constitutional rule overrides a U.S. constitutional rule in a case before a U.S. court. Canadian law is supreme in Canada in exactly the same way that U.S. law is supreme in the U.S. However, just because a domestic legal order is autonomous from other domestic legal orders (and the international legal system), this does not necessarily mean that a domestic court will be blind or deaf to the norms existing in such external legal systems, and many commentators have sought to explain the various ways in which a domestic court can see or hear external norms.

Joan Larsen (2004), for example, has argued that the U.S. Supreme Court has "used foreign and international law for three distinct purposes: expository, empirical, and substantive" (p. 1283). Larsen argues that it is justifiable to cite external laws in an expository sense in order to "contrast and thereby explain a domestic constitutional rule" (p. 1288). Using external laws for empirical purposes is also unproblematic for Larsen, as a consideration of the practical effects of a proposed rule is compatible with accepted approaches to constitutional interpretation. However, Larsen is much more wary of using external norms for "substantive" purposes, which involves using international and foreign laws to shape the content of a domestic constitutional rule. Larsen identifies two ways in which a court might use external laws in a "substantive" sense. First, the court might engage in "reason-borrowing." This refers to the process of using the reasons offered by foreign and international authorities in analogous cases to define and shape the domestic constitutional rule in question. The second variant of the substantive use of external laws is termed: "moral fact-finding." The court engages in "moral fact-finding" when it looks at the decisions reached by other courts in order to determine what the content of the domestic constitutional rule should be, regardless of the other courts' reasoning. Larsen's terminology is helpful for conceptualising, in part, the ways in which a court can conceivably use international and foreign norms.

Vicki Jackson (2005) provides three "models" for describing the relationships between domestic constitutions and law from external, or what she calls "transnational" (p. 109), sources. First, a court might adopt a "Convergence" Model, whereby the national constitutional provision and the external norm converge. The Convergence Model refers to the "implementation of international law" (p. 112) through national constitutions, and the external norm is used to direct the development of national law.[7] Second, there is the "Resistant" Model, whereby the court uses the national constitution to resist the invocation of external norms. In the United States, federalism is often "advanced as an affirmative reason to resist constitutionalising human rights norms derived from transnational sources" (pp. 113–114).[8] In between convergence and resistance lies the Engagement Model. The Engagement Model does not require a court to blindly follow the external norm, but it does not blind the court to that external norm either. Instead, under the Engagement Model,

Transnational sources are seen as interlocutors, offering a way of testing understanding of one's own traditions and possibilities by examining them in the reflection
of others' (p. 114).

Jackson asserts that it is this model that the Court adopted in *Roper v.
Simmons* (2005) – the Justices consulted external sources as a means of self-
reflection, in order to "interrogate their judgment" (p. 115). As will be
shown, though, the Engagement Model and the analysis that Jackson offers
is quite broad. There are different levels of interrogation available, and the
Engagement Model actually encompasses a number of other methods of
judicial domestication. For example, a judge can be said to be "engaging"
with external norms if they use such norms as empirical facts, or if they look
to the reasons employed by foreign courts in analogous cases. And as
Larsen has illustrated, these are two quite different methods of judicial
domestication. Therefore, any typology of judicial domestication must
explore the finer nuances of Jackson's engagement model.

Rather than describe possible purposes of, or approaches to judicial
domestication, Sujit Choudhry (1999) identifies three approaches to
constitutional interpretation that each in turn provides a normative
justification for then engaging in an analysis of comparative jurisprudence.
First, if a court takes a "universalist" approach to constitutional
interpretation, that court can be said to view all constitutions as "cut from
a universal cloth" (p. 825). Under such an approach, the principles and
norms in domestic constitutions are considered to transcend positive law,
thus allowing a judge to look at other, comparable constitutions. Second, a
court can take a "genealogical" approach to interpretation. This approach
differs from the "universalist" approach in that it views the provisions of a
national constitution as positive law. However, a genealogical interpretation
"holds that constitutions are often tied together by complicated relationships of descent and history, and that those relationships are sufficient
justification to import and apply" external norms (p. 825). Before engaging
in a comparative analysis, the court would have to identify a historical or
sociological link with the jurisdiction to which it is looking. Third,
Choudhry identifies a "dialogical" approach to constitutional interpretation, which is comparable to Jackson's analysis of the engagement model as
a means for self-reflection. By engaging in a comparable analysis of other
jurisdictions, courts are able to "identify the normative and factual
assumptions underlying their own constitutional jurisprudence" (p. 825).
Under this mode, as with the genealogical approach, a court is free to
disregard the external norm if the court decides that the external norm has
emerged from a fundamentally different legal and political order. In essence,

external norms are used as a means of self-reflection – a comparative analysis allows the court to determine the nature and normative scope of the rule in question, while also allowing the judge to critically assess their own reasoning and judgment. As with the accounts offered by Larsen and Jackson, Choudhry's analysis is part of the blind man's elephant. Taking these accounts together, though, allows for a typology of judicial domestication.

Implicit in all analyses is the distinction between (a) the *way* in which the court might consider external norms, and (b) the *effect* that such a consideration could have on the court's ultimate determination. These can be termed *methods* and *modes* of judicial domestication, respectively.

METHODS OF JUDICIAL DOMESTICATION

International Human Rights Law – Multilateral Treaties

Determinative
A court can consider itself bound by a particular treaty provision, and thus the treaty determines the decision of the court. As mentioned above, the United States traditionally exempts itself from the binding force of international human rights treaty law, and the Court has refrained from adopting Kelsen's monism.

Informative/Persuasive
A court can consider a treaty provision to be useful when interpreting its own domestic law. Such provisions can either be said to represent legal standards, or can be said to provide non-legal facts that are relevant to the court's determination. As such, treaty law is used as an interpretative aid, and informs the court of the content of its own domestic rule. This is particularly so when a court is considering a discrete treaty provision (such as the prohibition of the juvenile death penalty) when considering an open-ended domestic rule (such as the prohibition on "cruel and unusual punishments").

Confirmatory
A court can reach its own conclusion and then point to congruent treaty law to illustrate that the decision reached is generally considered to be a reasonable one. The treaty provision serves to confirm the reasonableness of the court's decision.

Inapplicable
A court may decide that it has no power to apply the treaty provision in question, and may also consider it inappropriate to consider such standards. This is especially likely in cases where the treaty provision that is being invoked by a litigant has not been transformed into domestic law, and the court takes a strict dualist approach to the relationship between international law and domestic law.

Comparative Death Penalty Laws and Practices of Foreign Countries

Empirical
A court can look at the factual consequences of decisions reached by foreign courts in analogous cases in order to evaluate the desirability of a proposed domestic legal rule. The foreign norm is used as evidence. For example, if it could be statistically proven that the abolition of the death penalty in South Africa led directly to a rise in homicide rates, the U.S. Supreme Court could use this fact as evidence that the abolition of the death penalty is not desirable.

Reason-Borrowing
A court can consider the reasons employed by foreign courts in analogous cases. It is perhaps inaccurate to say that the foreign legal rule is being domesticated judicially in such an instance, as the court is primarily examining the arguments that were articulated in the foreign court, and not necessarily the decision reached by that court.

Moral Fact-Finding
A court may cite the decisions of foreign courts in analogous cases as a reason for reaching a particular conclusion (i.e., other courts are abolishing the juvenile death penalty, so we should too). Moral fact-finding may also take place after the court's determination, in which case such norms are used in a confirmatory role (i.e., other courts are abolishing the juvenile death penalty, so it is reasonable for us to do so too).

Comparable Interpretation
A national court may be called upon to interpret a domestic provision which finds analogous provisions in the laws of other countries or in the international legal system. In such an instance, the court might consider how courts in other countries have interpreted those analogous provisions. An example is the "cruel and unusual punishments" clause of the United States Constitution

compared with the "cruel, inhuman or degrading treatment or punishment" clause of the European Convention on Human Rights. The European Court of Human Rights has interpreted the latter clause to include a prohibition of the "death row phenomenon," (*Soering v. United Kingdom*, 1989) and as such Justice Breyer has been keen to consider this when litigants have argued that the "death row phenomenon" violates the "cruel and unusual" clause of the U.S. Constitution. Although *Soering* was a decision of a regional, as opposed to domestic court, Breyer J. points out the Supreme Court of India has reached a similar conclusion, and thus this method of judicial domestication can be considered under comparative constitutionalism. This particular case, *Knight v. Florida* (1999), will be discussed in greater depth, later.

Expository

A court can use foreign laws in order to explain its own domestic law. In other words, a foreign legal rule is used to contrast and therefore explain a domestic legal rule. The foreign legal rule plays no role in the court's own reasoning or determination. Rather, it is used to explain the court's final decision.

Confirmatory

A court can reach its own conclusion, and then point to congruent decisions in foreign courts to illustrate that the decision reached is generally considered to be a reasonable one (i.e., other courts have abolished the death penalty for juvenile offenders, so it is reasonable for us to do so).

Irrelevant

A court may consider the laws of foreign countries to be irrelevant to its own determinations.

Modes of Judicial Domestication

The different methods of judicial domestication explained above can have varying effects on the domestic legal order. For example, a court may bring an international norm to bear *absolutely* on the domestic legal order if it decides that the international norm controls its decision. Alternatively, the court may adopt a method of judicial domestication that does not result in the international norm having any significant effect on the domestic legal order. Put another way, the *extent* to which the external norm is brought to bear on the domestic legal order varies according to which method of judicial domestication has been employed. The following sums up the various degrees of effect that the different methods of judicial domestication can have on the domestic legal order.

Absolute Judicial Domestication
When a court considers an external norm to be determinative, the court absolutely incorporates the external norm into the domestic legal order by declaring it to control the domestic law in question.

Strong Judicial Domestication
When a court finds an external norm to be particularly persuasive, the court's determination, although independent to the external norm, may be influenced by that norm to such an extent that, without it, the court may have reached an alternative conclusion.

Weak Judicial Domestication
When a court refers to external norms, but a closer reading of the judgment reveals that such norms played no part in the court's reasoning or final determination. The court would have reached the same conclusion regardless of the external norm.

No Judicial Domestication
When a court rejects outright the applicability and relevance of international and foreign standards of human rights.

The above analysis of the methods and modes of judicial domestication can be summarised as in Table 1.

Table 1.   Methods and Modes of Judicial Domestication.

Source of "non-American" Law	Method of Judicial Domestication	Mode of Judicial Domestication (JD)
International human rights law	Determinative	Absolute JD
	Informative/persuasive	Strong JD
	Confirmatory	Weak JD
	Inapplicable	No JD
Comparative death penalty practice	Empirical	Strong JD
	Reason-borrowing	Strong JD
	Moral fact-finding	Strong or weak JD
	Comparable interpretation	Strong or weak JD
	Expository	Weak JD
	Confirmatory	Weak JD
	Irrelevant	No JD

Judicial Domestication in Practice – An Analysis of the U.S. Supreme Court's Jurisprudence

The following examines which methods and corresponding modes of judicial domestication the U.S. Supreme Court has adopted when considering the constitutionality of the triumvirate areas of death penalty regulation. As will be shown, the Court has traditionally looked for a strong international consensus on an issue in order to buttress and confirm the reasonableness of its own findings.

The Triumvirate of Death Penalty Regulation

"When" The Death Penalty May Be Imposed
The idea that a punishment should be proportionate to a crime is a general theory in studies of crime and punishment. Therefore, given the seriousness and gravity of the death penalty, Article 6 of the ICCPR states that it should only be imposed for "the most serious crimes." Similarly, the United States Supreme Court has been concerned with proportionality. In *Coker v. Georgia* (1977), the Court held the death penalty to be a disproportionate punishment for rape, and therefore contrary to the Eighth Amendment prohibition on "cruel and unusual punishments." In doing so, the Court asserted:

> It is ... not irrelevant here that out of 60 major nations in the world surveyed in 1965, only 3 retained the death penalty for rape where death did not ensue. United Nations, Department of Economic and Social Affairs, Capital Punishment 40, 86 (1968) (*Coker* at 596, n. 10).

In other words, the Court carried out a comparative analysis of death penalty practice, and also referred to the findings of an international organisation. In *Enmund v. Florida* (1982), the Court noted that the "doctrine of felony murder has been abolished in England and India, severely restricted in Canada and a number of other Commonwealth countries, and is unknown in continental Europe" (*Enmund* at 796–797, n. 22). The extent to which these external norms affected the Court's determination, though, is limited. In both *Coker* and *Enmund*, references to external norms were relegated to footnotes, suggesting that such norms did not play a large part in the Court's reasoning or conclusions. The Court appears to have essentially used such norms in a weak, confirmatory role.

"Who" The Death Penalty May Be Imposed Upon
The gravity of the crime is not the only factor to consider when determining whether or not the death penalty is a disproportionate punishment. It is well established that the culpability of the offender must also be taken into account. In recent years, the Supreme Court has ruled that the death penalty is "cruel and unusual," and therefore unconstitutional, when imposed on offenders suffering from insanity, mental retardation, or who were under the age of 18 at the time of the crime. In each instance, external norms have been argued before, and considered by, the Court.

In *Ford v. Wainwright* (1986), the Court concluded that it is "cruel and unusual" to subject persons suffering from insanity to the death penalty, noting that:

> the natural abhorrence civilised societies feel at killing one who has no capacity to come to grips with his own conscience or deity is still valid today. And the intuition that such an execution simply offends humanity is evidently shared across this Nation. (*Ford*, at 409)

The reference by the Court to "civilised societies" is vague, and the external norm is only considered after the views of "this Nation" have been determined. The external norm is said to be already "shared" by America, and thus the Court cannot be said to have brought the external norm to bear on the domestic legal order.

Sixteen years after *Ford*, in *Atkins v. Virginia* (2002), the Court struck down the death penalty for mentally retarded offenders. After finding a "national consensus" against the practice of imposing the death penalty on mentally retarded offenders, as evidenced by the various pieces of state legislation that outlawed such a practice, the Court noted that the legislative conclusions of such states reflected the "opinions of the worldwide community" (*Atkins*, at 316–317, n. 21), a reference that drew some stinging criticism from the dissenting Justices. However, it would be wrong to overemphasise the role that worldwide opinion played in the Court's analysis. Mention of the opinions of the worldwide community is made in a footnote, and is expressly used in a weak confirmatory manner – it reaffirms the reasonableness of the democratic decisions of state legislatures.

The Court's changing attitude towards the relevance of international and foreign law to its Eighth Amendment determinations is illustrated well in its juvenile death penalty jurisprudence. *Thompson v. Oklahoma*, decided in 1988, represented an approach by the Court that took account of international standards. In striking down the death penalty for offenders under the age of 16, the Court noted the congruent laws and practices of "other nations that share our Anglo-American heritage, and ... the leading members of the Western European community" (*Thompson v. Oklahoma*, 1998, at 830). Justice O'Connor concurred with the plurality, finding it particularly significant that three major human rights treaties – including Article 68 of the Geneva Convention Relative to the Protection of Civilian Persons in Time of War (Fourth Geneva Convention) – explicitly prohibited the death penalty for juvenile offenders (*Thompson*, at 851).

Just a year later, though, the Supreme Court reversed its stance on the applicability of external norms to its Eighth Amendment analysis. In *Stanford v. Kentucky* (1989), Justice Scalia famously asserted that international laws and practices were irrelevant to the Court's Eighth Amendment analysis when upholding the constitutionality of the death penalty for offenders aged 17 and under, stating that:

> We emphasize that it is *American* conceptions of decency that are dispositive, rejecting the contention of petitioners and their various amici ... that the sentencing practices of other countries are relevant. (492 US 361, 369 (1989) at n. 1)

In 2005, though, the Court revisited the issue presented in *Stanford*: is it contrary to the Eighth Amendment to sentence offenders under the age of 18 to death? In *Roper v. Simmons*, the Court outlawed the death penalty for juvenile offenders. In doing so, the Court also expounded its latest approach to interpreting the Eighth Amendment. As in *Atkins*, the Court first found a national consensus against such a practice by examining state legislation outlawing the death penalty for juvenile offenders, and by examining the actual number of death sentences imposed on juvenile offenders. The Justices then also applied their own independent "proportionality analysis" in order to determine whether juveniles' reduced mental capacity rendered them less culpable than adult murderers, and therefore less deserving of the death penalty (*Roper*, at 568–575). After carrying out the "national consensus" test and the "proportionality analysis," the Court devoted an unprecedented section of the judgment to a discussion of international and foreign norms regarding the juvenile death penalty (*Roper*, at 575–578).

With regard to international human rights law, the Court drew attention to the prohibitions of the juvenile death penalty in the following treaties: Article 37(a) of the United Nations CRC, Article 6(5) of the ICCPR, Article 4(5) of the ACHR, and Article 5(3) of the African Charter on the Rights and Welfare of the Child. It is interesting that the Court chose to only refer to four treaties that do not bind the United States. The Court neglected to mention the prohibition in Article 68 of the Fourth Geneva Convention,[9] a treaty to which the U.S. is a party to, with no reservation to said Article, and

failed to acknowledge the Inter-American Commission on Human Rights'
(IACHR) finding that the prohibition of the juvenile death penalty has
attained the status of a jus cogens norm of international law, thus binding
the U.S. notwithstanding lack of consent (*Domingues v. United States*, 2002,
at para 85). The Court cast itself as duly respectful of international law,
while avoiding the difficult question of whether the Court is actually *bound*
by the prohibition of the juvenile death penalty in international law. Such
norms were thus used in a merely confirmatory manner, and the Court
evaded any questions of the binding or persuasive quality of such norms.
This is of particular interest and importance because it highlights the
conservatism of the court.

The Court also considered the death penalty practice of other countries,
acknowledging that virtually all other countries in the world have formally
outlawed the death penalty for juvenile offenders. It is unclear exactly how
the Court employs such laws and practices in its final judgment, though. At
first, Justice Kennedy, writing for the majority, appears to assign a weak
confirmatory role to such laws and practices:

> Our determination that the death penalty is disproportionate punishment for offenders
> under 18 finds *confirmation* in the stark reality that the United States is the only country
> in the world that continues to give official sanction to the juvenile death penalty. (*Roper*,
> at 575, emphasis added)

In other words, the invocation of external laws and practice came after
the Court's own determination, and played no part in the development of
the Court's determination. However, there is also evidence of the court
engaging in reason-borrowing and moral fact-finding, with suggestions that
the practices of other countries *assisted* the court in its determination, rather
than merely confirming the reasonableness of its independent determination.
For example, it is said that

> the Court has [historically] referred to the laws of other countries and to international
> authorities as *instructive* for its interpretation of the Eighth Amendment's prohibition of
> 'cruel and unusual punishments.' (*Roper*, at 575, emphasis added)

The Court is not clear whether such laws are instructive, or whether such
laws provide confirmation of the Justices' own findings.

Similarly, the Court appears to look at the *reasons* employed by other
countries for abolishing the juvenile death penalty. With respect to the
United Kingdom, the Court says: "[the U.K.] recognised the disproportionate nature of the juvenile death penalty; and it abolished that penalty"
(*Roper*, at 577). Mention is also made of the "international opinion against

the juvenile death penalty, resting in large part on the understanding that the instability and emotional imbalance of young people may often be a factor in the crime" (*Roper*, at 578). Ultimately, though, the Court seems to be using the reasons employed by other jurisdictions as a means of buttressing its own findings in its proportionality analysis. The discussion of international and foreign law comes at the end of the judgment, after the court has engaged in a survey of national practice, and after the court has engaged in its own independent proportionality analysis, based in large part on the scientific evidence offered by U.S. experts (Brief of Amici Curiae American Medical Association et al., 2006; Brief of Amici Curiae American Psychological Association et al., 2006). It is not clear whether the Court would have referred to the reasoning of foreign jurisdictions if those reasons did not concur with the Court's own finding. Justice O'Connor's dissenting opinion sums this up:

> the existence of an international consensus ... can serve to confirm the reasonableness of a consonant and genuine American consensus. (*Roper*, at 605)

However, because Justice O'Connor could not find an American consensus against the juvenile death penalty,

> the evidence of an international consensus does not alter my determination that the Eighth Amendment does not, at this time, forbid capital punishment of 17-year-old murderers. (*Roper*, at 604)

In this second area of death penalty regulation, then, the Court essentially assigns a weak confirmatory role to external norms. With respect to the argument propounded in this Article, it would appear that even if there was an international consensus creating an abolition norm, such an international consensus would not "alter [the Court's] determination" that U.S. state laws do not point to a national consensus in favour of abolition.[10]

"How" the Death Penalty Is Administered

The manner in which the death penalty is imposed is subject to regulation in both international law and in the laws of domestic countries, and has also been addressed by the United States Supreme Court. In the context of the Eighth Amendment, the Court has been asked to consider whether prolonged detention on death row constitutes cruel and unusual punishment.

Foreign courts and regional human rights courts have addressed the issue of the length of time spent on death row awaiting execution. In *Soering v. United Kingdom*, the European Court of Human Rights ruled that the extradition of *Soering* to the United States, where he faced a real possibility of facing the death penalty, would violate his right to freedom from cruel, inhuman or degrading treatment or punishment, as protected by Article 3 of the ECHR. In short, the Court found that conditions on death row, including the length of time spent awaiting execution, could amount to "cruel punishment." However, in 1998, the United States Supreme Court denied cert in *Knight v. Florida* (1999), in which petitioner argued that nearly 25 years on death row constituted "cruel and unusual" punishment as per the Eighth Amendment to the Constitution. Dissenting from this denial of cert, Justice Breyer argued that the Court should listen to the merits of petitioner's claim. Justice Breyer appeared particularly concerned with the fact that:

> A growing number of courts outside the United States – *courts that accept or assume the lawfulness of the death penalty* – have held that lengthy delay in administering a *lawful* death penalty renders ultimate execution inhuman, degrading, or unusually cruel. (*Knight*, at 995, emphasis in original)

After assessing the judgments of the Privy Council, the Supreme Court of India, the Supreme Court of Zimbabwe, and the European Court of Human Rights, Breyer J. acknowledged that such foreign authorities are not binding. Nonetheless, he opined that it is helpful to consider the findings of courts that have "considered roughly comparable questions under roughly comparable legal standards" (*Knight*, at 997). Breyer J. appears to be willing to engage in the "comparable interpretation" method of judicial domestication described above. However, Justice Thomas' view prevailed, as it did three years later in *Foster v. Florida* (2002), where petitioner also argued that lengthy incarceration on death row constituted "cruel and unusual" punishment. Rejecting this petition, Justice Thomas stated that the Court "should not impose foreign moods, fads, or fashions on Americans" (*Foster*, at 990, n*). Thomas J. was not just rejecting the applicability of external norms, though. In *Knight*, he went further and suggested that petitioner's recourse to international and foreign authorities actually provided evidence that his claim had no merit in American law. If petitioner could find support for his proposition in

> the American constitutional tradition or in this Court's precedent … [then] … it would be unnecessary for proponents of the claim to rely on the European Court of Human Rights, the Supreme Court of Zimbabwe, the Supreme Court of India, or the Privy Council. (*Knight*, at 990)

In other words, recourse to external norms is not only unnecessary or unhelpful, but also evidence that the claim has no merit in the domestic legal system.

The statements of both Justice Breyer and Justice Thomas are important to the central point of this chapter. Clearly, if Justice Thomas' view prevails, the idea of using external norms will lead abolitionists nowhere. Prima facie, Justice Breyer's stance is more promising to abolitionists who invoke external norms. However, Justice Breyer's comments may also inadvertently sustain the retention of the death penalty. Note his words: *"courts that accept or assume the lawfulness of the death penalty."* If the Supreme Court were to adopt Justice Breyer's methodology, then the judicial domestication of external death penalty norms would only serve to regulate the death penalty, not abolish it. Justice Breyer says specifically that the Court need only look at the jurisprudence of courts that retain, but regulate, the death penalty.

In sum, international and comparative law is used primarily in a weak confirmatory role. Importantly, the Court seems to select the external norms that (a) support its own conclusion and (b) do not require a discussion of whether, or to what extent, such law is binding on the Court. As explained in the next section, the Court's chosen method of judicial domestication leads to the conclusion that non-domestic norms will not lead to the abolition of the death penalty, and may actually strengthen its retention.

POTENTIAL CONSEQUENCES OF THE COURT'S CURRENT APPROACH TO JUDICIAL DOMESTICATION

This chapter has so far considered two discrete, yet interrelated issues – the current status of the death penalty worldwide and the Supreme Court's current approach to judicial domestication. It will be recalled that the following conclusions were reached with respect to these two issues: first, it cannot be said that there is a significantly strong abolition norm in the international community; second, the Supreme Court primarily considers international and comparative law in a weak, confirmatory manner.

The final part of this chapter grapples with the potential consequences of these findings. First, I illustrate the perhaps obvious conclusion that the Court's invocation of external norms will not assist it with finding the death penalty contrary to "evolving standards of decency." Although this conclusion has been elucidated elsewhere, specifically by Laurence Rothenberg (2004), I take a different stance to Rothenberg by arguing that it is not so much the *weakness* of the abolition norm worldwide that is the issue, but rather it is the Court's *chosen method* of judicial domestication that would prevent such a finding. Second, and more significantly, I argue that this current state of affairs might lead to a strengthening of the normative acceptance of the death penalty in the United States. In essence, I argue that the perceived threat to state sovereignty that judicial domestication by the federal court poses might result in attempts to retain the death penalty as a means of reasserting state autonomy.

The Court's Current Approach to Judicial Domestication Will Not Lead to a Finding that the Death Penalty Violates "Evolving Standards of Decency"

As long as the Supreme Court uses external norms in a merely confirmatory manner, it is unlikely that the Court would find that the worldwide trend towards abolition provides evidence that such a punishment offends "evolving standards of decency" and is therefore in contravention of the Eighth Amendment. The Court looks for a strong international consensus in order to buttress its own findings, and there simply is no strong international consensus on abolition of the death penalty. Although Rothenberg has illustrated this well, the essence of his argument lies in the weakness of the abolition norm in international and foreign law. The experience of the judicial abolition of the death penalty in South Africa, however, provides an illuminating example of how it is not so much the strength of the norm that affects the Court's decision, but rather the Court's chosen method of judicial domestication, which rests largely on the Court's chosen method of constitutional interpretation.

In *State v. Makwanyane and Another* (1995), the Constitutional Court of South Africa engaged in a process of judicial domestication that ultimately assisted the Court in finding the death penalty to be contrary to the constitutional prohibition on cruel, inhuman or degrading punishment. In doing so, the Court explicitly overcame the problem identified earlier in this chapter, namely, the weakness of any abolition norm in international law and the laws of foreign jurisdictions. Prima facie, *Makwanyane* provides hope for abolitionists who seek to use international and foreign prohibitions on the death penalty to further efforts to abolish the death penalty in the U.S. However, for the following four reasons, the decision of the South African Court is not easily transferable to the U.S.

The first three reasons are sociological and political. First, at the time *Makwanyane* was decided, South Africa as a whole was determined to move away from Apartheid, and it is arguable that the death penalty was a symbol of the state violence that characterized Apartheid. The United States has no such recent history that it is trying to move away from. Second, the South African Court could not look to its historical, internal traditions as (a) the new Constitutional Court had no domestic jurisprudence from which to draw and (b) to look at the jurisprudence of South African courts that operated under Apartheid would be to affirm the legal tradition under Apartheid. President Chaskalson explicitly notes:

> Comparative 'bill of rights' jurisprudence will no doubt be of importance, particularly in the early stages of a transition when there is no developed indigenous jurisprudence in this branch of the law on which to draw (para 37).

The U.S. Supreme Court has, it is arguable, enough indigenous jurisprudence on which to draw. Third, as a fledging Republic, South Africa at that time was seeking the approval of the worldwide community. It is hardly contentious to assert that new nations must seek the respect of other countries,[11] and if the Court had ignored, for example, European practice and had retained the death penalty, it is likely that South Africa would have incurred criticism from Europe, just as the use of the death penalty in the U.S. presently incurs. On the other hand, South Africa had nothing to lose and everything to gain from abolition. Abolition earned the respect of Europe and did not incur any criticisms. Again, as a nation with a highly developed legal system, the United States does not need to gain legitimacy from the international community.

The fourth and, in my view, most critical reason why the United States Supreme Court cannot "reason-borrow" and follow the steps of the South African Court, and find the death penalty unconstitutional, lies in the *method* of the South African Court in (a) utilising external norms, and, importantly, (b) *interpreting its own domestic constitution*. Sujit Choudhry (1999) has addressed this point, and I will sum up his analysis here. In short, the South African Court was able to find the death penalty unlawful, notwithstanding the lack of an abolition norm, primarily because of the Court's chosen approach to domestic constitutional interpretation, which Choudhry describes as "complex universalism" (pp. 851–855). The South African Court had to explain why it was deviating from the international acceptance of the legality of the death penalty. In its discussion of American jurisprudence, the Court noted that, at the time it was drawn up, the U.S. Constitution explicitly recognised the death penalty as lawful. In contrast, the South African Constitution remained silent on the issue. Thus, a textual approach to constitutional interpretation was not available to the South African Court, therefore enabling the Court to adopt an alternative approach to constitutional interpretation, and thus deviate from American jurisprudence. As President Chaskalson says

> [I]t would no doubt have been better if the framers of the Constitution had stated specifically, either that the death sentence is not a competent penalty, or that it is permissible in circumstances permitted by law. This, however, was not done and it has been left to this Court to decide whether the penalty is consistent with the provisions of the Constitution (para. 5).

This statement appears at the beginning of the judgment, and the importance of this will be explained below.

As a textual analysis of the domestic constitution was not possible, the Constitutional Court of South Africa chose to interpret the relevant part of the constitution in light of international standards. When looking at the validation for the death penalty in instruments of international human rights law, the Court noted that the United Nations Human Rights Committee had not found the extradition of a suspect to the U.S. (where there was a real possibility that the suspect would face the death penalty) to violate the right to life under the ICCPR. Similarly, in *Soering*, the European Court of Human Rights did not bar extradition because the death penalty was unlawful per se, but rather because of the "cruel" and "inhuman" way in which the death penalty was administered. Thus, according to the Court, even international authorities explicitly permitted the death penalty. However, the Court was able to free itself from this retention norm by analysing the international norms in a particular way. President Chaskalson quotes Article 6(6) of the ICCPR, which states a desire for eventual abolition of the death penalty. According to Chaskalson, the "fact that the International Covenant sanctions capital punishment must be seen in this context. It tolerates but does not provide justification for the death penalty" (para. 66). This freed the Court from any argument that the death penalty was *justified* or demanded by international law.

With the lack of justification in mind, the Court was able to then assess the consequences that the regulation norm could have on its own constitutional interpretation. President Chaskalson explains this:

> The fact that in both the United States and India, which sanction capital punishment, the highest Courts have intervened on constitutional grounds in particular cases to prevent the carrying out of death sentences, because in the particular circumstances of such cases, it would have been cruel to do so, *evidences the importance attached to the protection of life* and the strict scrutiny to which the imposition and carrying out of death sentences are subjected when a constitutional challenge is raised. The same concern is apparent in the decisions of the European Court of Human Rights and the United Nations Committee on Human Rights. (1995 (3) SA, para. 86, emphasis added)

A key point here is how the Court uses the regulation norm as evidence of the importance attached to the "protection of life." As Choudhry explains:

> the existence of 'the protection of life' as a transcendent legal principle helped President Chaskalson conclude that the death penalty amounted to cruel, inhuman, or degrading punishment (p. 855).

The death penalty is not justified, just tolerated, and the regulation norm was construed as an attempt to protect life. Applying the principle of the "protection of life," the Court was able to find the death penalty unconstitutional.

As such, the fourth reason why the South African experience is not transferable to the United States lies in the fundamentally different approaches to constitutional interpretation that the two Courts take. The South African Court first noted that it could not engage in a textual analysis of the South African Constitution because the constitution remained silent on the legality of the death penalty and, in light of this silence, the Court engaged in an analysis of external norms. In its analysis of external norms, the Court identified a transcendent principle of the protection of life, a principle that emerged from the regulation norm. Finally, the Court found this principle to be of importance when interpreting the constitutional prohibition on "cruel, inhuman or degrading punishment."

As illustrated above, though, the U.S. Supreme Court is not willing to adopt this rather generous approach to constitutional interpretation and, by extension, judicial domestication. The Court's death penalty jurisprudence shows a predominant concern with textual analysis, precedent, and Constitutional tradition in interpreting the Constitution, with external norms only playing a confirmatory role. Textual analysis would conclusively allow for the retention of the death penalty, as the Fifth and Fourteenth Amendments explicitly endorse the legality of the death penalty. Even if the Court did engage in an analysis of external norms, its current jurisprudence shows a stark conservatism when examining international and foreign laws, and a tendency to only "bean-count" the stance of international authorities and foreign countries on a particular death penalty practice. As such, the regulation norm would be interpreted as just that– a system of regulation, rather than as evidence of some other principle, such as the protection of life.

The above analysis of *Makwanyane* illustrates that the weakness of the abolition norm can be overcome by somewhat generous judicial interpretations of open-ended constitutional provisions. As such, it is possible to conclude that the main reason why the U.S. Supreme Court will not reach a similar conclusion to the South African Constitutional Court lies not in the weakness of any abolition norm, but rather in the manner in which the Supreme Court uses external norms. However, the issue does not end here. While abolitionists struggle to convince a reluctant court to adopt a more ambitious approach to constitutional interpretation, one that takes the regulation norm and turns it into an abolition norm, those who are concerned with the apparent threat to sovereignty that judicial domestication poses are in a prime position to consolidate the retention of the death penalty as a means of reasserting state autonomy.

Judicial Domestication Might Provoke States Into Retaining the Death Penalty

The idea that states in America may retain the death penalty as a means of asserting state sovereignty derives from the wealth of criticisms that have been levelled at the practice of judicial domestication. Although a number of reasons have been given for decrying the Court's invocation of external norms as "illegitimate" (Bradley & Goldsmith, 1997) and "dangerous" (*Lawrence v. Texas*, 2004, at 2472, Justice Scalia, dissenting), I am interested here in the following concerns: that the invocation by a federal court of external norms (a) presents a real threat to state (and national) sovereignty and represents an affront to basic tenets of democracy, and (b) is an affront to states' rights under the system of federalism.

The Threat to Sovereignty
The infiltration of external legal norms into the domestic legal order is seen to pose as much a threat to popular and legal sovereignty as the infiltration of a foreign army onto domestic soil would pose to territorial sovereignty. Alford (2004, p. 58) puts this succinctly: "Using global opinions as a means of constitutional interpretation dramatically undermines sovereignty by ... trump[ing] the democratic will." At a Congressional Hearing on the issue of the Court's invocation of external norms, Congressman Chabot echoed this sentiment

the judiciary not only is undermining the vision of our Founding Fathers but is chipping away at the core principles on which this country was founded, chipping away at our Nation's sovereignty and independence. (Hearing on House Resolution 97, 2005, p. 2)

Rothenberg (2004), too, has stated:

the sovereignty of the United States regarding a significant aspect of its criminal justice system is threatened ... by ... the insinuation of international and foreign law into U.S.

judicial decision-making regarding certain aspects of death penalty administration (pp. 547–548).

The threat to sovereignty is seen to be a very real and serious issue. Some commentators have even expressed the fear that recourse to foreign norms threatens the development of an American culture and legal order, and Carlos Rosenkrantz (2003, pp. 292–294) has argued that the Court's current practice impairs the development of a distinct, indigenous American constitutional legal order.

In response to this perceived threat to sovereignty, both the House of Representatives and the Senate have passed Resolutions calling for an end to the practice of judicial domestication (House Resolution 97, 2005; Senate Resolution 92, 2005), and there have also been calls to impeach the Justices who consult international and foreign laws in their constitutional analysis. For example, Edwin Vieira has stated that, for upholding "Marxist, Leninist, satanic principles drawn from foreign law" (Milbank, 2005), Justice Kennedy should be impeached. Title III of the Constitutional Restoration Act (2004) provides that judges who engage in citations of foreign law can be subject to impeachment (Cleveland, 2006, p. 4, n. 14). Such resolutions and calls for impeachment illustrate the depth of hostility that is felt towards this perceived threat to sovereignty, and, for the reasons below, it is submitted that this depth of hostility may manifest itself in a strengthening of the normative acceptance of the death penalty.

An Affront to State Rights
Franklin Zimring and Gordon Hawkins (1986) have illustrated the depth of hostility historically felt by states towards the federal court for interfering in the local administration of the death penalty. They write that the

doubling of the number of death sentences in the South in reaction to *Furman* [in which the U.S. Supreme Court temporarily abolished the death penalty] can be seen as the use of death penalty policy to express hostility toward the national government's power (p. 152).

Even when the federal court reinstated the death penalty in *Gregg v. Georgia* (1976), the Southern states imposed the death penalty with distinguishable vigour:

executions represent[ed] a manifestation of state autonomy that continues to influence state and local decision makers even when federal restraints on the freedom to execute have been removed (pp. 152–153).

According to Zimring and Hawkins, the death penalty is not just applied for penological reasons, but is also imposed because of the politically symbolic value that the death penalty represents for state autonomy: "the practice of execution has become almost as much a celebration of states' rights as a matter of criminal policy" (p. 152).

Although Zimring and Hawkins' study dates back to 1986, the principle that emerges from their analysis is relevant to modern times. Writing as recently as 2003, Zimring maintains the claim that "the special hostility towards federal courts ... continues a tradition of resentment towards federal courts in the South and the Southwest particularly" (Zimring, 2003, p. 80). It should be appreciated, though, that it is not just states in the South and Southwest that maintain the death penalty – California has the largest death row population in the United States, and Delaware has the second highest rate of executions per capita of all the states (Death Penalty Information Center, 2006). However, this does not detract from Zimring's general point: "[t]here is much natural hostility to federal norms and federal law enforcement in many American states." (2003, p. 80)

Zimring explains why some states feel antagonistic to the federal courts (2003, Chapter 4), and although it is beyond the scope of this chapter to comprehensively detail such reasons, it is sufficient to note that much of the antagonism lies in the desire felt by states to have control over their internal criminal law affairs, and the fact that federal involvement after a case has passed through the state system results in a delay, if not complete negation, of a state-chosen punishment being carried out.

Potential Consequences

If states have increased the use of the death penalty in response to the intervention by the federal court in *Furman*, there is every possibility that such states will increase the use of the death penalty in response to the perceived interventions by external norms. Just as states feel hostile to federal power, so states will feel threatened by the perceived threat to state (and national) sovereignty that the invocation of international and foreign norms poses. In fact, the invocation of external norms *by* the federal court represents a double attack on state autonomy – by interfering with state death penalty regimes *and* using external norms to do so, the federal court is adding insult to injury. As Roger Alford (2004, p. 61) has written:

> Reliance on global standards of decency undermines the sovereign limitations inherent in federalist restraints, limitations born out of respect for the reserved powers of the states to assess which punishments are appropriate for which crimes.

However, if the reason for a state's hostility to the federal court comes from a resentment that the federal court is questioning the competency of the state court, and is using laws that have not been democratically enacted, this leaves open the possibility that, as a normative matter, the use of international and foreign human rights law would be accepted if incorporated at the state level rather than the federal level, and by state courts rather than the federal courts. This brings to mind two occasions on which state courts have considered international and foreign human rights law. These cases must be considered before asserting that states feel inherently threatened by the insinuation of international and foreign human rights law.

In *Torres v. State of Oklahoma* (2004), the Oklahoma Court of Criminal Appeals stayed the execution of Mr. Torres in light of the International Court of Justice's ruling in Case Concerning Avena and Other Mexican Nationals (*Mexico v. United States of America*) (2004). The International Court of Justice (ICJ) had ruled that Avena and the other Mexican nationals on death row – including Torres – should have their convictions and sentences reviewed and reconsidered in light of the state authorities' failure to notify the defendants of their right to consular assistance under the Vienna Convention on Consular Relations (VCCR). Prima facie, it would appear that the Oklahoma Court of Criminal Appeals was bowing to the authority of the ICJ, with Judge Chapel stating that the Court "is bound by the Vienna Convention" and is obligated "to give effect" to the Convention (*Torres*, at 5). However, it would be wrong to suggest that the Court here was judicially invoking international and foreign human rights law in its death penalty jurisprudence. Judge Chapel explicitly states:

> I am not suggesting that the International Court of Justice has jurisdiction over this Court – far from it. However, in these unusual circumstances the issue of whether this Court must abide by that court's opinion in Torres's case is not ours to determine. The United States Senate and President have made that decision for us [by ratifying the Optional Protocol which] ... provides that the International Court of Justice is the forum for the resolution of disputes under the Vienna Convention. (*Torres*, at 2)

In other words, the Court of Criminal Appeals denied that it was judicially domesticating international and foreign human rights law. Rather, the Court suggested that the democratically elected branches of government – the Senate and the President – had brought such law to bear on the domestic legal order. As such, there was no issue of any threat to sovereignty or usurpation by the Court of the basic tenets of democracy.

The Missouri State Supreme Court adopted a similar line of reasoning in *State ex rel. Simmons v. Roper* (2003). In striking down Christopher Simmons' death sentence on the grounds that the death penalty for juvenile

offenders violated the Eighth Amendment to the Constitution, the Missouri
State Supreme Court stated that it was simply applying the U.S. Supreme
Court's approach to determining the content of the Eighth Amendment as
elucidated in *Atkins v. Virginia*, which included reference to the opinions of
the worldwide community. On this reading, the Missouri Supreme Court
was not judicially domesticating external norms, it was simply following the
instructions of the U.S. Supreme Court as laid out in *Atkins*.

In essence, then, it cannot be said that the state courts in Oklahoma and
Missouri were consulting international and foreign norms of their own
accord. Therefore, even in light of these cases, there remains the likelihood
of resentment being felt towards the federal branches for interfering in state
death penalty regimes by consulting international and foreign human rights
law. And, for the reasons outlined above, such resentment might lead
towards a state policy of maintaining the death penalty as a means of
reasserting state autonomy, as many states did post-*Furman*. Given that, in
the context of the Eighth Amendment, the U.S. Supreme Court places
predominant weight on a national consensus, states' retention of the death
penalty will not lead to a finding that such a punishment violates "evolving
standards of decency."

CONCLUSIONS

This chapter has highlighted the potential ramifications that increased
attention to external norms may have on the retention of the death penalty.
Of course, current statistics would suggest that there has not yet been any
discernible rise in death sentences and executions in direct response to the
Court's invocation of international and foreign norms. In fact, death
sentences and executions appear to falling annually (Death Penalty
Information Center, 2006). Furthermore, it is not suggested that prosecutors
seeking the death penalty, and jurors imposing the death penalty, would
make a conscious decision to increase the number of death sentences solely
because of the Supreme Court's attention to external norms. It is imperative
to remember that there are always a myriad of factors surrounding the
seeking and imposition of the death penalty, the crime and alleged criminal
being perhaps the two most significant factors. However, what this chapter
does show is that those who seek the abolition of the death penalty need to
consider exactly how they – and the Courts – use the worldwide trend
towards abolition. If a powerful state like America is ever going to abolish
the death penalty, it needs to *want* to abolish the death penalty, and not

be told to abolish it. At present, we have a situation where the resolve of those who reject the applicability of external norms is much stronger than the abolition norm or the Court's method of judicial domestication. Thus, while abolitionists struggle to convince a conservative Court to consider a weak abolition norm, those who fear a threat to sovereignty are in a better position to consolidate the death penalty in their individual states, and thus ensure that there is not a national consensus against the death penalty per se, thereby ensuring the survival of the death penalty in America.

NOTES

1. There are other avenues through which international and foreign norms can be brought to bear on the domestic legal order, other than the Eighth Amendment. A significant alternative avenue has been through the Vienna Convention on Consular Relations, a treaty which has been ratified by the U.S. and which demands that foreign nationals who are arrested are notified of their right to consular access. A succession of cases has dealt with the issue of foreign nationals on death row who were not notified of their right to consular access, resulting in calls for the quashing of the death sentence. While an important issue and certainly one that is relevant to my question, I have limited this chapter to dealing with the Court's Eighth Amendment jurisprudence. For an exceptionally useful analysis of how the Vienna Convention has been used as a portal through which international norms can be brought to bear on the domestic legal order, see McGuinness (2006).

2. See Office of the United Nations High Commissioner for Human Rights (2006) for status of ratifications.

3. The figure of 109 is calculated by adding the 71 that are retentionists in law and practice, the 27 who are retentionists in law but abolitionists in practice, and the 11 who have abolished it for ordinary crimes, but still retain the death penalty for "exceptional" crimes.

4. See Office of the United Nations High Commissioner for Human Rights, Declarations and Reservations to the ICCPR (2006) for status of reservations.

5. This is a necessarily rudimentary account of Kelsen. See Capps (2006) for a more critical account.

6. Although the Supreme Court's subsequent decision in *Sosa* brings this assertion into question, it is still clear that the Court is not wholeheartedly receptive to the applicability of customary international law.

7. The South African Bill of Rights is an example of this, Article 39(1) of which states: "When interpreting the Bill of Rights, a court, tribunal or forum ... (b) must consider international law; and (c) may consider foreign law."

8. Jackson's use of the word "transnational" is problematic here. Elsewhere, Koh ascribes the word "transnational" to the idea that, in human rights law, international and foreign laws have converged, thus creating a unitary transnational law. However, it is unclear if Jackson is using the term transnational to describe both

international and foreign law, and as explained earlier, it is not wise to consider the two in tandem.

9. Although this Convention applies to times of war, it is unlikely that the drafters intended lesser protections to apply during times of peace.

10. Although this was said by Justice O'Connor in her dissenting opinion, there is no indication in the opinion of the majority that a worldwide consensus would alter their determination had they found an incongruent national consensus.

11. Consider the words of the U.S. Declaration of Independence: "When, in the Course of human Events, it becomes necessary for one People to dissolve the Political Bands which have connected them with another ... a decent Respect to the Opinions of Mankind requires that they should declare the causes which compel them to the Separation." (Declaration of Independence, para 1–2, U.S., 1776)

ACKNOWLEDGMENTS

I would like to thank Dr. Pat Capps for his invaluable help, and Professor Austin Sarat and the anonymous reviewer for insightful comments on an earlier draught of this chapter.

REFERENCES

Alford, R. (2004). Misusing international sources to interpret the constitution. *American Journal of International Law, 98*, 57–69.

Alford, R. (2005). In search of a theory for constitutional comparativism. *UCLA Law Review, 52*, 639–714.

American Convention on Human Rights. (1969). Entered into force on November 22, 1144 UNTS 123.

Amnesty International. (2006). *Death penalty facts.* Retrieved on November 12 from http://www.amnesty.org.uk/content.asp?CategoryID = 10642.

Atkins v. Virginia. (2002). 536 US 304

Bradley, C., & Goldsmith, J. (1997). Customary international law as federal common law: A critique of the modern position. *Harvard Law Review, 110*, 815–876.

Brief of American Medical Association, American Psychiatric Association, American Academy of Psychiatry and the Law, American Society for Adolescent Psychiatry, American Academy of Child & Adolescent Psychiatry, National Association of Social Workers, Missouri Chapter of the National Association of Social Workers, National Mental Health Association as Amici Curiae in support of Respondent, filed in *Roper v. Simmons* (2006). Retrieved on November 12 from http://www.abanet.org/crimjust/juvjus/simmons/ama.pdf

Brief of American Psychological Association, Missouri Psychological Association as Amici Curiae in support of Respondent, filed in *Roper v. Simmons* (2006). Retrieved on November 12 from http://www.abanet.org/crimjust/juvjus/simmons/apa.pdf

Capps, P. (2006). Sovereignty and the identity of legal orders. In: C. Warbrick & S. Tierney (Eds), *Towards an 'international legal community'?* (pp. 19–75). London: BIICL.

Case Concerning Avena and Other Mexican Nationals. (2004). *Mexico v. United States of America* I.C.J. No. 128 (Judgment of March 31).

Childress, D., III. (2004). Using comparative constitutional law to resolve domestic federal questions. *Duke Law Journal, 53,* 193–222.

Choudhry, S. (1999). Globalization in search of justification: Toward a theory of comparative constitutional interpretation. *Indiana Law Journal, 74,* 819–892.

Cleveland, S. (2006). Our international constitution. *Yale Journal of International Law, 31,* 1–125.

Coker v. Georgia. (1977). 433 US 584.

Death Penalty Information Center. (2006). Retrieved on November 12 from http://www.deathpenaltyinfo.org

Dixon, M. (2000). *International law* (4th ed.). London: Blackstone Press.

Domingues v. United States. (2002). Case 12.285, Report No. 62/02, Inter-Am. C.H.R., Inter-American Commission on Human Rights.

Enmund v. Florida. (1982). 458 US 782.

European Convention on Human Rights. (1953). Entered into force March 9, ETS 005.

Ford v. Wainwright. (1986). 477 US 399.

Foster v. Florida. (2002). 537 US 990.

Glendon, M. A. (2001). *A world made new: Eleanor Roosevelt and the universal declaration of human rights.* New York: Random House.

Henkin, L. (1995). U.S. ratification of human rights conventions: The ghost of Senator Bricker. *American Journal of International Law, 89,* 341–350.

International Covenant on Civil and Political Rights. (1976). Entered into force March 23, 999 UNTS 171.

Jackson, V. (2005). Constitutional comparisons: Convergence, resistance, engagement. *Harvard Law Review, 119,* 109–128.

Kelsen, H. (1920) *Das Problem der Souveränität und die Theorie des Völkerrecht.* Tübingen: J. C. B. Mohr.

Knight v. Florida. (1999). 528 US 990.

Koh, H. (2002). Paying "decent respect" to world opinion on the death penalty. *University of California Davis Law Review, 35,* 1085–1132.

Larsen, J. (2004). Importing constitutional norms from a "wider civilization": Lawrence and the Rehnquist Court's use of foreign and international law in domestic constitutional interpretation. *Ohio State Law Journal, 65,* 1283–1328.

Lawrence v. Texas. (2004). 123 S. Ct. 2472.

McGuinness, M. (2006). Medellin, norm portals, and the horizontal integration of international human rights. *Notre Dame Law Review, 82,* 755–842.

Milbank, D. (2005). And the verdict on Justice Kennedy is: Guilty. *The Washington Post* (April 9, p. A03). Retrieved November 12, 2006 from http://www.washingtonpost.com/wp-dyn/articles/A38308-2005Apr8.html

Office of the United Nations High Commissioner for Human Rights. (2006). Declarations and reservations to the ICCPR. Retrieved on November 12 from http://www.ohchr.org/english/countries/ratification/4_1.htm

Office of the United Nations High Commissioner for Human Rights; Status of ratifications of human rights treaties. (2006). Retrieved on November 12, from http://www.ohchr.org/english/bodies/docs/RatificationStatus.pdf

Protocol No. 13 to the Convention for the Protection of Human Rights and Fundamental Freedoms Concerning the Abolition of the Death Penalty. (2003). As amended by Protocol 11, entered into force on January 7, ETS 187.

Protocol to the American Convention on Human Rights to Abolish the Death Penalty. (1990). Adopted on June 8, 29 ILM 1447.

Redgwell, C. (2003). US reservations to human rights treaties: All for one and none for all? In: M. Byers & G. Nolte (Eds), *United States hegemony and the foundations of international law*. Cambridge: Cambridge University Press.

Roper v. Simmons. (2005). 543 US 551.

Rosenkrantz, C. (2003). Against borrowing and other nonauthoritative uses of foreign law. *International Journal of Constitutional Law, 1*, 269–295.

Rothenberg, L. (2004). International law, U.S. sovereignty, and the death penalty. *Georgetown Journal of International Law, 35*, 547–596.

Second Optional Protocol to the International Covenant on Civil and Political Rights. (1989). December 15, art.1 1642 UNTS 414, 415.

Soering v. UnitedKingdom. (1989). 161 Eur. Ct. H.R. (ser. A), *reprinted in* 11 *Eur. Hum. Rts. Rep.* 439 (1989), 28 ILM 1063 (1989) (European Court of Human Rights).

Stanford v. Kentucky. (1989). 492 US 361.

State ex rel. Simmons v. Roper. (2003). 112 S. W. 3d 397 (en banc).

State v. Makwanyane and Another. (1995). (3) SA 391 (Constitutional Court of South Africa).

Steiker, J. (2006). United States: *Roper v. Simmons*. *International Journal of Constitutional Law, 4*, 163–171.

Thompson v. Oklahoma. (1988). 487 U.S. 815.

Torres v. State of Oklahoma. (2004). No. PCD-04-442 (Oklahoma Court of Criminal Appeals, May 13).

Trop v. Dulles. (1958). 356 US 86, 101.

Tushnet, M. (1999). The possibilities of comparative constitutional law. *Yale Law Journal, 108*, 1225–1311.

Universal Declaration of Human Rights. (1948). G.A. Res. 217A, U.N. GAOR, 3rd Session, U.N. Document A/810.

Hearing on House Resolution 97. (2005). *On the appropriate role of foreign judgments in the interpretation of the constitution of the United States: Hearing before the subcommittee on the constitution of the committee on the judiciary of the House of Representatives* (109th Cong., 1st Sess., July 19). Washington: Government Printing Office.

U.S. Senate Resolution 92. (2005). 109th Congress.

Waldron, J. (2005). Foreign law and the modern *Ius Gentium*. *Harvard Law Review, 119*, 129–147.

Zimring, F. (2003). *The contradictions of American capital punishment*. New York: Oxford University Press.

Zimring, F., & Hawkins, G. (1986). *Capital punishment and the American agenda*. Cambridge: Cambridge University Press.

DEATH, UNRAVELED

Jesse Cheng

ABSTRACT

This chapter explores knowledge practices around the subject of capital punishment. Capital sentencing jurisprudence and certain strands of academic scholarship on the death penalty have certain resonances with recent developments in reflexive cultural anthropology. Using the notion of productive unraveling, this chapter seeks to reinforce relations between these various knowledge practices by conceiving of them as situated on the same ground, already interwoven with one another. This chapter presents itself as both an example of and a call for the development of interconnections between these various kinds of expert knowledges concerning the death penalty.

INTRODUCTION

What is happening to thinking about the death penalty? I refer not to the institutions that do the practical work of capital punishment – the apprehending, the charging, the sentencing, and the executing. Rather, I am concerned about the knowledge practices that shape the analytical undertakings of both legal practitioners and academic commentators as they attempt to make sense of the practice of state killings. How is knowledge produced about the subject of capital punishment?

Special Issue: Is the Death Penalty Dying?
Studies in Law, Politics, and Society, Volume 42, 195–218
Copyright © 2008 by Elsevier Ltd.
ISSN: 1059-4337/doi:10.1016/S1059-4337(07)00407-3

In posing this question, I focus on two bodies of knowledge: the "practical" knowledge associated with the Supreme Court's capital sentencing jurisprudence, and the "scholarly" knowledge associated with certain strands of academic analysis on the death penalty in general. A key starting point of this chapter is that the simplistic dichotomy between "practice" and "scholarship," "application" and "academics" – and the privileging of the one over the other that the divide can imply – needs to be unsettled in favor of a more realistic view of the intricately interconnected nature of these various knowledge practices. Scholarly as well as practical analysis about the death penalty has historically shaped, and been shaped by, overlapping sets of moral, constitutional, and procedural considerations. Rather than focus on the substance of these questions – the morality, the constitutionality, and the procedure – I bring attention to the entwinements between "scholarly" and "practical" knowledge practices that make these questions intelligible in the first place.

I offer this as an instantiation of what the anthropologist Bill Maurer calls the "lateralization" of different analytical practices (Maurer, 2005b). The purpose of such an approach is "neither description as such, nor explanation as such, but dense lateralizations with objects and subjects that are already densely lateralized with each other and with the thing I [the anthropologist] call me and my work" (Maurer, 2005b, p. 17). Thus, this essay attempts not so much to offer a polished argument, but to sketch out a few working thoughts that delve into, draw from, reach out to, and thoroughly implicate themselves in traditional frames of analysis, even while refusing to be contained by them. In other words, I develop this analysis alongside my subjects, laterally, as opposed to "over" them, meta-analytically. Instead of claiming a privileged position of analysis vis-à-vis these other knowledges, this chapter attempts to puzzle things out with them. It casts some lateral lines with the hope of suggesting how crosscutting engagements that are already there provide opportunities for further engagement.

This may seem like an unusual approach for those unfamiliar with current developments in my own discipline of cultural anthropology, so I offer some elaboration here. In certain areas of social-scientific inquiry, phenomena have come to seem interesting – anthropologically and more generally – because of a heightened sense of unpredictability that attends unexpected and far flung connections, rapid change, and objects of analysis that refuse to stand still (Greenhouse, Mertz, & Warren, 2002; Harvey, 2005; Holmes & Marcus, 2005b; Tsing, 2005). The world appears ever more sophisticated in its interdependence and unruliness. In response to this state of affairs, anthropological subjects, particularly in fields of expertise (see, e.g., Boyer, 2005a; Mitchell, 2002; Miyazaki & Riles, 2005), take it upon themselves to employ their own techniques of analysis to make sense of contemporary conditions. If such approaches often seem to resonate with those developed in the qualitative social sciences, it is because these actors actively engage with and are influenced by academic conversations (Boyer, 2005b; Holmes & Marcus, 2005a; Riles, 2000; Strathern, 2004). In a sense, then, this already dialogic nature of analytical discourse places anthropologists on the same ground as those whom they would study; our analysis takes place alongside theirs, rather than over them.

The analytical approach of this chapter reflects a certain spirit among some reflexive anthropologists to "throw themselves wholly into their subjects, which, they find, often have already engulfed them" (Maurer, 2005a, p. 3). My goal, then, is not to present a step-by-step argument intended to establish the connections between me and my subjects through a process of proof. Instead, I submit that there is something to be analytically gained by beginning from the premise that current anthropological analysis, capital sentencing jurisprudence, and scholarship on the death penalty occupy the same ground, already entwined with one another under modern conditions as sophisticated practices of expert knowledge. This is not mere postulation. It is an observation based on my own ethnographic fieldwork with capital defense advocates, scholars of constitutional law, and academics who write about the death penalty. There are legal scholars who are practicing advocates, practicing advocates who are formally trained in cultural anthropology and other social sciences, social scientists who produce scholarship on capital punishment – and each of their respective doings affect the others in some manner. These sets of expert knowledge are already interrelated. This chapter attempts to reinforce those relations by suggesting possibilities for making sense of how we are all interwoven with one another, and how we might benefit from embracing and encouraging the mutually co-constitutive connections between our knowledge practices. In so doing, my intention is to encourage thinkers from these fields to further lateralize among themselves, with me, and with other analysts (also see Fischer, 2003; Marcus, 2002).

I implicate these various knowledge practices with each other by way of a notion that I think of as productive unraveling. By this, I point to a general analytical ethos characterized by a heightened sense of interconnectedness and complexity that the contemporary analyst perceives in her subjects, and in these subjects' relations with her. With this heightened sense comes an acceptance of the provisional nature of analysis as unexpected changes and connections are constantly discovered; analysis constantly has to undo itself. I note that the notion of "unraveling" carries no particular purchase in the discipline of cultural anthropology, although it certainly has resonances with so-called "postmodern" scholarship as well as various modes of deconstruction in the humanities, social sciences, and critical legal studies (see, e.g., Baudrillard, 1998; De Man, 1983; Derrida, 1974; Fish, 1999; Jameson, 1991; Kelman, 1987; Lyotard, 1984). But my purpose is not to differentiate anthropology, death penalty jurisprudence, and academic commentary by situating them in their respective contexts of development. Instead, I wish to suggest that they all occupy the same terrain by virtue of a rough, often unevenly theorized realization that the terrain they occupy is no longer properly their own – that they are increasingly interconnected, increasingly in flux, and increasingly interdependent on one another to make sense of their own practices. As I use it, then, the idea of unraveling justifies this chapter's lateralizing project by suggesting that its subjects are themselves primed for lateralization. Indeed, to some extent, they are already doing it.

These are sweeping strokes over broad territory – but the lateral lines sketched herein are merely suggestive. The moral, constitutional, and procedural questions ordinarily associated with capital punishment – whether it is right or wrong, under what conditions it is justified, what criteria ought to guide its application, who is to answer for its administration – must be understood in relation to the knowledge practices that produce them. But as producers of knowledge grow more aware of their dense interconnections, the play of unraveling takes on a life of its own. This, too, is an empirically based conclusion. If the practice of capital punishment generates a quantity of jurisprudential and scholarly analysis that is out of proportion with the issue's "real" import, however defined, it may be precisely because the sense of provisionality inspired by this unraveling spurs on a perpetual reconstitution of knowledge.

CAPITAL SENTENCING JURISPRUDENCE AND UNRAVELING IN ANTHROPOLOGY

In the case of *Lockett v. Ohio* (1978), the United States Supreme Court opened the door to an unprecedented range of evidence as mitigating factors in death penalty sentencing. The court held that the jury must be allowed to consider "any aspect of a defendant's character or record and any of the offences that the defendant proffers as a basis for a sentence less than death" (p. 604). In practical terms, this meant that the jury could not be denied "possession of the fullest information possible concerning the defendant's life" (p. 603).

A crisis was born–for in one fell swoop, the high court seemed to sabotage the spirit of a jurisprudential movement that, at its core, was about the place of criminal executions in modern civilization. Was the death penalty in the U.S. too arbitrary? Yes, it was (see *Furman v. Georgia*, 1972). Would the country need to take a timeout on state killings to figure things out? Yes, it would (see Banner, 2002, p. 244). Could capital punishment pass constitutional muster if the appropriate safeguards were put in place? Yes, eventually, it could – and, eventually, with the efforts of a whopping 35 states to revamp their statutory schemes or to create new ones, it did (see *Gregg v. Georgia*, 1976; *Jurek v. Texas*, 1976; *Proffitt v. Florida*, 1976; *Roberts v. Louisiana*, 1976; *Woodson v. North Carolina*, 1976). But now with the *Lockett* decision, the Supreme Court had suddenly gone soft, urging sentencing juries to feast on "the fullest information possible," when just two years before it had resolved to whip the system into shape through the disciplining work of procedure. As Justice Antonin Scalia remarked, saying that *Lockett* introduced an "inherent tension" in capital jurisprudence "is rather like saying that there was perhaps an inherent tension between the Allies and the Axis Powers in World War II" (*Walton v. Arizona*, 1990, p. 664).

For Justice Scalia, the nub of the conflict had to do with the need to guide the sentencer's discretion. Such guidance, he believed, was crucial for avoiding the freakishly arbitrary applications of the death penalty that *Furman* had found constitutionally infirm. As Scalia saw it, "curtailing or eliminating discretion in the sentencing of capital defendants was not only consistent with *Furman* but positively required by it" (*Walton v. Arizona*, 1990, p. 662). When the high court found capital punishment fit for reinstatement in 1976, it was because states had enacted procedures that appeared to solve the problem of unfettered discretion. *Lockett*, if taken seriously, would undo all of this; by swelling the ranks of "relevant" facts, it turned the sentencing trial into "an unconstrained and unguided evaluation of offender and offense" (*Walton v. Arizona*, 1990, p. 662). In other words, "the practice which in *Furman* had been described as the discretion to sentence to death and pronounced constitutionally prohibited, was ... renamed the discretion not to sentence to death and pronounced constitutionally required" (*Walton v. Arizona*, 1990, p. 662).

Thus it was that for Scalia, death penalty jurisprudence has come to be characterized by a fundamental inconsistency that must be resolved in favor of either procedural rigor or data-saturated contextualizing (Scalia sides with the former). In this section, however, I suggest a different perspective for understanding *Furman* and *Lockett*. *Lockett* opened the door to any potential evidence in mitigation precisely because there are infinite analytical connections that can be made in attempting to understand a defendant's life. The nature of these connections is paramount as advocates attempt to make a fully individualized presentation of the defendant's character, record, and circumstances of the offense, in accordance with the Eighth Amendment's emphasis on the "fundamental respect for humanity" (*Lockett v. Ohio*, 1978, p. 604). As various commentators have explained this apparent paradox (see, e.g., Hertz & Weisberg, 1981; Kirchmeier, 1998; Steiker & Steiker, 1992; Sundby, 1991), *Lockett*'s call for contextualization reflects a sense that there is more to be discovered, whereas the paring work of procedure required by *Furman* reflects the jurist's comfort with what he already knows. *Lockett*'s requirements underscore the significance of investigating the fullness of the defendant's humanity in all his individualized complexity, of being aware of one's own position in understanding and presenting information about another person's life, and of being allowed to pursue any avenue possible in establishing empathic connection with an audience. Another way to put this might be, *Lockett* represents a moment of crystallization when a sense of unraveling kicks in.

Visual Epistemologies in Cultural Anthropology

To better understand how unraveling set the conditions for this turn in capital sentencing jurisprudence, I reflect on certain developments that have influenced cultural anthropology as a point of comparison. Key thinkers have pointed out the discipline's complicity in promoting an epistemological orientation that privileges a tendency to conceive of the world in the form of bounded, manipulable objects. According to these reflexive analysts, such knowledge practices are founded on a trope of visuality. Below, I focus on works by Walter Ong, Marilyn Strathern, and Johannes Fabian as touchstones to offer a gist of these conversations.

Walter Ong tells how the rise of the written word "restructured consciousness" in Western thought, as compared to societies that retained oral communication as their primary means of exchanging ideas (Ong, 1977,

p. 17). The visualization of communication engendered a kind of alienating effect, "separating the knower from the external universe and then from himself" (Ong, 1977, p. 18). With the rise of the visualized word, knowledge came to resemble bounded units that inhabit space; these, in turn, could be shuffled around and deployed, much like physical objects that can be tangibly manipulated and put to use. In this sense, "objectification" is a kind of "estrangement," with its depersonalizing separation of subject-analyst from object-analysand (Keane, 2003, p. 223). Thus, a paragraph represents "a unit of thought visually advertised by an indentation" (Ong, 1977, p. 163); thought units can be understood as "'places' in the text and simultaneously topics of 'places' (*topoi, loci*) in the mind" (Ong, 1977, p. 166); and indexes become "visually serviceable" tools to order and arrange said thought units (Ong, 1977, p. 163).

To be clear, the broader critique that Ong helped to inspire conceives of visuality as a trope for knowledge. It is not necessarily the case that knowledge is actually manifested in visual form; the emphasis is on how the privileging of sight has produced a kind of epistemology that treats knowledge *as if* it is comprised of bounded, manipulable objects. Oral communication, by contrast, produces a different experience of knowing, "a kind of empathetic identification of knower and known, in which the object of knowledge and the total being of the knower enter into a kind of fusion" (Ong, 1977, p. 18). Ong traces this fusion to the simultaneity of knowledge's performance and knower's being. Unlike written texts, which can be inscribed and set aside for later use, oral knowledge transpires in the very moment of the knower's verbal utterance. Thus, knowledge and its bearers are as one–indivisible, because they are already whole.

Marilyn Strathern argues that certain Western knowledge practices are consumed by the idea that wholes are potentialities that need to be put together (Strathern, 1992). In other words, knowledge is not already whole. As she describes it, this epistemological view conceives of parts "out there" in the world that exist merely as parts. To know is to construct the whole of some phenomenon by locating its parts and drawing the right connections between them. Ong, too, agrees that manipulable units of knowledge are "thought of as pieces out of which a whole is constituted" (Ong, 1977). Together, these arguments suggest a direct link between visuality as the basis for a certain epistemological orientation, and the idea of knowledge construction as the manipulation of "useful" partial objects, the very usefulness of which derives from their ability to be pieced together and slotted into more complete wholes.[1]

Visuality's Self-Unraveling

According to these critiques, cultural anthropology is thoroughly implicated in this mode of knowledge production. Johannes Fabian has noted that objectifying moves "depend on distance, spatial and temporal .... [T]his means that the Other, as object of knowledge, must be separate, distinct, and preferably distant from the knower" (Fabian, 2002, p. 121). The self-realization of this distance sets up the insight that "[i]t has been the enactment of power relations between societies that sends out fieldworkers and societies that are the field" (Fabian, 2002, p. 122). As anthropologists came to recognize how their own knowledge enterprise perpetuated Eurocentric forms of domination, they realized that their own histories made them more intimately connected with their subjects than they would have liked to believe (see Asad, 1973). Anthropology was undergoing its own sort of unraveling (see Clifford, 1988; Clifford & Marcus, 1986; Marcus & Fischer, 1986). Once anthropologists questioned the soundness of parts, we were no longer so comfortable about fitting them together into wholes. Neither could we assume the soundness of wholes. As Susan Coutin puts it, "In that it critiques the authoritativeness of any single account, such a 'perspectival' approach is consistent with the reflexive turn in anthropology" (Coutin, 2005, p. 196).

What to do next is the elephant in the room, and this question sets the agenda for much thinking in the so-called postmodern or deconstructive developments in anthropology. For present purposes, however, I merely wish to identify a certain way that unraveling has manifested itself in the discipline – what Markus Schlecker and Eric Hirsch call the "crisis of context" (Schlecker & Hirsch, 2001). This is the realization that in a knowledge system of parts-and-wholes, the knower will always fail to know any whole in its entirety, because wholes can always themselves become parts of something more complete. New input has the effect not of reconstituting the system (see Luhmann, 1990; Maturana & Varela, 1980), but of exceeding its boundaries. It is always possible to draw more and more relations; it is always possible to bring in more and more parts. Where to draw the line? In a parts-and-wholes epistemology, there is no perfect answer. For many of those who derive their analytical practices from this tradition, the realization of this failure has provoked much reassessment of the assumptions that guide knowledge creation. One significant trend in contemporary cultural anthropology is to relinquish the project of bounding objects of analysis, attempting instead to implicate anthropological analysis in more diffuse and ambiguously defined fields of relations that are already implicated with one another (see, e.g., Choy, 2005; Fischer, 2005; Fortun, 2001). Such is the approach of this chapter.

"Drawing the Line" in Death Penalty Jurisprudence

Far from being a solely anthropological concern, I maintain that it is something like this question – where to draw the line? – that had Justice Scalia invoking Great War imagery to forecast the consequences of *Lockett.* If anything can be admitted as potential mitigation, then what about the defendant's life can jurors legitimately take to be mitigating? Everything? Some things? Which things? Scalia's worries have turned out to be somewhat justified. The Supreme Court has since held that the defendant's remorse and potential for rehabilitation can militate against death (*Hitchcock v. Dugger*, 1987), but that no decision against a death sentence can be founded merely on sentiment, conjecture, or sympathy (*California v. Brown*, 1987). Evidence of good behavior in jail can be admitted as a mitigating factor (*Skipper v. South Carolina*, 1986), but evidence of artistic ability cultivated while behind bars probably falls short (*Boyde v. California*, 1990). In some situations, the defense might be obligated to investigate certain aspects of the client's social history (*Williams v. Taylor*, 2000), but in other cases, it may be strategically reasonable (though rare indeed) for counsel not to present any mitigating evidence at all (*Wiggins v. Smith*, 2003).[2]

I believe that the conflict between *Furman* and *Lockett*, as Scalia describes it, exhibits something of a parallel in form with the anthropological problem of relating parts and wholes. How to decide what knowledge ought to be relevant in capital sentencing? With *Furman*'s doctrinal narrowing, privileged actors make this determination through the pronouncement of principles. The abstractions of these explanatory principles are readily taken to be totalizing representations, fit to represent the whole. On the other hand, *Lockett*'s substantive expansion lets the data build on itself. It always allows for the possibility that more or better or bigger parts are needed to stand in adequately for the whole, or that more or better or bigger relations are needed to tie the whole adequately together. The defendant's life is an unstable referent, constantly in flux, always calling for more connections to discover, evaluate, and present.

This parallel in form is itself an analytical connection, one that I have posited in my own role as analyst (see White, 1987). And yet, the possibility of discerning this parallel, I maintain, is a function of interrelated conditions of unraveling between me and my "subjects." In my ethnographic fieldwork, practitioners looking to fulfill the mandates of *Lockett* consulted with anthropologists, sociologists, psychologists, historians, geographers. Academic social scientists, in turn, dialogued with advocates about their methods of investigation. The lead counsel of *Furman* – an advocate-academic, and the co-author of a text that draws significantly on anthropological concepts of culture (see Amsterdam & Bruner, 2000) – told me that the social constructionist developments that shaped anthropology and other social sciences has seeped into the practice of capital defense. The mitigation investigation agency that served as my primary fieldsite is run by an anthropologist who tolerated my presence in good part because of my disciplinary affiliation.

Both anthropologists and the inheritors of *Lockett* have come to share the sense that what we analyze (anthropological subjects, death penalty defendants) presents itself to be in flux, malleable, and densely interconnected with other things – and that analysis, too, would do well to recognize change, adapt, and establish connections with other analysts. In short, had it not been for the fact that my "subjects" were willing to connect with me, I would not have been able to fully appreciate that legal practitioners, like anthropologists, are constantly looking for more connections. Those who attempt to fulfill *Lockett*'s mandates have already delved into other fields of knowledge, making their own lateral moves.

DEATH PENALTY SCHOLARSHIP

In this section, I suggest that the conditions of unraveling that have enabled intertwining between the Supreme Court's capital sentencing jurisprudence and cultural anthropology have also influenced certain developments in the historical trajectory of scholarship on the death penalty in general. With the idea of academic knowledge comes the idea of the disciplines; and with the idea of discipline comes the idea of bodies, gazed into a manipulable state of being by the objectifying eye (Foucault, 1975, 1980). Here, again, I suggest a parallel of form, born of the same circumstances of knowledges' awareness of their implications with each other in conditions of connectedness and complexity. Analytical objectification gets unsettled in favor of self-implication in densely interwoven fields of knowledge. In a way, the story of unraveling in capital punishment scholarship is really about a kind of unruliness that begins to overtake bodies of knowledge.

Again using my own discipline as a springboard, I focus first on cultural anthropology as one such body. The fact that there are so few anthropological works on the death penalty makes this scholarship easy to introduce to readers, who are likely, moreover, to be unfamiliar with how the discipline has approached the subject. Turning next to academic works in general, I then show how the same ethos of productive unraveling seems to have influenced important strands of death penalty scholarship. Finally, I narrow the focus once again, this time concentrating on academic analyses of capital sentencing "mitigation" – the substantive topic of the *Lockett* decision. By explaining developments in mitigation's knowledge practices, I set up the concluding thought of this chapter – that the side-by-side unraveling of capital sentencing jurisprudence, death penalty scholarship, and cultural anthropology bespeaks contemporary conditions under which knowledge practices are undoing the very idea of the death penalty.

Cultural Anthropology as Disciplinary Knowledge

If classic ethnographies broached the subject of capital punishment, it was typically by way of cursory anecdotal sketch. Boas wrote of an Eskimo who stole another man's wife (Boas, 1888, p. 668). Frazer traced the English custom of disemboweling traitors to ancient practices of human sacrifice to the Norse God Odin (Frazer, 1955, p. 290). Malinowski described a Trobriander who was shamed into taking a fatal leap from a coconut tree (Malinowski, 1926, pp. 77–78). Pospisil offered a tale of Kapauku Papuans who agreed to off a stingy villager after he refused to lend out his property (Pospisil, 1958, pp. 244–245). Rivers told of a Melanisian man sent adrift in a canoe who defied the chief's orders to break the bottom of the vessel and drown himself to death (Rivers, 1914, p. 306). And Speke's eyewitness account involved a Ugandan king who whimsically decided to take over the role of executioner, shooting a woman prisoner with a rifle (Speke, 1864, pp. 337–338).

Recently, more sustained studies have reflected the contending views within the discipline concerning the appropriate scope and breadth of anthropological inquiry. One commentator focused on a Balkan tribal society, concluding that the death penalty functions as a collective form of internal social control when attacks on neighboring group members carry a significant threat of retaliation (Boehm, 1985). Another author sifted through cross-cultural data from the Human Relations Area Files to argue that the "ultimate coercive sanction" is a universal phenomenon whose purpose is to maintain intra-societal harmony (Otterbein, 1986). Anthropological studies have alternately depicted the death penalty as a feature of politically decentralized tribes where retribution is a form of self-help (Dillon, 1980; Fried, 1967); a primitive manifestation of public law (Hoebel, 1954); or an indicator of political sophistication whereby the more complex the social system, the more likely leaders are able to establish their right to execute (Otterbein, 1986).

If ethnography has paid short shrift to the death penalty in general, it is no exaggeration to say that there exists virtually no anthropological investigation of capital punishment in the United States. Purdum and Paredes (1989) compared the ritualistic elements of American capital punishment to Aztec sacrifice, maintaining that the two share magico-functionalist elements of deity appeasement. And Colin Turnbull, a staunch death penalty opponent, used a popular press article to challenge the discipline to take on the "brutalization and dehumanization that take place on death row" (Turnbull, 1978, p. 51) – only to lament a decade later that the practitioners of our troubled science have embarrassed ourselves in our spectacular failure to care (Turnbull, 1989, p. 157).

Turnbull is a particularly interesting figure for the way in which he calls explicit attention to the performance of disciplinarity. One might say that much of the scholarship cited above is eminently anthropological; as representatives of an academic body of knowledge, they are quite disciplined about performing disciplinarity well. But Turnbull dares to question the very integrity of what constitutes the discipline in the first place, in the sense of both what makes the discipline truly whole and what makes it ethically sound. Anthropology, he declared, had to speak out for the value of life and the need to understand all of humanity. Included in that mix were those others who had been condemned right here at home. Unless the discipline turned its gaze back on its own national context, it could never be complete as an ethically coherent body of knowledge.

Bodily Forms of Knowledge

From the notion of anthropological knowledge as a body, I turn to the idea of bodies as they appear within knowledge. Here, I point to the clean, ordered structure of the case law summaries in Fig. 1.

This is what a law student would recognize as an "outline" – an organized display of case "squibs," each of which embodies some principle that each opinion is said to stand for. In this summary of some of the major U.S.

I. Death penalty overturned then reinstated

A. Road to *Furman*: Cases that led to the temporary abolition of death penalty.

> *Powell v. Alabama*, 287 U.S. 45 (1932): When defendants are not clearly assigned attorneys for death penalty (DP) trial, this is denial of counsel in violation of 14th Amendment due process.

> *Trop v. Dulles*, 356 U.S. 86 (1958): Articulated notion of "evolving standard of decency that marked the progress of a maturing society." Not a DP case.

> *McGautha v. California*, 402 U.S. 183 (1971): Does not violate fundamental standards of fairness under 14th Amendment due process to allow full discretion to juries; impossible to avoid some arbitrariness. "[J]urors confronted with the truly awesome responsibility of decreeing death for a fellow human [would] act with due regard for the consequences of their decision."

> *Furman v. Georgia*, 408 U.S. 238 (1972): Before this decision, virtually every DP statutory scheme afforded complete discretion to jurors. This decision directly placed administration of DP under Supreme Court's purview. Brennan and Marshall—8th Amendment prohibits death penalty. White, Douglas, and Powell—death not unconstitutional *per se* under 8th; death applied too arbitrarily.

B. *Gregg* and its quartet: Established provisional nature of Court's capital punishment jurisprudence, increasing involvement in regulation. Two key principles—"evolving standards of decency," and "dignity of man."

> *Gregg v. Georgia*, 428 U.S. 153 (1976), *Jurek v. Texas*, 428 U.S. 262 (1976), *Proffitt v. Florida*, 428 U.S. 242 (1976): Upheld new DP statutes that guided sentencer discretion—reinstated DP in those states. DP itself constitutional under 8th Amendment.

> *Roberts v. Louisiana*, 428 U.S. 325 (1976), *Woodson v. North Carolina*, 428 U.S. 280 (1976): Struck down new DP statutes that created capital offenses that mandated DP. Announced that consideration of mitigating circumstances is an instrumental part of individualized sentencing. Guilt alone is not sufficient condition for death—need bifurcated trial.

II. Mitigation

A. Early history of mitigation: Two *Gregg* cases and *Lockett* struck down mandatory DP and introduced idea of individualization.

> *Jurek v. Texas*, 428 U.S. 262 (1976): Plurality opinion, "what is essential is that the jury have before it all possible information about the individual defendant whose fate it must determine."

> *Woodson v. North Carolina*, 428 U.S. 280 (1976): Plurality opinion, belief in "the fundamental respect for humanity underlying the 8th Amendment requires consideration of the character and record of the individual offender" in a capital case.

> *Lockett v. Ohio*, 438 U.S. 586 (1978): Plurality opinion, but effectively established modern, wider-ranging notion of mitigation. Must allow evidence of "any aspect of a defendant's character or record and any of the circumstances of the offenses that the defendant proffers as a basis for a sentence less than death." Ohio statute assumed that since aggravating factors needed to be clearly specified, same applied to mitigating factors. This was violation of 8th Amendment.

B. Expansion of mitigation: Following decisions seem to consider any and all evidence as mitigating individualization evidence.

> *Eddings v. Oklahoma*, 455 U.S. 104 (1982): Majority adopted the plurality rule in *Lockett*. Oklahoma court had refused to allow defendant's family history, emotional disturbance, and youth as mitigating factors.

> *Skipper v. South Carolina*, 476 U.S. 1 (1986): State must allow consideration of defendant's good behavior in jail as mitigation.

Fig. 1. Case Squibs.

Hitchcock v. Dugger, 481 U.S. 393 (1987): Scalia reversed death sentence because jury limited from considering "innocence of significant prior criminal activity or violent behavior," "potential for rehabilitation," and "voluntary surrender to authorities."

Penry v. Lynaugh, 492 U.S. 302 (1989): Texas capital statute as applied impermissibly restricted consideration of defendant's mental retardation as mitigation. Texas allowed consideration of mitigation evidence only in context of specific questions (whether defendant committed crime deliberately, whether he would be dangerous in future, etc.). "Special issue" scheme—has given rise to sub-specialty in capital litigation, even though this matter is peripheral in the big picture.

Williams v. Taylor, 529 U.S. 362 (2000): Ineffective assistance of counsel when lawyers fail to investigate parents' imprisonment for neglect of defendant, institutionalization with child welfare. Defendant confessed to crime, but death sentence reversed.

Wiggins v. Smith, 539 U.S. 510 (2003): 6th Amendment effective assistance of counsel under *Strickland* requires investigations to be conducted in accordance with ABA Guidelines. Counsel must consider presenting medical history, educational history, employment and training history, family and social history, prior adult and juvenile correctional experience, and religious and cultural influences.

C. Qualification of appropriate mitigation: But Court has also indicated some discomfort about uncircumscribed mitigation. Appears to want to focus on reason rather than sentiment:

Skipper v. South Carolina, 476 U.S. 1 (1986): Dicta, Court had "no quarrel" with the idea that "how often [the defendant] will take a shower" can have be irrelevant to sentencing.

California v. Brown, 479 U.S. 538 (1987): Jury cannot be swayed by "mere sentiment, conjecture, sympathy" if unrelated to evidence presented. Since such sympathy or public sentiment is irrelevant to mitigation evidence, this principle does not violate 8th Amendment under *Lockett*.

Franklin v. Lynaugh, 487 U.S. 164 (1988): Jury's residual doubt about defendant's guilt is not mitigating factor, because not related to defendant's character, record, or circumstances of offense. The possibility of factual error applies to every criminal case, does not apply to particular individual attribute of defendant.

Walton v. Arizona, 497 U.S. 639 (1990): Scalia's concurrence—no longer will uphold *Lockett's* allowance of all mitigating evidence. To say there is an "inherent tension" between *Furman* and *Lockett/Woodson* "is rather like saying that there was perhaps an inherent tension between the Allied and the Axis Powers in World War II."

Boyde v. California, 494 U.S. 370 (1990): Suggested but did not announce that consideration of artistic ability (here, defendant's prize for dance choreography in prison) not indispensable to individualized sentencing. Relevant if it speaks to future dangerousness, but not if it speaks to defendant's intrinsic worth.

Fig. 1.   (Continued)

Supreme Court opinions leading up to and affected by the *Lockett* decision, it is legal doctrine – generalized principles and rules – that are the "found objects" of the lawyer's analytical practices (see Riles, 2004, p. 781). Although the orderly form of doctrinal principle lends an appearance of orderliness to the rule of law (Riles, 2004, p. 778–784), some commentators argue that the substance of the high court's Eighth Amendment jurisprudence achieves nothing more than purposeful obfuscation, putting a brake on state killings while satisfying the public's bloodlust (Banner, 2002; Weisberg, 1983). Other commentators would contend that the case law is not so unruly, that it is actually more consistent – more disciplined – than it appears (Bilionis, 1993).

The policy debates that inform much of the legal and philosophical scholarship on capital punishment deploy "bodies" of principles in a particular form, too. This is the form of opposition. It seems that we are either for or against the death penalty. So it is *either* that human life has infinite worth, and the right to life is inalienable, and capital punishment is cruel and unusual, and religion does not support the death penalty, and no amount of procedural safeguarding can ever prevent the execution of innocent people, and death does not deter crime, and the public does not understand that the system is fraught with prejudice and error, and retribution is never a justification for punishment, and the rest of the civilized world is against it – *or* that the worth of the victim's life must be affirmed, and religion supports the death penalty, and the execution of guilty defendants is not any less just simply because the condemned individuals happen to be ethnic minorities, and death does indeed deter crime, and the public fully understands and overwhelmingly supports the system, and retribution is a perfectly good justification for punishment, and criminal punishment is an internal issue of state sovereignty (see, e.g., Bedau, 1999; Black, 1981; Camus, 1961; Hood, 2001; Radin, 1980; Steiker & Steiker, 1998; van den Haag, 1986).

Indeed, many bodies of works within the death penalty scholarship are notable for how easily sets or subsets of them can be plugged into policy analysis, or an opening argument, or some theoretical debate. There are doctrinal analyses of whether judicial interpretations of case law function as adequate means to professed ends (Steiker & Steiker, 1995; Weisberg, 1983). There are empirical arguments about public beliefs (Bowers, 1993), juror beliefs (Tiersma, 1995), deterrent effects (Weisberg, 2005), racial discrepancies (Baldus, Woodworth, & Pulaski, 1990; Pierce & Radelet, 2005), and procedural flaws (Black, 1981; Goodpaster, 1983; Radin, 1980; White, 1993). Another prominent form of ordered bodies in the death penalty literature is that anthropologically familiar construct of unilineal extension. In one version of this, bodies of practices are bounded and ordered on a chain of increasingly civilized behavior. As mankind rides off into the horizon of progress, the barbaric rituals of capital punishment are deemed sure to fall (Amsterdam, 1982; Gorecki, 1983).

But unruliness has set in. Peter Fitzpatrick (1999) draws from Derrida's "Force of Law" to argue that the need to go beyond what is already known mandates the most profound sense of responsibility to the other. "A determination based on knowledge cannot ever be complete in some final resolution," Fitzpatrick says, for "[s]omething can always come from beyond, something 'more,' and reveal our overconfident conclusion to be not so" (Fitzpatrick, 1999, p. 123). Austin Sarat echoes these thoughts in holding that the very foundations of democracy require "a spirit of openness, or reversibility, or revision quite at odds with the confidence and commitment necessary to dispose of human life in a cold and deliberate way" (Sarat, 2001, p. 16). Capital punishment presumes that manipulable bodies can be made out of knowledge produced about human beings. But conditions of unraveling make these bodies unruly, agitating them with a sense of provisionality and the prospect of what cannot now be known.[3] In the world of death penalty sentencing, perhaps nowhere is this more apparent in the active consciousness than in capital "mitigation" – that area of advocacy that makes it its business to seek "the fullest information possible concerning the defendant's life" (*Lockett v. Ohio*, 1978, p. 603).

Mitigation and Representation

Mitigation specialists see themselves constructing representations. Indeed, the practice of capital mitigation traffics in constructions of them. Advocates troop on and do their job in the face of defense counsel's glaring incompetence (Tomes, 1997). They coax and cajole family members into cooperating (Leonard, 2003), asking them to take the stand and muddle through language that cannot possibly capture what they feel. They find ways to circumvent the client's own pleas to be put to death (Carter, 1987). They take their client's existence, shot through with violence, and mutilate ("cut") it again and again through countless deformities of representation, all in the name of "justice" (Derrida, 1992).

Some of the relevant academic literature is preoccupied with the apparent need to reconcile what might be called representations of cause with representations of effect. There is, for example, the prosecution's allocation of individual responsibility versus the defense's determinist claims about the influences of social upbringing (Alfieri, 1996); the procedural need to establish the causal relevance of evidence versus the moral need to understand the dispersed effects of complex contextual conditions (Hertz & Weisberg, 1981; Sundby, 1991); and the idea of mitigation as a moral imperative, a motivating good in itself, versus the idea of mitigation as a cost–benefit analysis, concerned with the logistics of administration (Bilionis, 1991). But mitigation's practitioners trouble this clear separation of cause and effect. If the death penalty banks on "the notion that people who commit capital crimes are less than human" (Haney, 1995, p. 548), then the work of mitigation is to show that the human condition is at once to act, and to be acted upon (Leonard, 2003).

Thus, we see works that self-consciously defy the dichotomies that the legal structure would slot actors into – government versus defense, agency versus determinism, cause versus effect. Some commentators parlay the individualism of agency into an argument to recognize the full extent of the defendant's individuality (Steiker & Steiker, 1992). They may even extend the notion of 'individualization' itself, making it a family affair (King & Norgard, 1999). Others, coming from the opposite direction, argue that effect-producing conditions – rotten social background (Delgado, 1985), for instance, or structural racism (Haney, 2004), or disease-like factors of social environs (Kirchmeier, 2004) – are nevertheless compatible with the acknowledgement of individual wrongdoing that jurors tend to find mitigating (Garvey, 1998).

For mitigation's advocates, then, it is not simply a case of layering deterministic fact upon deterministic fact, counterposing environmental effect to agentive causation. This would be simply to add more context, to tack on more parts or to make wholes bigger. But these practitioners are well aware that the "complete" whole can never truly be so. Thus, rather than make advocacy an issue of objectification, mitigation actually recasts expectations of context into processes of discovering interrelatedness between various actors – advocates, defendants, his loved ones, academics, mental health experts, and victims – and of understanding the defendant in his full individualized complexity. The literature describes this in terms of establishing empathic connections. Another way to put it might be, the practice and academic analysis of mitigation is thoroughly implicated in developments of capital sentencing jurisprudence, where a sense of unraveling has kicked in.

CONCLUSION: DEATH, UNRAVELED

One effect of lateralizing capital sentencing jurisprudence with academic commentary, and these with cultural anthropology, is that familiar frameworks get productively reformulated. Questions about whether capital punishment is right or wrong, or whether there are circumstances under which it can be applied justly, or what moral, constitutional, or procedural issues ought to figure most prominently in the debate, now sit alongside a self-assessing contemplation of how knowledge practices make sense of the death penalty. The fields of knowledge described in this chapter recognize themselves to be already implicated in each other, and in each other's analytical concerns. Instead of claiming a privileged position of analysis vis-à-vis other knowledges, thinkers from these fields attempt to puzzle things out with them.

Such efforts shape and are shaped by the questions of morality, constitutionality, and procedure that have traditionally framed conversations about the death penalty, even while they refuse to be bound by them. What is there to be learned about the individualized facts of a defendant's life? About broader socio-economic trends? About ethical considerations? About historical applications of principles of legal doctrine? With the orientation toward provisionality has come the feeling that all these questions are bound with one another, the analysts who ask them, and the entwined knowledge practices that make their asking possible. Under modern conditions of unraveling, marked by a heightened sense of interconnectedness and complexity with respect to analysis and its subjects, analysts think twice about any claim that would definitively pronounce what, exactly, the death penalty is, and what place it merits in criminal sentencing. Thus, the point is not that American society still allows capital punishment to take place, regardless of whether it should or should not. The point is that under current knowledge practices, analysts and advocates can and do think twice, thrice, four times, even though, as Justice Scalia points out, brute logic would seem to indicate that they do not have to.

There *is* something different about the subject of capital punishment; the sheer quantity of analysis generated about it is a testament to the productiveness of its unraveling. So even though I have sidestepped the question of whether the death penalty is dying, I am suggesting that efforts to make sense of it remain very much alive, and contain much vitality in its generative potential. To borrow a quote again from Turnbull, the anthropologist: "The argument is not for or against public executions, or even for or against the death penalty, but rather for a removal of [] ignorance by a depth of understanding of the total institution and its effect on the whole society" (Turnbull, 1989, p. 157). For him, abolition would be a natural byproduct of the lively ferment of knowledge's play. Should his forecast ever prove true, the self-implication of analysis in conditions of unraveling may very well have something to do with how the death penalty comes undone.

NOTES

1. Hayden White's (1973) seminal work on the use of certain tropes to organize plot structures – in particular, he identified metaphor, synecdoche, metonymy, and irony – paved the way for further examination of the relationship between analytical holism and its representation in key Western textual forms (see, e.g., Bruner, 1986[1982]; Marcus & Cushman, 1982; Thornton, 1988). Martin Jay (1993) offers a more general discussion on the relationship between visuality and dominant knowledge practices rooted in French Enlightenment projects.

2. The Wiggins decision itself stands for the considerable amount of investigation that defense counsel must undertake in order to establish a sufficient foundation of information upon which to base decisions of legal strategy. The American Bar Association's *Guidelines for the Appointment and Performance of Death Counsel in Death Penalty Case*s – explicitly embraced by the majority in Wiggins – indicates that "penalty phase preparation requires extensive and generally unparalleled investigation into personal and family history" (American Bar Association, 2003, p. 82). Among the things that counsel is required to consider are:

(1) Medical history (including hospitalizations, mental and physical illness or injury, alcohol and drug use, pre-natal and birth trauma, malnutrition, developmental delays, and neurological damage); (2) Family and social history (including physical, sexual, or emotional abuse; family history of mental illness, cognitive impairments, substance abuse, or domestic violence; poverty, familial instability, neighborhood environment, and peer influence); other traumatic events such as exposure to criminal violence, the loss of a loved one or a natural disaster; experiences of racism or other social or ethnic bias; cultural or religious influences; failures of government or social intervention (e.g., failure to intervene or provide necessary services, placement in poor quality foster care or juvenile detention facilities); (3) Educational history (including achievement, performance, behavior, and activities), special educational needs (including cognitive limitations and learning disabilities) and opportunity or lack thereof, and activities; (4) Military service (including length and type of service, conduct, special training, combat exposure, and health and mental health services); (5) Employment and training history (including skills and performance, and barriers to employability); (6) Prior juvenile and adult correctional experience (including conduct while under supervision, in institutions of education or training, and regarding clinical services) (American Bar Association, 2003, p. 83).

3. In fact, I would find unruliness in some of the apparently "disciplined" scholarship cited above – analyses that are intended to agitate, even as they are deliberately made intelligible and operational within existing disciplinary and advocacy structures (I think of Amsterdam's work in particular).

ACKNOWLEDGMENTS

Many thanks to Austin Sarat and the anonymous reviewers for their comments, and to Tom Boellstorff, Leo Chávez, Susan Coutin, Eric

Freedman, Bill Maurer, and Diego Vigil for their various contributions to this chapter.

REFERENCES CITED

LEGAL CASES AND GUIDELINES

American Bar Association. (2003). *Guidelines for the appointment and performance of defense counsel in death penalty cases.* Retrieved on April 3, 2007, from http://www.abanet.org/deathpenalty/resources/docs/2003Guidelines.pdf
Boyde v. California. (1990). 494 U.S. 370.
California v. Brown. (1987). 479 U.S. 538.
Furman v. Georgia. (1972). 408 U.S. 238.
Gregg v. Georgia. (1976). 428 U.S. 153.
Hitchcock v. Dugger. (1987). 481 U.S. 393.
Jurek v. Texas. (1976). 428 U.S. 262.
Lockett v. Ohio. (1978). 438 U.S. 586.
Proffitt v. Florida. (1976). 428 U.S. 242.
Roberts v. Louisiana. (1976). 428 U.S. 325.
Skipper v. South Carolina. (1986). 476 U.S. 1.
Walton v. Arizona. (1990). 497 U.S. 639.
Wiggins v. Smith. (2003). 539 U.S. 510.
Williams v. Taylor. (2000). 529 U.S. 362.
Woodson v. North Carolina. (1976). 428 U.S. 280.

SOURCES

Alfieri, A. V. (1996). Mitigation, mercy, and delay: The moral politics of death penalty abolitionists. *Harvard Civil Rights–Civil Liberties Law Review, 31,* 325–352.
Amsterdam, A. G. (1982). Capital punishment. In: H. A. Bedau (Ed.), *The death penalty in America* (3rd ed., pp. 346–358). Oxford: Oxford University Press.
Amsterdam, A. G., & Bruner, J. (2000). *Minding the law.* Cambridge, MA: Harvard University Press.
Asad, T. (Ed.) (1973). *Anthropology and the colonial encounter.* Amherst, NY: Humanity Books.
Baldus, D. C., Woodworth, G., & Pulaski, C. A., Jr. (1990). *Equal justice and the death penalty: A legal and empirical analysis.* Boston: Northeastern University Press.
Banner, S. (2002). *The death penalty: An American history.* Cambridge, MA: Harvard University Press.
Baudrillard, J. (1998). *Selected writings.* Palo Alto, CA: Stanford University Press.
Bedau, H. A. (1999). Abolishing the death penalty even for the worst murderers. In: A. Sarat (Ed.), *The killing state: Capital punishment in law, politics, and culture* (pp. 40–59). Oxford: Oxford University Press.

Bilionis, L. D. (1991). Moral appropriateness, capital punishment, and the *Lockett* doctrine. *Journal of Criminal Law and Criminology, 82*, 283–333.

Bilionis, L. D. (1993). Legitimating death. *Michigan Law Review, 91*, 1643–1702.

Black, C. L., Jr. (1981). *Capital punishment: The inevitability of caprice and mistake* (2nd ed.). New York: W.W. Norton & Company.

Boas, F. (1888). *The central Eskimos (No. Annual Report 6)*. Washington, DC: Bureau of American Ethnology.

Boehm, C. (1985). Execution within the clan as an extreme form of ostracism. *Social Science Information, 24*(2), 309–321.

Bowers, W. (1993). Capital punishment and contemporary values: People's misgivings and the court's misperceptions. *Law and Society Review, 27*(1), 157–176.

Boyer, D. (2005a). The corporeality of expertise. *Ethnos, 70*(2), 243–266.

Boyer, D. (2005b). *Spirit and system: Media, intellectuals, and the dialectic in modern German culture*. Chicago: University of Chicago Press.

Bruner, E. M. (1986[1982]). Ethnography as narrative. In: V. Turner & E. M. Bruner (Eds), *The Anthropology of experience* (pp. 139–155). Urbana, IL: University of Illinois Press.

Camus, A. (1961). Reflections on the guillotine. In: J. O'Brien (Ed.), *Resistance, rebellion, and death* (pp. 173–234). New York: Alfred A. Knopf.

Carter, L. E. (1987). Maintaining systemic integrity in capital cases: The use of court-appointed counsel to present mitigating evidence when the defendant advocates death. *Tennessee Law Review, 55*, 95–152.

Choy, T. K. (2005). Articulated knowledges: Environmental forms after universality's demise. *American Anthropologist, 107*(1), 5–18.

Clifford, J. (1988). *The predicament of culture: Twentieth-century ethnography, literature and art*. Cambridge, MA: Harvard University Press.

Clifford, J., & Marcus, G. E. (Eds). (1986). *Writing culture: The poetics and politics of ethnography*. Berkeley, CA: University of California Press.

Coutin, S. B. (2005). Being en route. *American Anthropologist, 107*(2), 195–206.

De Man, P. (1983). *Blindness and insight* (2nd ed.). Minneapolis: University of Minnesota Press.

Delgado, R. (1985). 'Rotten social background': Should the criminal law recognize a defense of severe environmental deprivation? *Law and Inequality, 3*, 9–90.

Derrida, J. (1974). *Of grammatology*. Baltimore, MD: Johns Hopkins University Press.

Derrida, J. (1992). Force of law: The 'mystical foundation of authority'. In: D. G. Carlson (Ed.), *Deconstruction and the possibility of justice* (pp. 3–67). London: Routledge.

Dillon, R. G. (1980). Capital punishment in egalitarian society: The Meta' case. *Journal of Anthropological Research, 36*(4), 437–452.

Fabian, J. (2002). *Time and the other: How anthropology makes it object*. New York: Columbia University Press.

Fischer, M. M. J. (2003). *Emergent forms of life and the anthropological voice*. Durham, NC: Duke University Press.

Fischer, M. M. J. (2005). Technoscientific infrastructures and emergent forms of life: A commentary. *American Anthropologist, 107*(1), 55–61.

Fish, S. (1999). *The Stanley Fish reader*. Oxford: Blackwell Publishers.

Fitzpatrick, P. (1999). 'Always more to do': Capital punishment and the (de)composition of law. In: A. Sarat (Ed.), *The killing state: Capital punishment in law, politics, and culture* (pp. 117–136). Oxford: Oxford University Press.

Fortun, K. (2001). *Advocacy after Bhopal: Environmentalism, disaster, new global origins.* Chicago: University of Chicago Press.

Foucault, M. (1975). *Discipline and punish: The birth of the prison.* New York: Vintage Books.

Foucault, M. (1980). *Power/knowledge: Selected interviews and other writings, 1972–1977.* New York: Pantheon Books.

Frazer, S. J. G. (1955). *The golden bough: A study in magic and religion, Part IV: Adonis Attis Osiris: Studies in the history of oriental religion* (Vol. 1, 3rd ed.). New York: Macmillan.

Fried, M. (1967). *The evolution of political society: An essay in political anthropology.* New York: Random House.

Garvey, S. P. (1998). Aggravation and mitigation in capital cases: What do jurors think? *Columbia Law Review, 98,* 1538–1576.

Goodpaster, G. (1983). The trial for life: Effective assistance of counsel in death penalty cases. *New York University Law Review, 58,* 299–362.

Gorecki, J. (1983). *Capital punishment: Criminal law and social evolution.* New York: Columbia University Press.

Greenhouse, C. J., Mertz, E., & Warren, K. B. (Eds). (2002). *Ethnography in unstable places: Everyday lives in contexts of dramatic political change.* Durham, NC: Duke University Press.

van den Haag, E. (1986). The ultimate punishment: A defense. *Harvard Law Review, 99,* 1662–1669.

Haney, C. (1995). The social context of capital murder: Social histories and the logic of mitigation. *Santa Clara Law Review, 35,* 547–609.

Haney, C. (2004). Condemning the other in death penalty trials: Biographical racism, structural mitigation, and the empathetic divide. *DePaul Law Review, 53,* 1557–1589.

Harvey, D. (2005). *A brief history of neoliberalism.* New York: Oxford University Press.

Hertz, R., & Weisberg, R. (1981). In mitigation of the penalty of death: *Lockett v. Ohio* and the capital defendant's right to consideration of mitigating circumstances. *California Law Review, 69,* 317–376.

Hoebel, E. A. (1954). *The law of primitive man: A study in comparative legal dynamics.* Cambridge, MA: Harvard University Press.

Holmes, D. R., & Marcus, G. E. (2005a). Cultures of expertise and the management of globalization: Toward the re-functioning of ethnography. In: A. Ong & S. J. Collier (Eds), *Global assemblages: Technology, politics, and ethics as anthropological problems* (pp. 235–252). Malden, MA: Blackwell Publishing.

Holmes, D. R., & Marcus, G. E. (2005b). Fast-capitalism: Para-ethnography and the rise of the symbolic analyst. In: M. Fisher & G. Downey (Eds), *Frontiers of capital: Ethnographic perspectives on the new economy* (pp. 33–57). Durham, NC: Duke University Press.

Hood, R. (2001). Capital punishment: A global perspective. *Punishment and Society, 3*(3), 331–354.

Jameson, F. (1991). *Postmodernism, or, the cultural logic of late capitalism.* Durham, NC: Duke University Press.

Jay, M. (1993). *Downcast eyes: The denigration of vision in twentieth-century French thought.* Berkeley, CA: University of California Press.

Keane, W. (2003). Self-interpretation, agency, and the objects of anthropology: Reflections on a genealogy. *Comparative Studies in Society and History, 45*(2), 222–248.

Kelman, M. (1987). *A guide to critical legal studies.* Cambridge, MA: Harvard University Press.

King, R., & Norgard, K. (1999). What about our families? Using the impact on death row defendants' family members as a mitigating factor in death penalty sentencing hearings. *Florida State University Law Review, 26,* 1119–1176.

Kirchmeier, J. L. (1998). Aggravating and mitigating factors: The paradox of today's arbitrary and mandatory capital punishment scheme. *William and Mary Bill of Rights Journal, 6,* 345–459.

Kirchmeier, J. L. (2004). A tear in the eye of the law: Mitigating factors and the progression toward a disease theory of criminal justice. *Oregon Law Review, 83,* 631–730.

Leonard, P. B. (2003). A new profession for an old need: Why a mitigation specialist must be included on the capital defense team. *Hofstra Law Review, 31,* 1143–1155.

Luhmann, N. (1990). *Essays on self-reference.* New York: Columbia University Press.

Lyotard, J. F. (1984). In: G. Bennington & B. Massumi (Eds), *The postmodern condition: A report on knowledge.* Manchester: Manchester University Press.

Malinowski, B. (1926). *Crime and custom in savage society.* London: Routledge.

Marcus, G. E. (2002). Beyond Malinowski and after *Writing Culture*: On the future of cultural anthropology and the predicament of ethnography. *Australian Journal of Anthropology, 13*(2), 191–199.

Marcus, G. E., & Cushman, D. (1982). Ethnographies as texts. *Annual Review of Anthropology, 11,* 25–69.

Marcus, G. E., & Fischer, M. M. J. (1986). *Anthropology as cultural critique: An experimental moment in the human sciences.* Chicago: University of Chicago Press.

Maturana, H. R., & Varela, F. J. (1980). *Autopoiesis and cognition: The realization of the living.* Dordrecht: D. Reidel Publishing.

Maurer, B. (2005a). Introduction to 'ethnographic emergences'. *American Anthropologist, 107*(1), 1–4.

Maurer, B. (2005b). *Mutual life, limited: Islamic banking, alternative currencies, lateral reason.* Princeton, NJ: Princeton University Press.

Mitchell, T. (2002). *Rule of experts: Egypt, techno-politics, modernity.* Berkeley, CA: University of California Press.

Miyazaki, H., & Riles, A. (2005). Failure as an endpoint. In: A. Ong & S. J. Collier (Eds), *Global assemblages: Technology, politics, and ethics as anthropological problems* (pp. 320–331). Malden, MA: Blackwell Publishing.

Ong, W. (1977). *Interfaces of the word: Studies in the evolution of consciousness and culture.* Ithaca, NY: Cornell University Press.

Otterbein, K. F. (1986). *The ultimate coercive sanction: A cross-cultural study of capital punishment.* New Haven, CT: HRAF Press.

Pierce, G., & Radelet, M. L. (2005). The impact of legally inappropriate factors on death sentencing for California homicides, 1990–1999. *Santa Clara Law Review, 46,* 1–47.

Pospisil, L. (1958). *Kapauku Papuans and their law.* New Haven, CT: Yale University Press.

Purdum, E. D., & Paredes, J. A. (1989). Rituals of death: Capital punishment and human sacrifice. In: M. L. Radelet (Ed.), *Facing the death penalty: Essays on a cruel and unusual punishment* (pp. 139–155). Philadelphia: Temple University Press.

Radin, M. J. (1980). Cruel punishment and respect for persons: Super due process for death. *Southern California Law Review, 53,* 1143–1185.

Riles, A. (2000). *The network inside-out.* Ann Arbor, MI: University of Michigan Press.

Riles, A. (2004). Property as legal knowledge: Means and ends. *Journal of the Royal Anthropological Institute N.S., 10,* 775–795.

Rivers, W. H. R. (1914). *The history of Melanesian society*. Cambridge: Cambridge University Press.

Sarat, A. (2001). *When the state kills: Capital punishment and the American condition*. Princeton, NJ: Princeton University Press.

Schlecker, M., & Hirsch, E. (2001). Incomplete knowledge: Ethnography and the crisis of context in studies of media, science and technology. *History of the Human Sciences, 14*(1), 69–87.

Speke, J. H. (1864). *Journal of the discovery of the source of the Nile*. New York: Harper & Brothers.

Steiker, C. S., & Steiker, J. M. (1992). Let God sort them out? Refining the individualization requirement in capital sentencing. *Yale Law Journal, 102*, 835–870.

Steiker, C. S., & Steiker, J. M. (1995). Sober second thoughts: Reflections on two decades of constitutional regulation of capital punishment. *Harvard Law Review, 109*, 355–438.

Steiker, C. S., & Steiker, J. M. (1998). Defending categorical exemptions to the death penalty: Reflections on the ABA's resolutions concerning the execution of juveniles and persons with mental retardation. *Law and Contemporary Problems, 61*(4), 89–104.

Strathern, M. (1992). *After nature: English kinship in the late twentieth century*. Cambridge: Cambridge University Press.

Strathern, M. (2004). *Commons and borderlands: Working papers on interdisciplinarity, accountability and the flow of knowledge*. Oxon: Sean Kingston Publishing.

Sundby, S. E. (1991). The *Lockett* paradox: Reconciling guided discretion and unguided mitigation in capital sentencing. *UCLA Law Review, 38*, 1147–1208.

Thornton, R. (1988). The rhetoric of ethnographic holism. *Cultural Anthropology, 3*, 285–303.

Tiersma, P. M. (1995). Dictionaries and death: Do capital jurors understand mitigation? *Utah Law Review, 1995*, 1–49.

Tomes, J. P. (1997). Damned if you do, damned if you don't': The use of mitigation experts in death penalty litigation. *American Journal of Criminal Law, 24*, 359–399.

Tsing, A. L. (2005). *Friction: An ethnography of global connection*. Princeton, NJ: Princeton University Press.

Turnbull, C. (1978). Death by decree: An anthropological approach to capital punishment. *Natural History, 87*(5), 50–67.

Turnbull, C. (1989). The death penalty and anthropology. In: M. L. Radelet (Ed.), *Facing the death penalty: Essays on a cruel and unusual punishment* (pp. 156–168). Philadelphia: Temple University Press.

Weisberg, R. (1983). Deregulating death. *The Supreme Court Review, 1983*, 305–395.

Weisberg, R. (2005). The death penalty meets social science: Deterrence and jury behavior under new scrutiny. *Annual Review of Law and Social Science, 1*, 151–170.

White, H. (1973). *Metahistory*. Baltimore, MD: Johns Hopkins University Press.

White, H. (1987). *The content of the form: Narrative discourse and historical representation*. Baltimore, MD: Johns Hopkins University Press.

White, W. S. (1993). Effective assistance of counsel in capital cases: The evolving standard of care. *University of Illinois Law Review, 1993*, 323–378.

SET UP A CONTINUATION ORDER TODAY!

Did you know that you can set up a continuation order on all Elsevier-JAI series and have each new volume sent directly to you upon publication? For details on how to set up a **continuation order**, contact your nearest regional sales office listed below.

To view related series in Political Science, please visit:

www.elsevier.com/politicalscience

30% Discount for Authors on All Books!

A 30% discount is available to Elsevier book and journal contributors on all books *(except multi-volume reference works)*.

To claim your discount, full payment is required with your order, which must be sent directly to the publisher at the nearest regional sales office above.